WE'RE NOT OK

In the United States, only 6 percent of the 1.5 million faculty in degree-granting postsecondary institutions are Black. While many institutions promote the idea of diversity in recruitment, research has shown that little progress has been made in diversifying the faculty ranks, especially at research-intensive institutions. This book shares the experiences of Black faculty to take the reader on a journey, from the obstacles to securing a full-time faculty position to the unique struggles of being Black educators at predominantly white institutions, with discussion of the deterrents to inclusion, retention, and mental well-being that are encountered along the way. The book provides practical strategies and recommendations for graduate students, faculty, administrators, and changemakers to make strides in diversity, equity, and inclusion. More than a presentation of statistics and anecdotes, it initiates a dialogue intended to usher actual change that will benefit Black faculty, their students, and their institutions.

ANTIJA M. ALLEN is an assistant professor of psychology at Pellissippi State Community College, a faculty development specialist, an anti-racism advocate, and a Maxine Smith leadership fellow.

JUSTIN T. STEWART is a faculty career coach at Allen Ivy Prep Consulting, a former entertainment journalist, and a member of the Black Organizers, Leaders, and Doers (BOLD) network.

WE'RE NOT OK

Black Faculty Experiences and Higher Education Strategies

EDITED BY

ANTIJA M. ALLEN

Pellissippi State Community College

JUSTIN T. STEWART

Allen Ivy Prep Consulting

CAMBRIDGE UNIVERSITY PRESS

CAMBRIDGE
UNIVERSITY PRESS

University Printing House, Cambridge CB2 8BS, United Kingdom

One Liberty Plaza, 20th Floor, New York, NY 10006, USA

477 Williamstown Road, Port Melbourne, VIC 3207, Australia

314–321, 3rd Floor, Plot 3, Splendor Forum, Jasola District Centre,
New Delhi – 110025, India

103 Penang Road, #05–06/07, Visioncrest Commercial, Singapore 238467

Cambridge University Press is part of the University of Cambridge.

It furthers the University's mission by disseminating knowledge in the pursuit of
education, learning, and research at the highest international levels of excellence.

www.cambridge.org
Information on this title: www.cambridge.org/9781316513347
DOI: 10.1017/9781009064668

© Cambridge University Press 2022

First published 2022

A catalogue record for this publication is available from the British Library.

ISBN 978-1-316-51334-7 Hardback
ISBN 978-1-009-07356-1 Paperback

Contents

Contributors

TEMPESTT R. ADAMS, Appalachian State University

ANTIJA M. ALLEN, Pellissippi State Community College

TYRA M. BANKS, University of St. Augustine for Health Sciences

REGINA BANKS-HALL, Cleary University

KATHY-ANN C. HERNANDEZ, Eastern University

NYESHA JAMES, Winton Woods City Schools

LARISSA MALONE, University of Southern Maine

SHAQUILLE O'NEAL MARSH, Pellissippi State Community College

OLIVIA MILLER, Guilford County Schools

ANICA CAMELA MULZAC, Sarah Lawrence College

TERI PLATT, Clark Atlanta University

DERRICK ROBINSON, Myedvantage Career and Consulting Services

NARKETTA SPARKMAN-KEY, Old Dominion University

JUSTIN T. STEWART, Allen Ivy Prep Consulting

JEAN SWINDLE, East Tennessee State University

SHUNTAY Z. TARVER, Old Dominion University

ANTIONE D. TOMLIN, Anne Arundel Community College

BRIAN K. WILLIAMS, North Carolina Agricultural and Technical State University

NAKESHIA N. WILLIAMS, Hollins University

Acknowledgments

Justin T. Stewart

To my mother, Thia Stewart, as the saying goes, none of this would be possible without you. Whether you are aware, or this is unbeknownst to you, your strength and commitment have been traits I have continued to follow throughout my personal and professional life. Your sacrifices have afforded me the resources I need to do better and accomplish the goals I set for myself. Guess I can check another goal off the list. Thanks Ma.

To my co-editor, Antija M. Allen, there aren't enough words to express my gratitude and appreciation in letting me ride shotgun throughout this process with you. Stretching back to our beginnings with Allen Ivy Prep Consulting, you have offered me an abundance of opportunity and, most importantly, your unwavering trust and confidence in my ability. This journey has definitely been quite a roller coaster, and I both admire and am inspired by your unrelenting dedication to getting this subject out to a wider audience. To collaborate with you on a project of this magnitude remains surreal, it is an experience that will be hard to top. I will never stop marveling at such a milestone in my life and an accolade in our partnership. We wrote a book!

To my wife, Sakinah, where do I truly begin? You have, and continue to be, the voice of reason and motivation to push forward. Always lending your ear, and perspective, this road that we continue to pave together has challenged me to bring my best version in whatever I strive for. Knowing my passion for writing, your support has kept me active within this space, even when my career has pulled me further away from it. Through the laughs and through the tears, you offer patience, reminding me that I can tackle anything, even when I think otherwise, and help me climb out of the holes I may put myself in. For this, I will forever be indebted.

Antija M. Allen

To my mother, Evelyne Moore-Cisse, your work ethic is truly contagious, and your support is endless. Without your love, constant words of encouragement, and willingness to lighten the load for me in any way you could, I don't think I would have been able to complete this project. I am grateful to you and for you.

To my co-editor, Justin T. Stewart, it is rare that I work with someone who can match my energy when it comes to getting things done and even rarer when I meet someone like you who surpasses it to the point where I feel like a slacker. I knew from working side by side with you at Allen Ivy Prep Consulting that you were not only a super-talented editor, but also an amazing partner. That's why when this book project landed on my heart, I knew there was only one person I wanted to ask to take this journey with me. Your patience, preciseness, consistency, and humor are what really got us to the finish line. You are a brilliant writer, and it has truly been an honor to take this ride with you. Thank you, thank you, thank you.

To my husband, Maurice, and children (Lily, Preston, Demetri, and Isaiah), thank you for being so patient with me as I followed my passion. Your love, smiles, welcome distractions, and insistence on celebrating every milestone along the way are what always kept me going. I am so lucky to have you all.

To my friends, my village, my tribe, thank you for always being there for me and cheering me on. I have no clue what I ever did to deserve you, but I am thankful.

***

To Cambridge University Press. We are grateful for your interest in our project and for providing us a platform to share our stories collectively. This has enabled us to elevate the voices and experiences of Black and Brown faculty and will serve as a call to action to usher in real change.

To the contributing authors. Thank you for your vulnerability in sharing your experiences in higher education and trusting us to handle this material delicately to ensure these topics were given the proper spotlight as we inch closer toward change for current and future faculty of color.

Breaking Our Silence

Antija M. Allen

When I first started teaching as an adjunct Psychology Instructor eighteen years ago, I taught at an institution where most professors, staff, and students were either Black or Hispanic. At that time, my only "real issue" was the fact that I looked much younger than I was, which resulted in me frequently being mistaken for a student. More an inconvenience than a struggle, for many years I knew that I was experiencing ageism, but as I grew older and moved into more predominantly white spaces, my experience began to change. I went from being one of several faculty of color to being one of very few people of color at the institution. Instead of being mistaken for a student, I was now being mistaken for the one staff or faculty member who was also a Black female.

According to the National Center for Education Statistics (2019), in fall 2017 there were 1.5 million faculty in degree-granting postsecondary institutions. Of this population, 53 percent were full-time and 47 percent were part-time. Demographically, 76 percent of full-time faculty were either white males or females, while only 3 percent were Black males and 3 percent were Black females. This research reveals that while many institutions tout the idea of diversity recruitment, not much progress has been made to diversify faculty ranks, especially at research-intensive institutions (Hazelrigg, 2019). In fact, professors are more likely than their students to be white (Flaherty, 2019).

This data makes it evident that there is an imbalance of diversity, resulting in unique experiences for Black faculty working in spaces as either the only Black faculty or being one in a limited population. Many times, this lack of representation will find Black faculty:

- feeling they do not belong or are not welcome (for example, lack of inclusion) at their institution;
- adapting their behaviors or identity (for example, code switching) to keep their white counterparts at ease;

- facing stressors (for example, microaggressions, microinvalidations, overt racism) that can lead to burnout and/or health (mental or physical) issues that, when compounded, will be detrimental in their professional and personal lives.

The idea that all Black faculty would share the same experiences is a fallacy, and the insinuation is as dangerous as assuming that all Black people are the same. In fact, not all Black people prefer the term "Black," which is why the contributing authors of this book will use several terms to refer to *Black faculty* such as: African American, minority, BIPOC (Black Indigenous People of Color), and People of Color (POC). With full awareness that Black faculty experiences are not monolithic, this book intends to serve as a voice and even a light for those who have endured (and are enduring) struggles and discrimination because of their race or, in some cases, because of the intersectionality of their race, sex, gender, sexuality, age, ability, and/or social status.

The purpose of this book is to:

- bring awareness to obstacles faced by Black faculty members in a predominantly white postsecondary institution;
- invite dialogue with the intent of ushering actual change that can benefit Black faculty, students, and institutions;
- identify positive or negative factors that impact the inclusion and retention of Black faculty;
- offer practical strategies, tips, and helpful hints to guide faculty, staff, and administrators.

While working at one institution, I remember frequently being greeted with big smiles and asked, "How's your brother?" While I do have an older brother, it is not something I tend to publicize with people I have never met before. Completely confused and usually in a hurry to get to my class or office to meet a student, I would just reply "He's fine," with a big smile, which always seemed to bring them relief. One day, I had time on my hands and a white colleague thrilled to see me asked the same question:

> "How's your brother?"
> "He's fine," I replied, "but I don't think you know my brother."
> "Of course, I do! He went to school here!"
> "No, my brother has never gone to this school."

Immediately, a look of confusion overcame her face and she suddenly seemed to be in a hurry, rushing off with a nervous smile. Later, bumping into a Black female staff member in the restroom, I asked if she had a brother, to which she replied yes. I then asked if he went to school here and she, of course, replied yes. At that point, I let her know that people had been mistaking me for her, and a state of confusion was now plastered on her face. Something quite evident to us, that apparently was not clear to several of our white colleagues, was that we looked nothing alike. The fact that there were so few Black female employees, I thought would have made it easier to distinguish between us. I would love to say that this was an isolated event and only happened at that institution, but no, I am still confused with my Black female colleagues, even on Zoom where names are displayed under our faces. To have spent months, and sometimes years, working closely with peers that I believed I had developed a bond with, this "innocent mistake" was truly disappointing.

This leads me to a topic that this book will address throughout, *inclusion*. Once an institution has hired a Black faculty member, there is this illusion of racial *diversity* being achieved, but a handful of People of Color among hundreds of white employees is not racial diversity, which is an issue that will be explored in later chapters. Once a Black person has been hired as full-time faculty, like any new hire, there is a desire to feel connected to the institution and their colleagues. Usually that connection comes from feeling welcomed, valued, seen, and heard. Imagine spending months working side by side with a colleague on a committee, only to realize that this person you thought you had connected with could not tell you apart from someone they had only had contact with a handful of times.

In the chapters that follow, several barriers to inclusion will be discussed including *microaggressions*. Microaggressions, a term introduced in the 1970s and defined as "subtle, stunning, often automatic, and nonverbal exchanges which are 'put downs'" (Pierce et al., 1978: 66), was used to describe subtle discrimination that Black Americans faced, primarily regarding stereotypical media portrayals (Nadal, 2018). The subtlety of microaggressions baffled me for many years. A white colleague or student would make a statement about me that seemed harmless, but somehow left me feeling uneasy. The most common are comments regarding my intellect, with white students referring to me as "intelligent" on evaluations or white colleagues raving about how "smart" I am during meetings. I say with certainty that if I were to react with anger or frustration, the commenter would insist that they were giving me a compliment.

Perpetrators of microaggressions presume that their behaviors are innocuous or well intentioned, while targets of microaggressions perceive perpetrators' behaviors as biased or malicious (Nadal, 2018). There are some who will read this unsure as to how being called intelligent is somehow negative. Having a student in my class or fellow faculty member tell me I am intelligent is the same as a Black individual being told they are "so articulate" or "speak so well." The covert message behind these statements is one of astonishment, similar to saying, "I cannot believe that a Black person is able to speak like this" or "I didn't know Black people were this intelligent." Sometimes, I feel like I am (or have been) regarded in my workplaces as if I'm a unicorn that they are amazed actually exists.

Many years ago during a job interview, two white women were asking me a series of the usual interview questions. One woman turned to me and asked, "How is it that you were able to get hired at such prestigious institutions," and then began to rattle off the places I had been employed at as if I was not aware of what was on my résumé. While I was thrown by the question, she asked it as if it was a normal question that is commonly asked of all interviewees. I sat there and actually explained why I was qualified to work at places like New York University and the Albert Einstein College of Medicine. While that incident was at least a decade ago, to this day it still bothers me. Strangely, I'm not as troubled that they asked me the question as much as I am that I took the time to answer it, as if they had the right to ask. By answering, I was giving them permission to ask other Black people with glowing résumés to defend their credentials.

I know there is a segment of the population that does not believe that much of what this book focuses on is real, perhaps considering that this entire book is just based on the delusions of some that discrimination against Black faculty is prevalent in higher education. In Part I, Chapter 5 Derrick Robinson will examine such *microinvalidations*, which K. L. Nadal has defined as:

> Verbal communications that dismiss, refute, or undermine the lived experiences of people of various marginalized groups. Microinvalidations can include situations in which people of color are told that they need to stop complaining about racism. Microaggression perpetrators assume that their perspective is the only possibility – thus invalidating the target's perspective and reality. (Nadal, 2018: 45)

Microaggressions are upsetting, no matter how subtle they may be. Like emotional abuse, they may not leave signs of physical harm, but the effect is just as painful. Then to be told that your experience is invalid is even more traumatic. These negative experiences significantly impact both psychological and physiological health, requiring adaptive coping strategies to ensure healthy psychological functioning (DeCuir-Gunby et al., 2020).

Therefore, in addition to sharing Black faculty experiences, *mental health wellness* is another focal point of this book. One goal of this book is to prevent or lessen the mental burdens that Black faculty carry by making administrators (existing and future) aware of their negative experiences and equipping them with practical strategies for how to address them. We are aware that there are Black faculty who will read this book and may be struggling with the trauma of systemic racism, the stress of the current COVID-19 pandemic, and may still be reeling from the constant killings of unarmed Black individuals. This is why, in Part II, we provide strategies for mental health that are directed at the faculty themselves.

Experiencing racial microaggressions can cause Black faculty to choose maladaptive coping strategies. Maladaptive coping strategies are negative or unhealthy methods that may increase stress because this form of coping is defined by attempts to remove stressors mentally, emotionally, and physically. According to DeCuir-Gunby et al. (2020), "this form of coping can result in the following: the suppression or internalization of feelings (for example, social withdrawal, self-criticism), physiological consequences (for example, high blood pressure), feeling isolated, and refusing to directly confront the racism experienced (for example, problem avoidance), among others" (p. 494).

I remember during my first week of work at an institution I will not name, I was being introduced to my new colleagues. At one point, they introduced me to a Black staff member, I'll call "Alicia." When Alicia's white male supervisor introduced her, he said, "This is Alicia, she's a good one," to which I immediately knew what that meant. She was quiet, did what she was told, and never complained. It seemed as if he was setting the tone for how Black employees were supposed to behave. I could be mistaken and for all I know that may have simply been Alicia's personality, but it was not mine. Yet I conformed, and I was "a good one." Then one day I realized I was not being fully my authentic self, which was not helpful to me, my students, or the institution, and I decided that I was no longer going to stay silent and be "good" for the sake of others' comfort at the cost of my own.

In general, when individuals are unhappy at their workplace, they decide to stick it out, either hoping it will get better or surrendering to the fact that it may never improve, while others will remain only until they have devised an exit strategy. This leads me to the final focal point of this book, *retention*. Too often, administrators who express an interest in the diversity, equity, and inclusion of faculty of color, will spend a great deal of time assessing Black faculty experiences. Employee satisfaction is measured through focus groups, confidential interviews, ad hoc committees, or surveys. Unfortunately, after data has been collected and reviewed, promises of future action are made, but rarely are any concrete plans implemented. In fact, there may be no mention of the data again unless it becomes a global issue like the protests and outrage that gained worldwide attention after the killings of George Floyd and Breonna Taylor.

What is disturbing is that following the data gathering, if there is any movement around an action plan, faculty of color are frequently tasked with the development and execution of the plan. Although retention will be touched upon throughout the book, Part III has chapters dedicated to both strategies for inclusion and retention of Black faculty, which go hand and hand, since, as the saying goes, "No one wants to stay where they're not wanted." The final chapter of this book provides profiles of model programs that have shown promise in diversity, equity, and inclusion (DEI). Institutions are encouraged to conduct a needs assessment prior to incorporating the various strategies recommended in that chapter and throughout the book.

For much of my time at predominantly white institutions (PWIs), I would (and still at times) feel the weight of being overloaded with work that was beautifully packaged as service to the college. I sat at tables that I was invited to, but then felt invisible as I listened to people talk around and at me, while never asking for my input. I often felt silenced when I did speak, sharing expertise that I thought was requested, but quickly realized I was there to diversify the group, not add to the discussion. There were countless times where I bit my tongue, instead of speaking up in disagreement, because I did not want to appear like the "angry Black woman." Remember, I am usually the only one or one of very few: they do not always see me as Antija or Dr. Allen, but sometimes as a representative for Black people or Black women. As such, I would never want to misrepresent my race and provide them with a reason not to hire more Black people.

I have asked the authors of this book to share their experiences, obstacles their colleagues have faced, and data they have gathered about Black faculty through their research. I could not expect them to be fearless in their willingness to contribute to this book without being the same. This is why this introduction not only presents what to expect from this book, but also reflects my own experiences as a Black faculty member over the years.

Exposing the negative experiences of faculty in PWIs can be risky for Black or Brown people because, despite what some may believe, systemic racism is very real, especially for those who are contingent or non-tenured faculty. As former civil rights leader and Representative John Lewis tweeted (2018): "Do not get lost in a sea of despair. Be hopeful, be optimistic. Our struggle is not the struggle of a day, a week, a month, or a year, it is the struggle of a lifetime. Never, ever be afraid to make some noise and get in good trouble, necessary trouble." For those of us who may feel alone, excluded, marginalized, and silenced, this book could be the catalyst for change. That's what makes this book worth the risk because we're not OK!

REFERENCES

DeCuir-Gunby, J. T., Johnson, O. T., Edwards, C. W., McCoy, W. N. & White, A. M. (2020). African American professionals in higher education: Experiencing and coping with racial microaggressions. *Race Ethnicity and Education*, 23(4), 492–508. doi: 10.1080/13613324.2019.1579706

Flaherty, C. (2019). Professors still more likely than students to be white. *Inside Higher Ed*. August 1. insidehighered.com

Hazelrigg, N. (2019). Slow going on faculty diversity. *Inside Higher Ed*. July 2. insidehighered.com

Lewis, J. @lrepjohnlewis (June 27, 2018). Do not get lost in a sea of despair. https://twitter.com/repjohnlewis/status/1011991303599607808

Nadal, K. L. (2018). *Microaggressions and Traumatic Stress: Theory, research, and clinical treatment*. Washington, DC: American Psychological Association.

National Center for Education Statistics (NCES) (2019). *The Condition of Education 2019*. Washington, DC: US Department of Education. https://nces.ed.gov/pubsearch/pubsinfo.asp?pubid=2019144

Pierce, C., Carew, J., Pierce-Gonzalez, D. & Willis, D. (1978). An experiment in racism: TV commercials. In Pierce, C. (ed.), *Television and Education*. Beverly Hills, CA: Sage, 62–88.

PART I

Experiences – The Journey from Student to Faculty

CHAPTER I

Why Are You Talking White? Code-Switching in Academia

Justin T. Stewart

Introduction

Inequities in representation associated with race are substantial across the United States of America, as evidenced by the lack of African-American faculty in colleges and universities. In fall 2018, of the 1.5 million faculty in degree-granting postsecondary institutions, 54 percent were full-time, and 46 percent were part-time. Of the full-time, roughly 75 percent were made up of white males and white females, while Black males, Black females, Hispanic males, and Hispanic females accounted for 3 percent each (National Center for Education Statistics, 2020: 150–3). Such a low percentage relative to the population illustrates the limited diversity among professors in higher education. Among faculty of color working at predominantly white institutions (PWIs), concerns regarding tenure, advancement, and retention remain constant as they fight to dispel any negative perceptions, fueled by biases, to be accepted and legitimized by their white colleagues and students. The manifestation of these perceptions has created hostile environments, with both covert and overt acts of racism directed at the intelligence and ability of Black faculty, all of which have proven to diminish paths to future opportunities. With these societal perceptions, a lack of representation and a sense of isolation, Black faculty feel pressure to resist their cultural identity and are challenged on how to approach the idea of being authentic within the classroom.

America is fascinated by the culture of Black people, but that admiration is not always present in the engagement of Black people. From a consumer base, Black culture's mainstream popularization has inspired lingo, fashion, entertainment, and overall lifestyle within the US. (Harris, 2019). The legacy of Jim Crow laws, the Great Migration, the civil rights movement, and now Black Lives Matter, however, has repeatedly demonstrated how the country perceives the people within this culture, being treated, at best, as second-class citizens. The strength of media outlets is also influential in groups developing negative opinions about one another based on prejudices and stereotypical portrayals, along with creating a social caste system that promotes structural racism. This hierarchy has been a factor in the self-consciousness of African Americans – being the lower tier and made to feel as though they are lesser than. Descriptors like "violent," "aggressive," "loud," "poor," "ghetto," "angry," "emotional," and "unintelligent" have profiled Black men and women in a history that can be traced back to the Minstrel Shows and Blackface of the nineteenth century (Clark, 2019). In a society where others are threatened by skin color, and complexion can be prioritized over character, Black people have found themselves at risk on a professional and personal level. As a defense mechanism, these marginalized groups have been raised to suppress their holistic selves in the presence of white culture, sometimes regarded as the "dominant culture," from adolescence onward.

Existing with the "double consciousness" identified by sociologist W. E. B. Du Bois, Black people are observing themselves through the eyes of the majority (Du Bois, 1903). Some feel this to be a requirement to present themselves in a manner that is "socially acceptable." Conflicted, however, by the assumptions of what others expect you to be, as opposed to who you are, these individuals are obligated to hide aspects of their natural presentation in professional settings while adapting to standards mandated by a white, male culture. Unfortunately, this often feels like a prerequisite for a Black person to be successful in America. While some debate this as superficial and performative, others deem it a necessary evil to establish credibility within predominantly white spaces.

When defining a professional or a leader, what are the qualities, traits, or images that come to mind? When picturing a professor, what does that individual look and sound like, and how do they behave? What does Google *show* you? Our perspectives, and the standards fulfilling these descriptions, can be problematic for outliers outside this prototype, and as a result, an unnecessary amount of pressure is applied to these perceived outsiders to fit into what is deemed acceptable (Stitham, 2020). These implicit biases are components of institutional racism and sexism, which has seeped into the fabric of higher education, impacting minority and female faculty.

Teaching at PWIs, and being immersed in a predominantly white culture, requires a sense of duality for African-American faculty to thrive. As the minority of the staff at these institutions, cultural expressions understood within their community do not easily translate for those unfamiliar with that community. Although culture is a foundational component of personal identity, the potential ramifications of this expression can be a gamble. Carefully navigating their actions throughout these professional spaces, where the idea of "Blackness" can be mischaracterized as inappropriate, finding a way to hide in plain sight and mask aspects of their individuality is critical to being viewed as a competent professional. In turn, this can be an exchange to unlock doors and enable access to the securities that further advance his or her career.

There is raised awareness, and a degree of tact, for Black faculty to exercise context and use the appropriate language with the appropriate audience. They must consciously bite their tongue, or be in tune with their emotions, to avoid the perception of overreacting, which can cause their points to be dismissed. The concept of "Blackness," and what it represents, is unfamiliar territory for white people and the expression of passion can be confused with being "disruptive," "aggressive," or "difficult." In a *Race, Ethnicity and Education* paper, Ebony O. McGee and Lasana Kazembe studied the experiences of thirty-three Black faculty members presenting research in academic settings. Twenty-four of those participating reported being subjected to comments regarding their "passion" or energy level. One respondent reported hearing; "He was so energetic and lively with his expressions. . . . Actually, he was so enthusiastic I thought he was going to do a little dance." Another reported hearing that he really needed to "tone it down a little" from a white colleague who said the audience might think his passion was "making up for a lack of research subjectivity" (McGee & Kazember, 2015).

As a guest on *Inside the Actor's Studio,* comedian and entertainer Dave Chappelle once said, "Every Black American is bilingual. All of them! We speak street vernacular and we speak 'job interview'. There's a certain way I gotta speak to have access" (Lipton, 2006). Known for his reflective comedy, such a dose of reality has served in holding a mirror to the state of society. The manner in which a person speaks in personal settings versus professional settings dictates how that individual wants to be perceived or how secure he or she feels within a certain environment. A 2019 survey revealed that 85 percent of Black adults sometimes feel the need to code-switch. Of those participants, 48 percent, with at least a four-year college degree, expressed the need to code-switch, compared to 37 percent without a college degree. Citing negative stereotypes regarding African Americans as the cause, these opinions have left them stigmatized, requiring additional effort to prove themselves, and be accepted in the workplace (Dunn, 2019).

Code-switching, a term introduced in 1954 by sociolinguist Einar Haugen, is described as language alterations, or the mixing of various dialects. Once considered a substandard usage of language, code-switching occurs when speakers alternate between languages or dialects within a single conversation. According to William B. Gudykunst, code-switching facilitates several functions: To mask fluency and memory in a second language; move between formal and informal conversation; exert power over another; and align with and unify among familiar groups in certain settings (Gudykunst, 2004: 1–40). Since Haugen, linguists have studied code-switching to identify *when* it occurs, while psychologists examined *why* it occurs, with particular interest in members of minority ethnic groups.

The act of altering language is not a new phenomenon, as people shift several times in a single day based on their interactions. There is a difference in how we communicate with parents, lovers, children, friends, and strangers. While still presenting yourself, there are certain aspects that are more prominent based on the dynamics of the relationship that boil down to context. The difference, when compared to code-switching, is a sense of authenticity, which is generally not the case with code-switching. As culture is not accepted holistically, the native tongue and expression of African Americans can be detrimental in certain white spaces. And while donning this mask can be seen as playing a character, it lessens the chances of faculty being categorized by a caricature and placates any presumptions another cultural group may have.

Throughout colleges and universities, some Black faculty have resorted to code-switching to assimilate with their white counterparts. By adopting white traits, conscious shifts in speech and presentation help to avert any stereotypes projected by peers and students. In many PWIs, Black faculty make up a small population, and being the token can add pressures to be *the* standard for all of their culture. "Talking white" can ease narratives, and in return, improve their prospects for future success and longevity in academia. As societal norms are dictated by the majority white culture, the idea of "whiteness" is the benchmark of normalcy and credibility.

Faculty of color, however, face a crossroads on whether the risk is worth the reward. The experiences of code-switching, positive and negative, differ from individual to individual. Downplaying ethnic traits has increased the perception of professionalism and the likelihood of being hired. By avoiding stereotypes, minorities can also be identified as having leadership qualities and afforded such opportunities. The other side of the coin, however, carries the burden of identity crisis, appearing "fake" with colleagues of your culture by projecting a false image to avoid being labeled the prototypical Black person. Simultaneously combatting stereotypes and trying to "fit in", Black faculty spend an inordinate amount of time proving themselves to white people across all levels, from leadership to peers to students. These pressures can lead to burnout for these professors, overcompensating to prove their value to the institution. In making the choice to be or not to be, it begs the question; do you have to be inauthentic to be accepted?

Meeting "the Qualifications"

Whereas earlier applications of code-switching primarily related to spoken language, modern usages have evolved, capturing various forms of language that define self-presentation including speech, appearance, behavior, and expression. This has also been applied to showcase qualifications and experience in job searches.

Marybeth Gasman, a higher education professor at the University of Pennsylvania who studies institutions with high minority enrollment, has described the lack of desire for institutions to hire Black faculty, shining a light on the selection process:

> I have learned that faculty will bend rules, knock down walls, and build bridges to hire those they really want (often white colleagues) but when it comes to hiring faculty of color, they have to 'play by the rules' and get angry when any exceptions are made. Let me tell you a secret – exceptions are made for white people constantly in the academy; exceptions are the rule in academe. (Gasman, 2016)

An article for *The Hechinger Report* in September 2016 detailed the experiences of Felicia Commodore, an African-American woman with a doctorate in higher education and a slew of published articles. Commodore expressed the difficulties she was having securing a college teaching job, having been regularly rejected. Questioning if race played a factor, she intentionally toned down her cover letter, downplaying any racial references. Having substituted terms like "African-American communities" with "cultural communities," she was conflicted when she then started to receive more traction from prospective institutions, stating "I wondered whether I wanted to be in a field, academia, where you have to whitewash yourself." Starting fall of 2016 as an associate professor of education at Old Dominion University at a crossroads, feeling that she had to compromise her identity to be in academia, Commodore understood what was needed to secure a job. Ironically, Commodore would add that, before working on her master's degree, she had never come across a Black tenure-track professor (Krupnick, 2016).

Minority job applicants, in an attempt to increase the likelihood of landing a position, are reported to "whiten" résumés. Deleting references to their race, they increase their chances in the job market. Research conducted by Katherine A. DeCelles, a professor of Organizational Behavior at the University of Toronto, identified bias against minorities during the résumé process at companies across the US. Co-authoring the September 2016 article "Whitened Résumés: Race and Self-Presentation in the Labor Market" in *Administrative Science Quarterly,* as part of a two-year study, the findings of DeCelles and her colleagues revealed that "whitened" résumés results in more job call-backs for African Americans.

In one study, researchers created résumés for Black and Asian applicants, distributing them to 1,600 entry-level jobs throughout 16 metropolitan sections of the US. Some résumés intentionally reference minority status for an applicant, while others were whitened. Additional techniques involved adopting Americanized names, with Asian applicants substituting "Luke" for "Lei," and Black applicants toning down affiliations to Black organizations. This scrubbing also applied to accolades, with a Black college senior omitting a prestigious scholarship from his résumé due to fear of his race being discovered. Data from these studies revealed 25 percent of Black candidates received callbacks with whitened résumés, compared to the 10 percent who left ethnic cues. The difference was also visible for Asians, with 21 percent callbacks for whitened résumés, contrasted to 11.5 percent without. Ironically, some of the companies that were part of the research identified as being pro-diversity (Gerdeman, 2017). Of these "equal opportunity employers," DeCelles noted that discrimination still exists in these organizations, and while they are not intentionally setting up these minority applicants, there is a clear disconnect in their diversity values versus the person screening resumes:

> This is a major point of our research – that you are at an even greater risk for discrimination when applying with a pro-diversity employer because you're being more transparent. Those companies have the same rate of discrimination, which makes you more vulnerable when you expose yourself to those companies. (cited in Gerdeman, 2017)

The Standards of American English: The Sound of Success

In the 2018 film *Sorry to Bother You,* African-American protagonist, Cassius Green, is a telemarketer struggling to make sales with customers. Seeking help, Langston, his colleague and fellow African American, advises that he use his "white voice."

> You want to make some money here? Then read the script with your white voice . . . It's sounding like you don't have a care. Got your bills paid. You're happy about your future. You're about ready to jump in your Ferrari after you get off this call. Put some real breath in there. Breezy like . . . I don't really need this money. You've never been fired, only laid off. It's not really a white voice, it's what they wish they sounded like. So, it's like what they think they're supposed to sound like. (Riley, 2018)

Cassius immediately excels in his newfound persona, climbing the ranks and gaining access to newer opportunities. He is, however, unable to lean away from his "white voice" and is urged by another Black co-worker, who has similarly ascended, never to stop using it. By presenting a favorable version of himself, one that made white executives feel comfortable, Cassius is afforded the opportunity to be successful. The central idea of a satirical film – that a voice can propel a person further than their skin tone – is the reality for many African Americans in the workplace. Director Boots Riley, spoke as a guest on *CBS This Morning*, expounding further and stating:

> Everything is a performance. In the movie, the white voice that they use is this sort of mythical thing that says 'Everything is okay'. That's like the performance of whiteness for some folks. (CBS This Morning, 2018)

The idea of adopting a "white voice," and what a person thinks they should sound like, is a tool to reach the desired outcome. Within traditionally white spaces, "sticking to the script" has enabled Black and other racialized communities to navigate effectively to gain access to opportunities. Whether this tactic is right or wrong is a subjective judgment, but for many, playing the game and leveraging politics within the work environment can be an enabler to reach the desired outcome of career advancement. In a study conducted by Shiri Lev-Ari, a psycholinguist at the Max Planck Institute of Psycholinguists in Nijmegen, it was determined that "we're less likely to believe something if it's said with a foreign accent" (cited in Erard, 2016). When exposed to non-native speaker accents – and taxed with the additional effort of processing unfamiliar speech – our brains are prompted to discriminate against that speaker. Conclusions about a person's profile relating to level of income, education, or social standing, can be drawn based on linguistic biases (Erard, 2016).

While some argue that the English language has been "bastardized," evidenced by its variations in dialects and the ability to manipulate and introduce new terminology through slang, Standard American English (SAE) still holds overall preeminence. African Americans, while native English speakers, encounter biases due to the dialect shared within their communities, generally referred to as African-American Vernacular English (AAVE) or Black English. Not widely accepted outside this culture, it has been described as "broken English" or speaking with "poor grammar," and is regarded as a display of low intelligence or lack of education (Retta, 2019). J. Michael Terry, an associate professor in the Department of Linguistics at the University of North Carolina at Chapel Hill, has identified an unequal valuation of languages in different spaces: "Those characteristics of language that become associated with people of color have such negative connotations and are viewed from the outside as being somehow not only different from but defective. And that's part and parcel of a view that says that people of color are somehow defective" (cited in Wesley, 2021). He added that while many people deviate from SAE, some deviations are marked in terms of class and do not count against you in the same way as those that are racially and ethnically marked.

Fluidity in conversation – being able to adapt speech to a particular audience – has been viewed as a strength that is used to great benefit by some Black faculty. To many, the ability to connect effectively with people from different social skills is a valuable trait. In Harris, 2019, professors shared their personal experiences, with some finding benefits and others expressing frustrations. Georgetown sociology professor Michael Eric Dyson has stated that he frequently code-switches in many of his speeches across the globe, going from "highfalutin theoretical discourse down to gut bucket reality." Dyson feels it is a necessity for the protection and preservation of Black culture: "We have to speak in front of white folk who understand what we are saying so we have to be covert with it" (Harris, 2019).

Business psychologist and coach Dione Mahaffey has leveraged the practice throughout her career. While tiresome, she understands the need to negotiate within white spaces:

> It's exhausting, but I wouldn't go as far to call it inauthentic, because it's an authentic part of the Black American experience. Code-switching does not employ an inauthentic version of self, rather, it calls upon certain aspects of our identity in place of others, depending on the space or circumstance. It's exhausting because we can actually feel the difference. (Harris, 2019)

Mahaffey continues to describe code-switching as an exchange, requiring give and take. She has used these performative niceties to her advantage when working in white spaces to learn what she needs, secure what she requires, and use it to create and build.

While this assimilation to standard language has proven to be successful for some, opposition remains toward the practice, with many perceiving "talking white" as a suppression of cultural expression. Derrick Harriell, poet and associate professor of English and African-American Studies at the University of Mississippi, has expressed his regrets with code-switching and has since made the decision to stop:

> I know certain forms of code-switching have been responsible for saving our lives as Black people and key to our survival, so in that way, I'm not judgmental. I understand that my ability to not code-switch is a privilege, but it's also a privilege my people died for, therefore for me, I have to [be myself] or else I feel as if I'm doing my ancestors a disservice. Amongst the Black community, there are those rejecting the notion of conformity in code-switching, feeling the sacrifice is too much. Culture is a foundational and an integral part of identity that should be expressed, but these shifts require an individual to dilute the idea of being the "best version of me." (Harris, 2019)

Myles Durkee, assistant professor of psychology at the University of Michigan, has done extensive research on racial code-switching, and detailed the added burden that code-switching can create for Black professionals:

> We actually find in our data with Black professionals that those who tend to code-switch more frequently, also report significantly more workplace fatigue and burnout from their current positions. Simply, because they have to be a different person and mask all the cultural assets that they probably value and appreciate internally. But they realize that those same traits aren't valued in their workplace. So they have to bring a completely different person to the workplace and basically keep that personality on throughout the workday. That can just be draining and likely will lead to mental health consequences, Durkee said. (Gill, 2021)

Token Black Faculty: The Pressures of Fitting In

As an outlier in PWIs, Black faculty face increasing insecurity, due to a lack of representation. This insecurity stems from the pressures of being one of a few, if not the only, faculty of color, which can cause these individuals to have higher visibility and be singled out for their racial identity. According to the National Science Foundation, only 6.4 percent of US citizen or permanent resident research doctoral recipients were Black and 6.5 percent were Hispanic (Krupnick, 2016). Additionally, while 13.3 percent of education doctorates are awarded to Blacks, they receive 3.5 percent of doctorates in the physical sciences. This disparity in representation creates an environment where these faculty members find themselves overworked in areas including diversity initiatives and hiring committees. As a small fraction of the community, being one of a few, if not the only, faculty of color, these tokenized Black professors implement code-switching to help avert any discrimination based on assumptions associated with their cultural identity.

Dating back to 2008, Black women in faculty positions remain underrepresented, showing little or no growth. African-American women were only 2 percent of all women faculty members in PhD departments, 3 percent of women faculty members in bachelors-only departments and 0 percent in masters-only departments (Porter & Ivie, 2019). Feelings of isolation and alienation have prompted these faculty to minimize their presence among male colleagues. In May 2020, *The Physics Teacher* journal reported that Black female faculty working in physics experience hyper-visibility, and as a coping mechanism, alter their behavior to counter any discrimination based on gender and racial stereotypes (Dickens, Jones & Hall, 2020). Women resort to "identity shifting" and intentionally change their behavior to appear less physically feminine and become more masculine verbally, or make other behavioral changes to be accepted. Assimilating to a predominantly white male culture, women have changed the tone of their voice to prevent it being mistaken for threatening. This shifting has yielded benefits for Black female faculty navigating these spaces, enabling them to make connections and build networks (Dickens, Jones & Hall, 2020).

While these strategies have been leveraged to counteract negative assumptions of what a Black man or woman is, or should be, within the workplace, having to become a minimized version has led to internal obstacles. Marla Baskerville Watkins, Aneka Simmons, and Elizabeth Umphress detailed these challenges in an analysis of eighty studies of token employees that had been undertaken between 1991 and 2016. Watkins commented that:

> Our review showed that tokens have higher levels of depression and stress. They're more likely to experience discrimination and sexual harassment than women and racial minorities who are working in more balanced environments. Research shows people are less satisfied and less committed at their jobs if they're tokens. Companies should be concerned about this, said Watkins. (Academy of Management, 2020)

In GaNun (2020), Black professors at the University of Georgia (UGA) detailed their perspectives as students and as faculty in academia. Working at UGA, these faculty members are part of an underrepresented Black population. Reported for fall 2019, only 5 percent of full-time faculty at the institution identified as Black or African American. Among these faculty is Paige Carmichael, a professor of pathology in UGA's College of Veterinary Medicine, where she has spent her entire teaching career, dating back to the 1990s. As the first African American in her department, Carmichael cited previous instances of microaggressions, to which she used code-switching in an attempt to fit in with the accepted majority. When expressing herself in feeling the need to suppress aspects of her heritage of culture, Carmichael has felt even further diminished due to the responses:

> I have heard somebody say to me, "Well, I had no idea you felt that way, Paige, I don't see you as Black." And I don't know what that means, because if you don't, then you're not seeing all of me, and if you're not seeing all of me, what else are you missing? (GaNun, 2020)

Challenges of Identity within the Classroom

Based on the low percentages of African-American faculty within PWIs, it would not be far-fetched if a student never had a Black professor, and remained accustomed to the traditional image of a professor solely as a white man instead. With limited or no experience of a Black person ever being the authority in the classroom, Black professors are often subject to negative attitudes and inappropriate behavior from students. While performing their duties in the classroom, they must actively manage their engagement within the classroom to resist the pressure to confirm or disprove students' beliefs that are projected onto them relating to their competence and capacity to be those students' professor.

Manya Whitaker, an associate professor of Education at Colorado College, has described "stereotype threat" as the experience of confronting negative stereotypes about race, ethnicity, gender, sexual orientation, or social status (Whitaker, 2017). Considered a social psychological construct, Whitaker details how people are, or feel themselves to be, at risk of conforming to stereotypes about their social group. Whitaker identifies women faculty who are members of racial minority groups as being most at risk of becoming stereotype threatened, experiencing anxiety about confirming or disproving the beliefs of students.

Whitaker further discusses how students' personal beliefs of what a professor should be and look like could be projected in the classroom. These descriptions can hold true for the traditional, older white male professor, but they are only a *part* of the faculty population, not *the* faculty population. Those that do not fit these criteria are challenged by expectations based on sexual and racial biases:

> To complicate matters, students have different expectations for faculty of different ethnic and racial backgrounds. Asian professors, for example, are supposed to be meek but very intelligent while Black professors are expected to be loud and aggressive. Males and females also face far different challenges in the classroom. Men are stereotyped as smarter than women so it's no wonder that students often challenge women about their qualifications, and evaluate them more harshly than men. (Whitaker, 2017)

In these instances, Whitaker indicates that these faculty of color and female faculty generally take one of two approaches: (a) confirm students' stereotypes; (b) disprove their beliefs. In confirming stereotypes, professors are avoiding tension that can come from challenging these perceptions from students, and instead opt to behave in a manner that aligns with the expectation of that student. Black female professors have leveraged false characteristics to become the loud, sexualized Black woman primed and prepped for an argument. In exchange for "method acting," they are better able to build a strong "relationship" with non-Black students. In disproving beliefs, which is the more common approach, with a weight of self-awareness related to cultural expectations, these professors consciously counter negative tropes. While not blatantly challenging these beliefs, they intentionally play counter to what their assumed behavior should be. The "aggressive" Black male professor, for example, will maintain distance from students, be mindful of his tone and avoid any explicit language.

While these tactics are understandable, Whitaker implores her own approach to simply be herself; a Black, young, Southern female who enjoys football. It is less about combatting what she is perceived as, and more about being intentional when describing who she is. Understanding that students are selective in accepting certain aspects of their professor, being herself, unapologetically, has helped to establish the foundation of these relationships.

Blurring the Lines: Your Personal Space or Your Professional Space

The impacts of COVID-19, and the requirement of keeping people socially distant, necessitated a transition from the usual on-site environment to a remote one for many workers. The home, a previous place of refuge, has become the office, which has presented a hurdle for code-switching as the boundaries of personal and professional space have become blurred. Our personal environments have been breached, now front and center with constant meetings over Webex, Zoom, Skype, and other web conferencing applications. The trigger that was presented when entering the physical office is more difficult now that our private space teeters the line on being the virtual office. Although the convenience of being at home has been embraced, there are additional obstacles as a result of these "living at work" arrangements.

Previously able to choose what they wanted to share, Black faculty are more out in the open with their personal lives on display once the Brady Bunch boxes appear for these virtual meetings. According to McCluney & Roberts (2020), working from home has signaled the need for code-switching to evolve, with BIPOC making their physical spaces "whiter." The use of virtual backgrounds or choosing not to turn on the camera are tactics adopted to avoid having at-home lives on display. McCluney, an assistant professor of organization behavior at the School of Industrial and Labor Relations at Cornell University, has described her fear of having her own cultural identity mischaracterized or misunderstood by colleagues due to having African cultural artwork on display that features bare-chested figures.

Shonda Buchanan, author and professor, shared her initial experiences in "Zooming While Black" as she transitioned to working from home. Accustomed to a more relaxed presentation at home, where she had full reign and freedom to be her *full* self, she has had to maintain awareness now that her living space is being broadcast to professional colleagues:

> As soon as my image leapt onto the videoconferencing screen, it dawned on me, a smiling African-American woman wearing a sleek, multicolored headband, that I was probably a little too relaxed in my appearance. I also realized that my colleagues, mostly white and Asian, were seeing me for the first time in my natural, fuss-free cultural state. In the classroom, I wear slacks or a skirt, a blouse, maybe a shawl. My hair is always neatly pulled back. I am prepared for that space. I have cultivated my image there over 18 years of university-level teaching – operating with the understanding that I am a role model by default. As such, I represent Black women and girls everywhere. But in a virtual space, with just my cute smile, unruly locs and quickly typed questions in the chat box, I felt odd and spatially closer than I'd ever been to my colleagues. A little more exposed. A little more vulnerable. Zoom offered a window into our private spaces, and closing off mine, like some others had done, wasn't an option. (Buchanan, 2020)

Buchanan continues that while she feels anxious on certain aspects of her cultural identity being amplified through this virtual window, her colleagues, mostly white and Asian, were not concerned at all with their own presentation.

Having a Seat at the Table

One could ask the question: Why is there still a need to code-switch? Surely, the culture of institutions has diversified enough for conformity to be no longer required. While somewhat true on a social level, the demographics of higher-ranking positions at colleges and universities tell a different story. According to 2017 data from the College and University Professional Association for Human Resources, white people held the majority of administrative positions (American Council on Education, no date). These positions include top executive officers, senior institutional officers, academic deans, institutional administrators, and heads of divisions, departments, and centers. With white employees accounting for more than 75 percent of higher education professionals, African-American employees made up less than 15 percent. Although the amount of Black faculty has steadily increased, the positions of power remain occupied, in abundance, by white employees, specifically white males. As the environments of PWIs do not disproportionately impact these individuals, they are less inclined, or incentivized, to dismantle these systems and advocate change. With limited diversity among executive leadership, the discussions, perspectives, and ultimately, actions, are skewed, making progress more laborious without the perspectives of the marginalized groups that are affected.

PWIs must make a shift in broadening their understanding of the plights of Black faculty within these colleges and universities to truly become allies. As guest speaker on the YouTube series *Women in Colour,* Nicole Neverson, a professor of sociology at Ryerson University, shares some of her internal struggles challenging her peers as the minority:

> When you're navigating a lot of these white spaces that are telling you your body is not a part of this space, or it's an unfamiliar body in this space, you sort of have to adopt the language and the movements of whoever has normalized that space. So, it's a very tricky thing and, on one hand it is survival, on the other hand, the way that I look at it, is it keeps on communicating to me who I am. And it keeps communicating to me the spaces where, as Vanessa said, I have to insert myself more. You make choices on "Okay, am I going to say something in this meeting? Am

I going to use the physical and emotional energy that I have, to break it down for these people and tell them that this idea that they've just proposed, it's no good?" And, it's actually not great for most students and it's only going to serve a certain type of student, and not all, or be more inclusive. (Women in Colour, 2020)

There have been reports, dissertations and articles detailing when and why code-switching is used for people of color, but discussions should also identify organizations that create these environments to necessitate this strategy. In Lloyd & Washington 2020, Courtney L. McCluney speaks at length on the subject, based on extensive research she has conducted with a colleague:

I think what makes code-switching a unique phenomenon, that institutions are responsible for creating the need and pressure to code-switch, is that it becomes attached to things that are not necessarily relevant for our given situation. So, I think about this a lot of times in the workplace where currently, in more states in this country, you can fire someone for wearing their hair in its natural state. There are no legal protections at the Federal level protecting someone's hair texture from being discriminated against and being considered unprofessional. (Lloyd & Washington, 2020)

While legislation from the CROWN Act (Create a Respectful and Open Workplace for Natural Hair), a law passed in California in 2019 that prohibits discrimination based on natural hair texture and style, is now under way in all states and federally, McCluney explains that it illustrates how code-switching requires individuals to deny natural aspects of themselves and, in continuing this adjustment, it provides validation of the stigma that is attributed to Black expression by not challenging it:

The problem with it is, over time, it can contribute to burnout. People are trying to learn to present themselves on top of doing their jobs, or existing in any given space, and that is quite mentally, physically, and emotionally exhausting. On the other hand, it also reinforces beliefs that the norms we have set in place in society are the default, and it is preferred. The norms are so preferred that even this Black person is adjusting how they speak and suggesting that the one right way of being is the white way of being. So, it reinforces the inequality that we are actually fighting against by code-switching and leaning into those ways of speaking, dressing, behaving, etc. (Lloyd & Washington, 2020)

Recommendations

Code-switching revolves around the need for African Americans to be legitimized within professional spaces that are predominantly white.

Existing at PWIs, this tool has enabled Black faculty to survive, as well as thrive, but it presents a gap in the infrastructure of these institutions in understanding culture, identity, and diversity, and has led to these professors feeling minimized, unsupported, and required to play a role to be accepted.

Through leadership acknowledging and monitoring any inherent bias against social class and cultural signals in faculty of color, there is an opportunity to re-evaluate expectations and welcome new methods of learning.

Elevating the Diversity of Campus Culture

This chapter has detailed the inequities for faculty of color throughout PWIs. Diversity, throughout all mediums of higher education, is a vital step in building a community that offers unique perspectives, along with showing that representation is a genuine priority.

In devising strategies for their respective institutions, leadership should:

- Assess the current diversity of senior leadership, hiring committees, and interview panels to ensure that all voices are present at the table and are representative of the campus population.
- Review policies and create criteria for the candidate interview process that seeks the most qualified individuals, while also promoting individuality.
- Invest in minority populations by visiting and recruiting talent from historically Black colleges and universities (HBCUs), and other under-represented cultural groups, to diversify the applicant pool of faculty prospects.
- Implement faculty developmental programs that expand scholarly activities to identify and develop leaders in the making.
- Host social networking events on campus that provide ongoing training for students, faculty, and non-academic staff to encourage interaction and discussion on diversity issues.

Implementing Cross-Cultural Groups and Events

As a minority at PWIs, Black faculty can feel, or be made to feel, like outsiders, struggling to fit in with standards that are not naturally representative of their respective cultures. PWIs should establish spaces within the workplace that encourage discussion on diversity-focused topics. These platforms should allow open dialogue to deconstruct implicit biases, which can help provide faculty of color the freedom and comfort to connect and freely express themselves without fear of reprimand. To drive efforts forward in creating a more inclusive environment, institutions should:

- Increase the amount of engagement channels to stimulate conversation among faculty with outlets such as Lunch and Learn sessions and Employee Resource Groups (ERGs) to champion diverse communities (for example, African American, Asian American, LGBTQIA+) and build cultural awareness and understanding across the campus population.
- Facilitate intimate focus groups/fireside chat sessions with a diverse panel of faculty and administration to share critical, thoughtful dialogue on experiences and challenges within the workplace.
- Partner with neighboring colleges and universities for networking events to expand professional connections and find new opportunities to connect with potential mentors and supportive colleagues.
- Administer quarterly surveys to faculty and administration through online platforms to gather feedback and insight that can identify opportunities to improve the work environment and increase overall job satisfaction.

Moving Forward as Black Faculty in PWIs

As a person of color at a PWI, the struggle of identity and authenticity remains the conundrum of being visibly Black while trying to avoid being the stereotypical Black. It is the difference between feeling safe or insecure in your own skin. The acceptance of appearance with the rejection of assumed behavior that comes with being Black has muted opportunities to learn how that culture can effectively be integrated into the workplace instead of imposing a single "white is right" standard.

For faculty of color, the demands of daily code-switching, juggling the presentation of yourself with teaching, and assessing the culture of your institution, will ultimately lead to a decision about remaining in or departing from that system. The need to be constantly "on" can be physically, emotionally, and psychologically exhausting in trying to express yourself without falling into negative cultural expectations. It is pertinent to observe and evaluate the environment within the institution thoroughly against the values that you hold for yourself. Achieving success may be your goal, but when this is at the expense of happiness, is it worth it? In developing your own sense of safety, you should be immersed in spaces that nurture who you are instead of feeling forced to overcompensate for what you are not. Ultimately, this decision rests with you.

REFERENCES

Academy of Management (2020). Research shows us workplaces need this level of diversity to prevent tokenism. *Fast Company*. https://bit.ly/3l1Mpsm

American Council on Education. Postsecondary faculty and staff. College and university administrator positions. https://bit.ly/3zlxIGI

Buchanan, S. (2020). Zooming while black. *Sisters Letter*. https://www.sistersletter.com/culture/zooming-while-black

CBS This Morning (2018) Director Boots Riley on the "mythical white voice" in "Sorry to Bother You". July 16. YouTube. https://www.youtube.com/watch?v=QooDl8UHvPU

Clark, A. (2019) How the history of blackface is rooted in racism. *History*. https://www.history.com/news/blackface-history-racism-origins

Dickens, D., Jones, M., Hall, N. (2019). Being a token black female faculty member in Physics: Exploring research on gendered racism, identity shifting as a coping strategy, and inclusivity in Physics. *The Physics Teacher*, 58(5), 335–7.

Du Bois, W. E. B. (1903). *The Souls of Black Folk: Essays and sketches*. Reprinted 1989. New York: Penguin Books.

Dunn, A. (2019). Younger, college-education black Americans are most likely to feel need to "code-switch". *Pew Research Center*, https://pewrsr.ch/32eMKBl

Erard, M. (2016). The reason you discriminate against foreign accents starts with what they do to your brain. *Quartz*. https://bit.ly/3cJyItm

GaNun, J. (2020). Being Black in the "ivory tower": UGA faculty members share experience in academia. *The Red & Black*. https://bit.ly/3nJ7noV

Gasman, M. (2016). The five things no one will tell you about why colleges don't hire more faculty of color. *The Hechinger Report*. https://bit.ly/3DLM7gv

Gerdeman, D. (2017). Minorities who "whiten" job resumes get more interviews. *Harvard Business School*. https://hbs.me/349H4JP

Gill, K. (2021). What is code-switching? How does it impact the Black community? *Local 4: Click On Detroit*. https://bit.ly/3r2AWfS

Gudykunst, W. B. (2004). *Bridging Differences: Effective intergroup communication*. Thousand Oaks, CA: Sage.

Harris, I. (2019). Code-switching is not trying to fit in to white culture, it's surviving it. *Yes!* https://bit.ly/3l13FoM

Krupnick, M. A. (2016). Colleges' promises to diversify face one challenge: Finding black faculty. *The Hechinger Report*. September 12. https://bit.ly/30SIhDF

Lipton, J. (2006) Dave Chappelle. *Inside the Actor's Studio*. YouTube. https://www.youtube.com/watch?v=7kVdcmdNjDE

Lloyd, C. & Washington, E. (2020). What's so bad about code-switching at work? *Cultural Competence: Gallup Center on Black Voices*. https://bit.ly/3HXkAvl

Matthew, P. A. (2016). What is faculty diversity worth to a university? *The Atlantic*, https://bit.ly/3CIIQgK

McCluney, C. & Roberts, L. (2020). Working from home while Black. *Harvard Business Review*. https://hbr.org/2020/06/working-from-home-while-black

McGee, E. O., Kazembre, L. (2015). Entertainers or education researchers? The challenges associated with presenting while black. *Race, Ethnicity and Education*. 19(1), 96–120. doi: 10.1080/13613324.2015.1069263

National Center for Education Statistics (NCES) (2020). *The Condition of Education 2020*. Washington, DC: US Department of Education. https://nces.ed.gov/pubsearch/pubsinfo.asp?pubid=2020144

Porter, A. M. & Ivie, R. (2019). *Women in Physics and Astronomy, 2019*. American Institute of Physics. https://bit.ly/34fpaWi

Retta, M. (2019) The mental health cost of code-switching on campus. *Teen Vogue*. https://bit.ly/3nHOJqb.

Stitham, K. (2020) How bias influences perception: Three lenses. *Transformative Readership*. https://bit.ly/3eKVMJj

Wesley, N. (2021). "A necessary evil": Code-switching calls for alteration of dialect. *The Daily Tar Heel*. https://bit.ly/3r1uyW9

Whitaker, M. (2017) Do their stereotypes affect your teaching? *The Chronicle of Higher Education*. March 22. www.chronicle.com

White, C. C. R. (2018) How African Americans have influenced style and culture. *TIME*. https://time.com/5134486/how-to-slay-black-fashion-influence

Women in Colour (2020) Black women in education: Barriers, competition, code-switching. September 3. https://www.youtube.com/watch?v=PgQaptpwjNE

CHAPTER 2

Classroom Dynamics: Uncovering Hidden Truths while Black

Shaquille O'Neal Marsh

"We must play by a different set of rules."

These were the opening words of a conversation I had with a Black male student about the reality of being a Black professional in higher education.

"That is not fair," the student protested, to which I had to respond:

"It may not be fair, but it is reality."

Introduction

When I was approached by the student about being Black in higher education, my emotional state shifted from sadness to curiosity. I experienced sadness because the conversation I was about to have with this student needed to inform him of hard truths about being Black in the academy. Then, I experienced curiosity because, for the first time in my academic career, I questioned if I was doing enough outreach to minority students who felt out of place in a higher education system that was not set up for them to succeed.

During the discussion, I talked about my experiences of being a Black college professor at predominantly white institutions (PWIs). To provide context, the student and I both earned undergraduate degrees from a PWI in a Southern state in the United States. However, the student sought information about my experiences from a working professional's standpoint, and not from a student's point of view. The opening line at the start of this chapter was difficult to say to the student. I wanted to instill confidence in the student that he could pursue a career in higher education at a PWI, but provide helpful information that will help him succeed once he completed graduate school and started his career.

As the conversation progressed, the student expressed interest in becoming a college professor. This part of the dialogue is where the questions became more specific for the student to answer. The reason for this is that Black students pursue graduate education with some choosing a career as a college professor and many, I would argue, are not prepared for a future in the academy. Moore, Hines-Martin & Gattis (2020) have stated that new Black faculty members are often unprepared to assume their roles upon graduation. A future where they are the first, or only, person who looks like them in their respective academic department(s). In fall 2018, the National Center for Education Statistics found among degree-granting postsecondary institutions, of full-time professors, 3 percent were Black males, Black females, Hispanic males, Asian/Pacific Islander females, while 53 percent were white males, and 27 percent were white females (2021).

I proceeded to have the student recall the number of Black professors he had studied under while an undergraduate. "Zero (0) professors, with his left hand motioning zero," he stated. I then told him to think about that number and reflect on why minorities may be reluctant to pursue a career in academia as a professor. I went on to tell him that, in my time in graduate school (masters and doctorate), I did not study under any Black professors. Zero.

Pursuing higher education can be a change agent for students, but the system itself can be resistant to change. This situation makes for a compelling dichotomy. As ethnic minorities and other marginalized groups seek higher education for opportunities to meet professional and personal goals, colleges and universities are not meeting the needs of these students. Kelly, Gayles & Williams (2017) state that the experience of Black faculty is one of the many factors that can contribute to a poor campus climate for marginalized students. If the marginalized faculty do not feel a sense of belonging at a PWI, how can marginalized students? The academy must examine itself to ensure that the needs of all students and faculty are being met.

Graduate schools in the US strive to provide students with opportunities to seek specialized knowledge in a particular area. While college is supposed to "even the playing field" for minorities, this may not be the case in all situations. Racism, microaggressions, loneliness, and expectations to fit within an academic department culture (which is more often than not white and male) await many Black students as they enter the academy. The book knowledge obtained in graduate school may improve Black students' qualifications to obtain an academic job, but graduate schools may not prepare Black students for the overt and covert ways that may keep them from advancing in their academic careers, even forcing some to leave the academy altogether.

The focus of this chapter is to provide insights into a Black faculty member's experiences of being Black in graduate school and teaching while Black at PWIs in the Southeastern United States. Additionally, hidden truths about being Black in the college classroom will be unveiled. The chapter will conclude with specific strategies in which diversity, equity, and inclusion programs at PWIs can help faculty and staff members assist undergraduate and graduate students develop inter-cultural competence. This may in turn mitigate the concealed realities for Black professors teaching in predominantly white college classrooms. Also, advice will be given to human resource departments and decision-making gatekeepers at PWIs on retaining Black faculty, who often do not feel supported.

Graduate School Experience and First Time Teaching at a Predominantly White Institution

I pursued my graduate education (masters and doctorate) from the same PWI. As a first-generation student, I decided the best way for me, as a Black male, to improve my socioeconomic status would be to pursue graduate education in the hope of leveling the playing field in obtaining a job once I left graduate school. I attended a PWI for my undergraduate education, so I thought that the student experience of attending a PWI for graduate school in the South would be no different. Morris & Monroe (2009) argue that most contemporary educational and social science studies ignore the South as a critical, cultural, political, and economic backdrop in Black education. The Pew Research Center found that in 2019 the Southern United States had the highest share of the country's Black population at 56 percent (Tamir, 2021).

My decision to attend a graduate school was not without the counsel of family, friends, and mentors helping me along the way. For the most part, almost everyone I talked to was supportive of my decision, but I did have people who advised against my move and made discouraging remarks about the decision. I recall one conversation with a fellow Black male who told me that I would not be welcomed into the academy because I was Black. Hurt and disappointed, for a moment, I did hesitate about pursuing graduate education. But, once I got over the initial discouragement, I gathered my thoughts and expressed to many around me that I desired to be a fighting example not only for Black students, but also for any students perceived to be different, who feel out of place or unwelcome in higher education.

I applied to several graduate programs and participated in two campus visits. I had a mental construct that all PWIs would be the same, in terms of campus culture and resources, but this was not my impression following the visits. This is why I encourage all students to follow the advice of guidance counselors, teachers, and administrators who encourage them to visit the college campus first before committing to attend the institution. There was a clear choice on which institution I wanted to attend due to the campus environment, professors, and staff. In addition, the academic, professional, and personal resources offered at this institution had a major impact on my decision to choose it to pursue my graduate education. Along with choosing this institution to pursue my graduate degree, I was fortunate to be awarded a graduate teaching assistantship to help pay for my education. Teaching is my passion, so being awarded an assistantship helped reaffirm my love of it.

Prior to the start of the academic year, all the graduate teaching assistants were required to attend a mandatory orientation to learn about the responsibilities of the job. Entering graduate school, I had a preconceived notion that I would see more students who looked like me, even at a PWI, but I was wrong.

At the first meeting for graduate teaching assistants, I realized that I was the sole minority in the room, but thought that was no problem, since this had been common when I was an undergraduate. Being the "token" Black guy had also been my norm while growing up in a predominantly white hometown.

Realizing that I was the "token," I worked hard to be visible in my department as a graduate student and teaching assistant. In my mind, I was going to prove to everyone that I belonged there and they (the graduate committee that had made the decision to admit me) had not wasted their money or time on a Black guy. I wanted to be successful and not disappoint anyone. Whenever potential new graduate students toured campus, I would be present to welcome them. If the department needed a volunteer for some event, I showed up and volunteered my time. I needed to feel like I belonged and was a part of the academy, even if it meant sacrificing time, energy, and even changing who I was, as a person, to fit in.

Being one of the few minority students in my graduate program, learning from my mostly white professors or teaching at the front of the room in front of mostly white undergraduate students, left me uncomfortable at times. This discomfort could be attributed to walking on campus and not seeing minorities in any positions of power such as faculty, staff, and senior administrators. When I did see a non-white person, it was often not as an academic, but in a service capacity, such as a janitor or cook. Be clear, I am not saying that these jobs are inferior. However, what I am saying is that seeing people that looked like me only in the capacity of physically serving others started to take a mental toll.

My graduate school experience foreshadowed my reality as I pursued a career as a college professor. I used this as motivation to tell myself that the path I was about to partake in would not be easy, but I am pursuing it for the Black and other minority students feeling out of place in higher education who will succeed me. If only one student, no matter who they are, has me as a teacher or sees me in the hallway and that helps propel that student into academia, I know I will have accomplished my goal to be the representation that student needs to become a higher education professional.

In terms of teaching, all graduate teaching assistants were required to attend training on teaching, conducted by the teaching and learning center at my institution. The training provided participants with specific strategies that could be used once they began teaching. This introduction was good for specific strategies that we could use once in the classroom, but it did not provide us with all the information, such as the student population these strategies were tested on. Graduate teaching assistants enter the classroom with an array of experiences and strategies that work on one student population, but may not work on another.

After this training, I realized that it did not focus on an important part of the teaching and learning process, the human component – the relationship between the instructor and the student. The training did not account for cultural differences among the students and the instructors. I took a course in intercultural communication as an undergraduate student. Reflecting on what I learned in the class, it made me aware of the cultural differences between my students and I. The teaching approach I use may not be effective in reaching my white students at a PWI: Is my teaching style too aggressive? Was my tone of voice threatening? Were my class activities too thought-provoking for students who may not care about learning new perspectives? Will I be viewed as another Black man with a social justice agenda? These questions, and more, ran through my mind and impacted how I approached teaching and managing my classroom. However, I did not realize that I was experiencing what is now known as "stereotype threat" and "imposter syndrome." Stereotype threat surmises that African-American students, when cognizant of the fact that a standardized test, task, or their mere presence, can in some way be perceived to measure their intelligence or value, will experience anxiety regarding their ability to perform in academic settings (Steele & Aronson, 1995). Imposter syndrome describes high-achieving individuals who, despite their objective successes, fail to internalize their accomplishments and have persistent self-doubt and fear of being exposed as a fraud or impostor (Kolligian & Sternberg, 1991). Also, "implicit bias" played a factor in why I felt this way. Beckles-Raymond (2020) defines implicit bias as our biases understood as (a) beyond our cognitive awareness and (b) beyond our control. These two factors in the classroom will be discussed later in the chapter.

Stereotype Threat in the Classroom at Predominantly White Institutions

Before I became an instructor of record, I was able to learn different teaching strategies by sitting in class sessions with different instructors. I was a recitation lab leader for a lecture class of 200 students, where I was responsible for covering the material learned in the lecture with fifty students. Each recitation lab had twenty-five students in it, so I led two recitation labs.

For the first time in my academic career as a recitation lab leader, I was faced with a group of students alone in an academic setting where I assigned grades for assignments. I had no prior training in classroom management, and I was worried about student complaints and attitudes toward me as a leader in the classroom. I took a class in conflict management in my undergraduate career, so I drew upon those tools. However, I did not have conflict management training in the classroom. Adding to this situation, I was a Black teacher in a classroom with mostly white students. Parker & Neville (2019) argue that opportunities for cross-racial interaction often occur in the classroom primarily between students rather than faculty, as the majority of faculty are white. Different cultural backgrounds and standpoints are all I could think about.

I decided almost immediately to take what I deemed the safest route to teaching students in the recitation labs: (a) Review and teach the material in a generic fashion so students did not complain about me to the instructor of record of the course or anyone in administration. (b) Provide examples that are not controversial or do not touch on hot button issues. I picked up these strategies in graduate school while a recitation lab leader, then as an instructor of record. I did not learn these strategies from past teachers; I learned these instinctually while learning to navigate teaching at a PWI instead. It developed as a survival mechanism for me to succeed in teaching while (being) Black. Even as a full-time faculty member, I use these strategies. I would argue that I could not reach my full teaching potential without implementing these strategies. Sad, but true. I do not want to be called in for a meeting with any supervisor stating that I had made anyone feel uncomfortable or that I had been unfair in grading any assignment, though that experience can happen no matter what the instructor does in the classroom. McGowan (2000) found that African-American faculty perceive that some white students are more ready to report their concerns and critiques to the professor or to that person's superior (supervisor or boss).

On top of not rocking the boat while teaching undergraduate students, I did not feel like I could contribute to the discussion in my graduate courses. I often felt out of place and like the stupid person in the room. I was experiencing imposter syndrome. Once this feeling of being an imposter faded, I found graduate work to be awesome because you get to explore new ideas more in depth. I wondered, as I pursued graduate work, why there was a lack of minorities (teachers and fellow students) in my program or at the institution overall. In my entire time in graduate school, I did not enroll in a course that was taught by a Black professor. It was also rare that I came into contact with or engaged in a conversation with other minority students.

During my first semester in graduate school, I questioned if I belonged at the institution. I questioned if I was smart enough to understand the complex ideas I was learning. I questioned if my professors viewed me differently, academically, as a student, since I was often the only Black male in the room. It did not help my confidence when, in my first semester of graduate school, a white male professor told me that I was not cut out to complete graduate work successfully. To me, this was coded language that I was not smart enough to complete graduate work at that institution where I was the minority. This led me to wanting to drop out of graduate school after my first semester. Tears flowed down my face and anger followed as I navigated this new terrain. It was evident to me that some instructors at the institution were not aware of cultural differences among their students. The apathy toward the differences among students was something that I did not expect as a graduate student. Outright hatred is not something that I respond to well as an individual.

With my pursuit of graduate education, I learned that to survive in academia, I had to develop thick skin and not let things bother me to the point of quitting. I learned to accept harsh criticism that would not only attack the work I produced, but who I am as a person. This interaction with my white male professor was foreshadowing what I was going to experience being Black and working at a PWI.

African Americans are often subject to stereotype threat within academic settings. When teaching at a PWI, Black faculty members may feel the pressure of not meeting the expectations of Black stereotypes. I have experienced stereotype threat at the three institutions I have taught at, two public two-year community colleges and one public four-year research-intensive land, sea, and space grant institution, all in the South. My experiences come from being a recitation lab leader, a graduate teaching assistant, an adjunct, and a full-time tenure track professor.

Stereotype threat has manifested itself in several ways for me at PWIs. For example, I know for some of my white students from the South, I may be the first, or only, Black professor who will be in front of the classroom serving as their teacher in their educational career. Redlining and hiring policies play a major role in why students may not experience having a teacher who is different from them, but this is a conversation for another day.

Stereotype Threat One: Skin Tone

The effort involved in not being viewed as the "scary Black man" takes a toll mentally and physically. This may be because I am a six-foot tall man with brown skin. Mentally, I prepare myself to not live up to any stereotype that is affiliated with being a Black man. Physically, I make sure to walk with an open body posture that seems inviting. I walk at a pace that seems like I am not rushed or hurried. I make eye contact and smile with every person I encounter to ensure the other person knows that I am not threatening. At the end of each day, my face hurts from all the smiling. In addition, I can relax and be my true self, which experiences both positive and negative emotions.

If I ever show negative emotions in the classroom, I feed into the media trope of the "scary Black man," someone who is going to harm others and comes across as threatening. Harper (2015) finds that Black males report that their white peers assume Black men have a scary or threatening appearance. Every time I walk into the classroom, I must make a conscious effort to perform to the best of my abilities.

When students evaluate the classes I teach, the comment that appears consistently is that I am intimidating. Though I do my best to smile, ask engaging questions, and allow students as much freedom to explore their ideas in the classroom, this comment has remained throughout my academic career. Having even one "off day" will result in negative student perceptions in the classroom. An "off day" could be not smiling each day or not physically feeling my best to teach. Each class session I try to establish a welcoming classroom where all viewpoints are heard. But, for me, my skin tone is often the first thing my students see. This is difficult to start off a class in the negative where I want students to grow academically, personally, and professionally.

Stereotype Threat Two: Attire

Just like women in the academy are criticized for their attire while teaching in the classroom, so am I as a Black professor. It seems to me that my white male colleagues can wear any attire they like and not lose credibility with students and colleagues. Over the course of my career, I have seen some of my white male colleagues wear Hawaiian shirts, wrinkled T-shirts, flip flops, tank tops, shorts, jackets with writing on them, and even pajamas, when going to teach their classes. I, however, am mindful to wear business casual attire when engaging with my colleagues and students.

Slater, Arguete & Mwaikinda (2017) examined the effects of professors' race and clothing style on student evaluations. They found that students, overall, rated white professors more favorably than Black professors. Also, students trusted Black professors more when the professor was dressed more formally, compared to casual clothing. My credibility as a Black professional working in higher education is tied to how I am dressed daily. If I were to be seen in any of the leisure attire mentioned, my credibility would be tarnished, not only by my students, but also by my colleagues.

Stereotype Threat Three: Speaking Style

The third stereotype threat that keeps me self-aware is my speaking style. Being from the South, most people may prejudge me and think that I am not educated or lack basic etiquette. As an undergraduate student, I was required to take a Voice and Diction class to graduate with my undergraduate degree. This class proved to be invaluable because I was able to learn to adapt my voice to different situations and settings. A form of code-switching, I often ask myself if I am being my true self. When I go back to my hometown, I am often challenged with balancing my smalltown background prior to attending college, and the post-college version of myself. I recall visiting my hometown's post office to send a letter, when the local clerk asked me where I was from. When I told the clerk that I was from the area, the person responded that I did not sound like I was.

Frustratingly, I am confronted with the stereotype threat of "talking Black" or "not talking Black." I have been called an "Oreo" by many Black and white students in my time in the academy. Moore and Toliver (2010) have argued that though a professor's skin may be Black, style of diction within an institution might cause him or her to simply look like a darker version of the faculty members as a whole. Some white students are surprised that I am articulate and can pronounce words "correctly." Some of my Black students are also surprised by this, but then tell me that I talk "white." In the classroom, these experiences make it challenging for me because it seems like I cannot relate or appeal to any of my students.

Stereotype Threat Four: Choosing When to Speak

A fourth stereotype threat is choosing when it is appropriate to speak up and correct something. In certain situations, students may say things that I deem inappropriate, such as demeaning language targeting certain groups of people. Sue et al. (2011) found that Black professors experienced an internal struggle between balancing their own values and beliefs with an attempt to remain objective when different racial dialogues occur. Most of the time, I do not say anything to a student who has made an inappropriate comment, and many may ask why. I am regularly the lone Black person in the room discussing a topic with a mostly white student population. I do not want to be viewed as the angry Black man while teaching, justifying suggestions that I am using the race card or that I only defend marginalized groups. If I am too assertive in defending a group of people, I could be viewed as a social justice warrior with an agenda.

Stereotype Threat Five: Educational Level Challenged

A fifth stereotype threat I am faced with is when students doubt that I have obtained the proper level of education to teach them and question my qualifications. Although I hold a doctorate degree, I had one situation where a white male student asked me to produce a copy of my master's degree certificate on the first day of class. Is it surprising that a student would even consider asking a teacher such a question?

Related to the stereotype threat of having students view me as less educated than my white counterparts, some white students often ignore my official title of "Doctor" (Dr.). Some of my white colleagues allow their students to call them by their first name, claiming it reduces the power dynamic. I have, however, heard many of my white students call some of my white colleagues Doctor, when they do not hold a doctorate degree. Why is this the case? Many white students may have interacted with white professors who have doctorate degrees. This is not the case for Black or minority professors. If minority professors do hold a doctorate degree, some white students may not acknowledge their title due to a lack of understanding, care, or even recognition that minorities can be as educated as anyone else. Recalling that less than 3 percent of the full-time professors in the academy are Black, it is unsurprising that some students can have difficulty calling me Doctor.

Some people may call me egotistical for making my students call me Doctor because they may think I am using it for power. It is easy to say that if that person has the power to choose whether to have their students call them by their first name or "Doctor Whoever," but no, I am not using it for power. For me, the title is used to honor and respect those who fought for the right for Black people to earn an education. When an entire culture of people, like Black people, were not able to obtain higher education in the country, the distinction of "Doctor" holds a special place in my heart because minorities had to overcome and continue to fight systemic racist barriers. Calling a professor of color who has earned a doctorate by their title is important because representation matters. It matters because minority professors with doctorates should be the norm, not an exception. The title of "Dr." matters because it can serve as a model for minority students to emulate. My hope is that the future doctors who come after me surpass what I have accomplished. The title of "Dr." potentially gives minorities a seat at the decision-making table of academia and therefore a positive impact on all of humanity.

Implicit Bias in the Classroom

Having implicit bias does not mean that someone is intentionally being malicious. Everyone has implicit biases, as it is formulated through our everyday lived experiences. The biases that we have are mental shortcuts to help us organize the world around us without taking up mental energy. We should however have the goal of ensuring that our implicit bias does not cloud our judgment about others as we interact.

How does this implicit bias play out in the classroom? The initial implicit bias may start well before any students arrive. The way people judge a person by a name can lead to implicit bias. A student may be more apt to take a professor's course who has a "white" sounding name than one who does not. This is supported by Mendez & Mendez (2018), which found that based on names, students preferred taking the courses of white faculty members rather than those of non-white faculty.

I remember an instance where a white female student would not take a class with a professor whose name was not a traditional "white" American name. I asked the student if she had had a previous class with the professor before and she said no. She said that she would not take a class with that specific professor because she has interacted with people on the phone from that professor's perceived ethnic/cultural background and she could not understand them. Therefore, she decided that since this was the case in those situations, the same must hold true for the teacher. This blunt honesty shook me to my core as I could only imagine how students regard me in the classroom without any previous experience of interacting with me. So, explain to me how obtaining a graduate degree helps level the playing field for minorities in higher education?

Parker & Neville (2019) found that white students who took a course with a Black professor were at the entrance phase of racial identity development, with little to no racial consciousness, when entering the college environment. Many students in the study stated they did not see color and believed that racism was no longer a societal issue. The color-blind mentality that many of the students exhibited demonstrated that implicit bias is a real issue that people need to confront in order for social change to occur.

Related to this lack of racial consciousness by some white students entering college, I remember an incident where I was discussing hate speech and the implications of it in a public speaking setting. A white male student stated that minority groups needed to stop being so sensitive. Being the only Black person in the room in front of my mostly white class, I asked him why he felt this way. He replied that that his father had been passed over for a promotion by a Black guy and the only reason the Black guy had got it was his race. The student stated that reverse racism is occurring and that it was not right. After that, the student stormed out of the room without allowing me to respond. The next day, the student dropped my class. In my experience, this does not happen often. Most students choose silence over speaking out when discussing racial issues (Sue et al., 2011). The student did not allow for civil discourse to occur, believing only that his standpoint was the right one and no one could tell him otherwise. This overt form of hostility is an example of some of the challenges that Black faculty face at PWIs when discussing complex societal issues with students.

It is natural for people to gravitate toward people who look and act similarly to themselves. This is called the "mere exposure effect." Zajonc (2001) defines it as the repeated exposure to a stimulus, increasing liking for that stimulus. A reality I am faced with being Black, at a PWI, is having students uncomfortable interacting with me in the same way they do with my white colleagues. Media portrayals of African Americans play a role in this interaction. If students constantly see Black people as criminals or violent on local and national news stations, they can easily mischaracterize and bring these impressions into the educational arena. As previously mentioned, on student evaluations, I consistently receive comments that I am "intimidating." No matter how much I smile, no matter how my voice communicates that I am trying to be welcoming, no matter how I structure a class, I know that society has deemed me as scary, and I may not reach as many students as I would like to.

The first day of classes highlights the implicit bias that students, unconsciously, exhibit toward me. Toward the end of the first day, I leave time for students to ask me questions about the class, the content, and concerns I should be aware of as their professor. Over the duration of my career as a college professor, I have noticed something about students and the amount of space they place between themselves and me. For my minority students, they are more likely to have a conversation with me, shake my hand, and stand closer to me when having a conversation. My white male students are more likely to have a conversation with me, not shake my hand, and leave space between us. My white female students are least likely to interact with me at all, instead sending an email to ask their questions. Accidental? I think not.

I discussed earlier how a stereotype threat I face includes speaking style. The same holds true for implicit bias toward my speaking style. When students remark on how articulate I am while speaking, I wonder why such a comment is being directed at me. Regionalisms, slang language, dialect, and idioms may play a role in how people perceive a person's education level. Some of my white students may not have interacted with a Black person in their entire lives before, so when they view a Black professor, they may not automatically associate that teacher as an intellectual.

Humans like patterns. They make it easier for us to make sense of the world around us. However, when a pattern does not match with our preconceived learned pattern, it can lead to uncomfortable situations. For me, it leads to students questioning my ability to teach them course material. One semester, on the first day of class, I recall a student asking my age and if I was able to teach college students. I told the student I hold a doctorate degree and specialize in the subject matter I am teaching them.

Toward the end of the semester, the student told me that my class was rigorous, and they had learned a great deal in my class. In this case, the implicit bias that had initially been exhibited became conscious and the behavior changed.

Strategies to Assist Diversity, Equity, and Inclusion Programs at Predominantly White Institutions

Cross-Cultural Events for Undergraduate Students

Students may enter the college environment not being exposed to cultures outside their own. It is recommended that First Year Experience faculty and staff includes cross-cultural events in their curriculum for undergraduate students. Glass & Westmont (2014) found that cultural events, leadership programs, and community service enhanced a sense of belongingness, buffered the effects of racism, and provided a secure base for the exploration of cross-cultural relationships for domestic and international students. Exposing students to different perspectives may help alleviate stereotype threat or implicit biases they have toward others who are different. In the First Year Experience curriculum, highlighting different cultural groups and their norms may lessen the anxiety of interacting with others.

Student Life departments could host events where different customs are highlighted. Be careful, however, with labeling it as a diversity initiative. Simply make it an integral and ordinary part of your Student Life Office to hold events that focus on cross-cultural/ethnic backgrounds. Instead of waiting until a particular month to celebrate Black History or Hispanic History months, hold events that feature different aspects of different cultures and normalize them.

Cross Cultural Communication Training for Graduate Teaching Assistants

I would advise graduate schools to implement cross-cultural communication training for graduate teaching assistants. Okoth & Mupinga (2007) argued that problems relating to cross-cultural communication are cultural differences that often arise in a multicultural classroom due to different cultural beliefs and myths. Students' interactions with teachers inside the classroom can make or break a student's motivation to pursue their goals. Cultural differences need to be accounted for when graduate teaching assistants and students interact with each other in the classroom.

Hiring Committee Selection Process Reviewed within Human
Resources Departments

Human Resources departments need to assess how they hire faculty, staff, and administrators. Reexamine who is being selected to serve on search committees. Sensoy & Diangelo (2017) argued that hiring committees protect whiteness rather than unsettle it. From my experience at PWIs, Black professors, staff, and administrators are asked to serve on hiring committees, but not lead a search committee. This inevitably poses the question of why we (Black professionals) cannot lead and make decisions. We know we are the "diversity" component of the committee. Encourage and/or appoint Black and minority faculty to lead search committees and other college-wide committees that are in part helping to shape the culture of the institution. Also, in this manner, Black professionals may feel more connected to the campus community instead of just being the diversity hire.

Also, think about the power dynamics that are happening within the search committees. Do some people have tenure, while others do not? Is someone's supervisor leading the search committee? The power dynamic plays a role in whether someone is going to stand up for someone who they think is qualified. Someone who does not have tenure may not say anything in fear of retaliation from those who do have it. If a supervisor is on the search committee, the employees who report to them may not speak up due to that person having the ability to fire someone or give an unfavorable review if the person disagrees. Ideally, when compiling search committees, they should be composed of people on the same organizational level, and not include anyone with the ability to affect others' employment. This is ultimately important because students want to see themselves in their professors.

Decision Making Gatekeepers Reexamined and Challenged at Levels
within the Institution

Notice who are the decision-makers in your organization. Do they have different ideas? Do they all look the same? If a higher education institution notices that all its decision-makers look, act, and think alike, there is a problem. Being a "yes" person will not yield progress for the institution. Procedural conflict is a good thing. Harris & Ellis (2020) report that the level of diversity present in a national higher education system plays an important role in enabling the system to respond to a variety of demands from society. Ideas and perspectives that are challenged benefit the college and the community greatly through innovative and fresh ideas to move an institution forward.

When students can see a diverse leadership team at the institution, they may be able to one day see themselves in that exact same seat. However, if the senior administration, deans, and department chairs all look the same, this may not be possible for students. Based upon the familiarity complex mentioned earlier in this chapter, people who are in positions of authority are more likely to promote and/or give more opportunities for growth to people who look like them. For Black professionals, this is a rare situation at a PWI. Recognizing talent and being willing to let that talent make mistakes and grow professionally could help Black professionals feel comfortable and, in turn, help them in assisting students' academic, professional, and personal growth.

REFERENCES

Beckles-Raymond, G. (2020). Implicit bias, (global) white ignorance, and bad faith: The problem of whiteness and anti-black racism. *Journal of Applied Philosophy*, 37(2), 169–89.

Glass, R. C. & Westmont, M. C. (2014). Comparative effects of belongingness on the academic success and cross-cultural interactions of domestic and international students. *International Journal of Intercultural Relations*, 38, 106–119.

Harper, S. R. (2015). Black male college achievers and resistant responses to racist stereotypes at predominantly white colleges and universities. *Harvard Educational Review*, 85(4), 646–74.

Harris, M. S. & Ellis, M. K. (2020). Measuring changes in institutional diversity: The US context. *Higher Education*, 79(2), 345–60.

Kelly, B. T., Gayles, J. G. & Williams, C. D. (2017). Recruitment without retention: A critical case of Black faculty unrest. *The Journal of Negro Education*, 86(3), 305–17.

Kolligian Jr, J. & Sternberg, R. J. (1991). Perceived fraudulence in young adults: Is there an "imposter syndrome"? *Journal of Personality Assessment*, 56(2), 308–26. https://doi.org/10.1207/s15327752jpa5602_10

McGowan, J. (2000). Multicultural teaching: African-American faculty classroom teaching experiences in predominantly white colleges and universities. *Multicultural Education*, 8(2), 19–22.

Mendez, M. J. & Mendez, P. J. (2018). What's in a name ... or a face? Student perceptions of faculty race. *Journal of Political Science*, 14(2), https://doi.org/10.1080/15512169.2017.1389282

Moore, E. S., Hines-Martin, P. V. & Gattis N. M. (2020). Paying it forward: The role of senior Black faculty in preparing junior faculty and Black doctoral students for career success. *The Journal of Negro Education*, 89(2), 146–57.

Moore, P. J. & Toliver, S. D. (2010). Intraracial dynamics of black professors' and black students' communication in traditionally white colleges and universities. *Journal of Black Studies*, 40(5), 932–45.

Morris, J. E. & Monroe, C. R. (2009). Why study the US south? The nexus of race and place in investigating black student achievement. *Educational Researcher*, 38(1), 21–36. https://doi.org/10.3102/0013189X08328876

National Center for Education Statistics (NCES). (2021). Fast facts. March 21. https://nces.ed.gov/fastfacts/display.asp?id=61

Okoth, A. E. & Mupinga, D. M. (2007). An evaluation of the international graduate teaching assistants training program. *Academy of Human Resource Development International Research Conference*. https://files.eric.ed.gov/fulltext/ED504334.pdf

Parker, T. L. & Neville, K. M. (2019). The influence of racial identity on white students' perceptions of African American faculty. *Review of Higher Education*, 42(3), 879–901.

Sensoy, Ö. & Diangelo, R. (2017). "We are all for diversity, but . . .": How faculty hiring committees reproduce whiteness and practical suggestions for how they can change. *Harvard Educational Review*, 87(4), 557–80.

Slater, J., Aruguete, M. & Mwaikinda, S. (2017). The effects of professors' race and clothing style on student evaluations. *The Journal of Negro Education*, 86(4), 494–502.

Steele, C & J. Aronson. (1995). Stereotype threat and the intellectual test performance of African Americans. *Journal of Personality and Social Psychology*, 69(5), 797–811.

Sue, D. W., Rivera, D. P., Watkins, N. L., Kim, R. H., Kim, S. & Williams, C. D. (2011). Racial dialogues: Challenges faculty of color face in the classroom. *Cultural Diversity & Ethnic Minority Psychology*, 17(3), 331–40.

Tamir, C. (2021). The growing diversity of Black America. *Pew Research Center*. https://pewrsr.ch/3DX5Ee6

Zajonc, R. B. (2001). Mere exposure: A gateway to the subliminal. *Current Directions in Psychological Science*, 10, 224–8.

CHAPTER 3

Systemic Racism, the Well-Known Secret Facing African-American Adjunct and Full-Time Faculty in Higher Education

Regina Banks-Hall and Olivia Miller

Background

The nexus of Black Lives Matter protests and a pandemic that dispropor-tionately impacts African Americans highlights the need to end systemic racism. The term systemic racism resurfaced to address police brutality and motives that normalize discrimination toward minorities. Systemic racism involves structures that manufacture prejudicial results for minorities, normalizing the process without justification. Several industries ignore the prevalent issues that stem from systemic racism and strategically utilize the law's components to enable their discriminatory actions. As higher education (HE) is one industry increasingly impacted by systemic racism, the aim of this chapter is to increase awareness and provide strategies to assist HE leaders counteract it.

Throughout 2020, the world struggled with a pandemic, civil unrest, and the reminder that stereotypes and racism toward minorities are ever-present. As minorities continue to suffer from bigotry and police brutality, there is no doubt that large sections of society consider African Americans a threat. George Floyd, a 46-year-old African-American male, died after being accused of using a counterfeit twenty-dollar bill. During detainment, Minneapolis Police officer Derek Chauvin had "placed his knee on Floyd's neck for nearly eight minutes while Floyd pleaded he could not breathe" (Levenson, 2021). In response to this horrific act, African Americans gathered to protest police brutality peacefully. The media, however, focused primarily on the violence that stemmed from counterprotesters and other individuals rather than racial injustice.

Pro-Trump supporters near the White House in January "stormed the US Capitol, seeming to overwhelm Capitol Police, who struggled to contain the violence" (Griffith & Hampton, 2021). The same white people subsequently negated the concept of "Black Lives Matters," arguing instead that "Blue Lives Matter." The idea of police fearing African Americans, who were peacefully protesting against racial injustice, correlates with systemic racism. Ironically, in other instances, such as the invasion of the Capitol by Trump supporters, protests seemed justified to many individuals previously opposed: white men and women suddenly ignored the concept of "Blue Lives Matter" and violently attacked police officers during the assault. The purpose of the invasion was an attempt to overturn President Trump's election defeat. Despite several election officials legally verifying the votes, these people protested and were not feared by law enforcement.

Contrary to the excessive force used during African Americans' protests, limited law enforcement was present, and leaders did not summon the National Guard. Sadly, many people received injuries, and five individuals died. Many argue that, if African Americans had attempted to invade the Capitol building, the outcome would have been different. Peaceful protests by African Americans always attracts an increased number of law enforcement officials. In many instances of Black Lives Matter protests, law enforcement officials have used excessive force or provoked the protesters. Thomas, Gabbatt & Barr (2020) noted "Police brutality against African-American protesters has been extensively documented in New York City, Seattle, Minneapolis, Los Angeles, etc." Once again, after many years of fighting for integration, a line of segregation and discrimination exists. Keneshia Grant, an associate professor of political science at Howard University, emphasized that the law enforcement system is designed to protect specific individuals (Griffith & Hampton, 2021).

Critical Race Theory

We have looked at the impact of systemic racism through the lens of Critical Race Theory (CRT) and are passionate about increasing awareness of systemic racism for improved social justice outcomes. During the mid-1970s, legal scholars Derrick Bell, Alan Freeman, and Richard Delgado developed CRT to examine African Americans' civil rights (Delgado & Stefancic, 1998). Other scholars have since used CRT to analyze racial inequities in higher education. Patton (2016) has argued the foundation of US higher education involves white supremacy, is linked to enslaving African Americans for capitalistic gains, and contains knowledge production rooted in racist ideologies. Sleeter (2017) adds that teacher education patterns involve educational policies and testing based on the white populations and fail to diversify or form strong pedagogical relationships with African-American students. Researchers have also argued that most white teachers exhibit bias toward African-American students.

Most colleges and universities hire faculty members to fulfill the affirmative action hiring requirement. This process includes stopping the process of hiring African Americans once the affirmative action goal has been met. Data obtained from the National Center for Education Statistics provides evidence of systemic racism. According to the NCES, in 2018, 1.5 million faculty were working in degree-granting postsecondary institutions. Of this number, 54 percent were full-time and 46 percent part-time. A further review of the data highlighted that among full-time professors, 53 percent were white males, 27 percent were white females, 8 percent were Asian/Pacific Islander males, and 3 percent were Asian/Pacific Islander females. Black males, Black females, and Hispanic males each accounted for 2 percent of full-time professors, and others 3 percent (NCES, 2018). Efforts should involve meaningful hiring efforts for African Americans versus fulfilling a quota or statistic. Qualified African Americans exhibit so much more in the workforce and deserve fair treatment and professional growth opportunities.

Systemic Racism in Higher Education

When looking at the concept of systemic racism in higher education, academic journals, and other publications mention African Americans proclaiming that systemic racism issues exist in higher education. In reviewing the problem, many people working in academia have acknowledged that the selection of faculty, staff, and students at PWIs perpetuates structural racism. Quillian et al. (2017) conducted a study that revealed white candidates receive, on average, 36 percent more callbacks than African-American candidates, a figure that has not changed since 1989. Secondly, it is vital to examine the first-year success rates for African-American students struggling to transition to college campuses' academic life. Eakins & Eakins (2017) emphasize that these issues may exist because PWIs fail to implement equitable educational systems for African-American students.

Most colleges and universities favor African-American athletes, but fail to acknowledge their intellectual capabilities. One example, shared by one author as an African-American college student-athlete, involved the coaches choosing majors for students of color. Specifically, African-American students with full scholarships majored in less rigorous subjects to focus on sports. PWIs also increase their recruitment for African-American athletes in revenue-generating sports, such as basketball and football. Such scenarios exhibit the idea that PWIs profit from African-American athletes, but fail to provide them with a meaningful education in anything else. Several studies indicate that African-American athletes have lower graduation success rates (GSRs) than their white peers. In 2016, a report by the National Collegiate Athletic Association (NCAA) revealed, "the GSR of African-American male college athletes at the Division I level was 70 percent, which was significantly lower than their peers: 87 percent for white males, 95 percent for white females, and 84 percent for African-American females" (Cooper, Nwadike & Macaulay, 2017: 221).

In other scenarios, several colleges and universities fail to acknowledge white supremacy on their campus. Taylor (2019) argued that a noose hung on a campus tree, and the "n-word" written on the Mary Lou Center, etc., exhibits white supremacy at Duke University. A Duke alumnus published a letter stating "Groups of color are better off when their men marry the women they have babies with and stay around to raise them, when they avoid drugs, stay out of trouble, and prefer a paycheck to a handout, and when they realize that 'acting white' by studying, say, is not a bad thing" (Clutts, 2020). Putting aside the question of why the magazine published such a statement, it nonetheless exhibits white privilege and a failure to consider African-American students' feelings at Duke University.

According to the Hechinger Report, African-American professors mention that they feel invisible at predominantly white schools. African-American professors believe they have been hired as "eye candy," and that they are either overlooked or scrutinized (Krupnick, 2018). Both authors support the findings in the Hechinger Report based on personal experiences of being left out of the decision-making process. The authors believe their opinions or ideas are dismissed, and they are constantly treated as if they are inferior. Often, when invited to a meeting to discuss new programs, assessments, or other administrative issues, the decision has already been made, and the process has been prepared and finalized. After having conversations with other African-American faculty or staff members at PWIs, a single theme emerged: Their feedback is excluded from consideration, and PWI campus leaders imply that we should be content with being employed by the university.

African-American faculty members on campuses work with significant disadvantages compared to their white colleagues. The disadvantages are sometimes not easily identified when a few African-American faculty members are promoted to Professor or secure tenure. While African

Americans account for 5.4 percent of full-time or tenured faculty at PWIs in the United States (Killough et al., 2017), social isolation and lack of collegiality continues for them: Willie J. Edwards and Henry H. Ross argue that African-American faculty "have sometimes found themselves having to decode the information from, and reactions of, their colleagues, thus adding to the stress experienced in an environment of isolation and with little to no collegiality" (Edwards & Ross, 2018: 144). It seems that the underlying issue, in this case, is providing African-American faculty members access to university resources. Louis et al. (2016) referred to this disadvantage as a racial microaggression that involves African-American faculty being made to feel invisible because they have failed to receive mentorship, are overworked with low-perceived value, and their qualifications are doubted by PWI leaders and white colleagues.

Addressing Systemic Racism

In looking at systemic racism issues in higher education, the challenge is determining how to chart a pathway forward. This pathway involves exploring leadership and strategic planning measures for colleges and universities to assist faculty and students in removing barriers that hinder success. We begin by looking at diversity, leadership, and multiculturalism through a different lens. The definition of diversity is one of the first challenges for universities and other organizations. Many people refer to diversity based on race or ethnicity without recognizing a broader appeal (Kamales & Knorr, 2019). However, to implement successful diversity initiatives, organizations must look at the concept of diversity and inclusion as assets that are vital to the organization's performance. By expanding the scope of diversity, organizational leaders can see the long-term vitality in leadership development and growth. Viewing diversity through a broader appeal enables organizational leaders to look at more than race, including differences in knowledge, skills, values, and community status. Diversity as an asset encompasses economic, education, and generational differences. Inclusion, as a counter asset, communicates that all individuals provide value to an organization. Within a university setting or organization, managing diversity involves coordinating and managing the organization's diversity (Tavakoli, 2015).

The leadership selection process in colleges and universities is critical to implement authentic diversity. The presence of diversity begins at the top of the house. Therefore, leaders of PWIs should recruit and retain leaders who study, understand, and acknowledge the importance of diversity.

These hiring efforts may include a combination of transactional leaders who build relationships based on culture and transformational leaders who thrive on organizational change (Adserias, Charleston & Jackson, 2017). Additionally, PWIs should examine all leadership areas, including the hiring and admissions department, for improved diversity. It is also essential for PWIs to develop diverse hiring and admission committees to ensure African-American candidates receive fair consideration for employment or admission.

Studies reveal that culturally engaging campuses increase African-American students' sense of belonging. Museus (2014) indicated that African-American students experience adverse campus climate and discrimination from faculty at PWIs. Neal & Georges (2020) have added that pandemics, such as COVID-19, extend inequalities in higher education and decrease African-American students' sense of belonging at PWIs. Therefore, PWI leaders must allocate funds to research methods to create cultural engagement for African-American students. Additionally, PWI leaders must encourage cultural events and activities to increase African-American students' sense of belonging. Finally, PWI leaders should strategically hire individuals with extensive awareness of cultural engagement.

Specific Strategies

University leaders must incorporate strategies that showcase diversity, inclusion, and multiculturalism (Kamales & Knorr, 2019). These strategies can be exhibited in the newsletter, website, emails, brochures, and other campus-related materials. A specific strategy could involve exploring the college or university's marketing plan. Most colleges and universities use advertising as a means of complying with diversity requirements. However, a genuine commitment to diversity would go beyond the status quo. We suggest that colleges and universities structure their marketing departments to include opportunities to improve diversity. Instead of marketing departments using African Americans as a crutch to attract minorities, they should consist of genuine information based on the strengths, weaknesses, and areas of opportunity for diversity. Therefore, valid research is vital to ensure colleges or universities do not mislead African Americans into believing institutions are diverse when significant room for improvement exists. Such efforts may inspire existing African-American students on campus to contribute with strategies to increase diversity.

Another strategy links to the need for colleges and universities to acknowledge the importance of encouraging African Americans to voice their opinions and concerns. We are confident that if colleges or universities listen to the voice of African Americans and other minorities, the campus diversity will be authentic. Therefore, we recommend that university leaders develop ways to inform African Americans that their voice matters. One solution might be to involve creating groups or platforms, such as a University African American Network or University Asian Network . These types of networks operate within organizations like the Ford Motor Company and Chrysler. A second solution might be to conduct surveys via email or text canvassing African Americans' perception of campus diversity. The social infrastructure and campus climate are positive when student and academic affairs align with diversity. A third solution is for leaders to hold focus groups with all student populations to ensure all students feel involved in the process.

Our next strategy is for colleges or universities to promote an open-door policy with specific instructions for students who face discrimination or other racial issues. To ensure the open-door policies are effective, university leaders must promptly address issues rather than ignore them to avoid backlash from the media. Therefore, we recommend that universities be transparent when diversity problems exist. Such matters may increase awareness of campus diversity issues and improve African-American students' trust at the college or university. Additionally, it may encourage other African Americans to apply for admission, thereby providing authentic growth in diversity.

Recommendations

As we continue to look at the impact of a multicultural environment, it is essential to look at the effect of diversity and inclusion on building the leadership skills of employees. One recommendation for looking at leadership's impact requires reviewing the university's mission and vision statement. The mission statement focuses on the university's values, and the vision outlines what the university aspires to be. As stated earlier, diversity, inclusion, and a multicultural atmosphere can be used as an asset for the organization (Tavakoli, 2015). After the university has realigned its mission and vision, key department leaders, working in conjunction with the Human Resources Department, can begin sharing the vision throughout the organization. By utilizing the university's mission and values statement, the organization can begin to realign its culture into a space that embraces multiculturalism (Kamales & Knorr 2019).

As faculty, staff, and other vital stakeholders begin to embrace the mission and vision statement to support a multicultural environment, the stakeholder's interaction with students, suppliers, and vendors will change. In conducting additional research on this topic, we recommend that leaders not just look at the impact of creating a diverse campus, but consider multiculturalism holistically with the creation of a significant strategic plan (Barber et al., 2020). For multicultural education to be successful, it is crucial to include the elements of critical literacy. According to Ira Shor (1999), critical literacy challenges the status quo to discover alternative social and self-development paths. University leaders must create a campus atmosphere where students and faculty question power within the academic society. For the student, it will take place within the classroom. For the faculty, it will take place in questioning the process used for promotion, tenure, support for scholarships, and research.

The next step for the realignment of the culture of PWIs requires leaders to begin a dialogue with employees and faculty members. This will open the door for support and buy-in by university personnel, who will then be empowered to start the conversation with students. The university can also begin to use multiculturalism in marketing, web resources, and correspondence with students and donors.

The second recommendation monitors openness. It will be essential to identify support and understanding of culture before investing heavily in programs. The goal after beginning the dialogue is to create an atmosphere where terms of diversity, inclusion, and multiculturalism become part of university speech. The goal is to take these words and incorporate them within the fabric of the university.

The third recommendation is expanding awareness. In coordination with the HR Department, focus should be on the knowledge elements of diversity, inclusion, and multiculturalism. Through awareness training, university leaders can highlight the importance of cultural differences in the workplace for employees and the value in having different employee perspectives. Awareness training can help employees see how these different perspectives can support all organization areas through decision-making and other workplace initiatives.

The fourth recommendation is to implement a training program for all personnel. Creating a campus atmosphere that embraces diversity, inclusion, and multiculturalism takes time. The university needs to develop training programs for faculty and staff. Within the training, university leaders can create activities where employees who feel excluded can see their value. These training program sessions can be utilized as opportunities to help employees learn how to recognize differences, and more importantly, embrace them.

The final recommendation requires a strategy for reinforcement. Creating a culture that fosters diversity, inclusion, and multiculturalism takes time. It requires a method for reinforcing the "why" and "how." The "why" centers on the need for diversity, inclusion, and multiculturalism. The "how" focuses on the process to get there. This recommendation is as essential as the others, since change initiatives can start strongly but gradually fade.

Conclusion

In concluding this chapter, we believe that university leaders can utilize the history of racism to transform their institutions into places that embrace diversity, inclusion, and multiculturalism. The history of racism includes slavery, issues in housing, voter suppression, lack of education, and wages. African-American faculty need reassurance that equity in university resources, promotions, and other employment issues, is provided. When looking at this issue from a minority student perspective, the ability to voice concerns and the atmosphere to thrive as students is essential. When university leaders acknowledge the impact of systemic racism, they can turn the page and create a new culture that embraces diversity, inclusion, and multiculturalism.

REFERENCES

Adserias, R. P., Charleston, L. J. & Jackson, J. F. (2017). What style of leadership is best suited to direct organizational change to fuel institutional diversity in higher education? *Race Ethnicity and Education*, 20(3), 315–31. doi:10.1080/13613324.2016.1260233

Barber, P. H., Hayes, T. B., Johnson, T. L. & Márquez-Magaña, L. (2020) Systemic racism in higher education. *Science*, 369, 1440–1. doi:10.1126/science. abd7140

Clutts, C. P. (2020) It's not all racism. *Duke Magazine*, 103(3), 5. https://alumni.duke.edu/magazine/issues/winter-2020

Cooper, J. N., Nwadike, A. & Macaulay, C. (2017). A critical race theory analysis of big-time college sports: Implications for culturally responsive and race-conscious sport leadership. *Journal of Issues in Intercollegiate Athletics*. http://csri-jiia.org/wp-content/uploads/2017/12/RA_2017_11.pdf

Delgado, R. & Stefancic, J. (1998). Critical race theory: Past, present, and future. *Current Legal Problems*, 51(1), 467–91. doi:10.1093/clp/51.1.467

Eakins, A. & Eakins Sr, S. L. (2017). African American students at predominantly white institutions: A collaborative style cohort recruitment & retention model.

Journal of Learning in Higher Education, 13(2), 51–7. https://files.eric.ed.gov/fu lltext/EJ1161827.pdf

Edwards, W. J. & Ross, H. H. (2018). What are they saying? Black faculty at predominantly white institutions of higher education. *Journal of Human Behavior in the Social Environment*, 28(2), 142–61. https://doi.org/10.1080/1091 1359.2017.1391731

Griffith, J. & Hampton, D. J. (2021). Capitol Police response to rioters draws claims of racist double standards. January 8. https://nbcnews.to/3D2Wk7e

Hiraldo, P. (2010). The role of critical race theory in higher education. *The Vermont Connection*, 31(1), 7. https://bit.ly/3I6WNc6

Kamales, N. & Knorr, H. (2019). Leaders with Managing Cultural Diversity and Communication. *Asia Pacific Journal of Religions and Cultures*, 3(1), 63–72. https://bit.ly/3D8OQ2y

Killough, A. L., Killough, E. G., Walker II, E. & Williams, O. (2017). Examining the delicate balance of maintaining one's blackness as a black professional on the predominantly white campus. *Journal of Best Practices in Health Professions Diversity: Research, Education and Policy*, 10(2), 81–110.

Krupnick, M. (2018). After colleges promised to increase it, hiring of black faculty declined. *The Hechinger Report*. October 2. https://bit.ly/3G1opxD

Levenson, E. (2021). Jury selection begins in Derek Chauvin's trial in the death of George Floyd. Here's what to expect. CNN. March 11. https://cnn.it/3FYp4jm

Louis, D. A., Rawls, G. J., Jackson-Smith, D., Chambers, G. A., Phillips, L. L. & Louis, S. L. (2016). Listening to our voices: Experiences of black faculty at predominantly white research universities with microaggression. *Journal of Black Studies*, 47(5), 454–74. doi:10.1177/0021934716632983

Museus, S. D. (2014). The culturally engaging campus environments (CECE) model: A new theory of success among racially diverse college student populations. In *Higher Education: Handbook of theory and research*. Dordrecht: Springer, 189–227.

National Center for Education Statistics (NCES) (2018). Race/ethnicity of college faculty. https://nces.ed.gov/fastfacts/display.asp?id=61

Neal, B. & Georges Jr, C. T. (2020). From integration to cultural consciousness: The call for culturally engaging environments on community college campuses. *Insights on Equity and Outcomes*, 23. https://files.eric.ed.gov/fulltext/ED609846 .pdf

Patton, L. D. (2016). Disrupting postsecondary prose: Toward a critical race theory of higher education. *Urban Education*, 51(3), 315–42. https://doi.org/ 10.1177/0042085915602542

Quillian, L., Pager, D., Hexel, O. & Midtbøen, A. H. (2017). Meta-analysis of field experiments shows no change in racial discrimination in hiring over time. *Proceedings of the National Academy of Sciences of the United States of America*, 114 (41), 10870–5. https://www.pnas.org/content/114/41/10870

Shor, I. (1999). What is critical literacy? *Journal of Pedagogy, Pluralism, and Practice*, 1(4), Article 2. https://digitalcommons.lesley.edu/jppp/vol1/iss4/2

Sleeter, C. E. (2017). Critical race theory and the whiteness of teacher education. *Urban Education*, 52(2), 155–69. doi:10.1177/0042085916668957

Tavakoli, M (2015) Diversity and inclusion drive success for today's leaders. *Talent Development*, 69(5), 46–51.

Taylor, D. (2019). What's wrong with Duke? White supremacy is the root. Duke Social Science Research Institute. August 20. https://bit.ly/3I74BdU

Thomas, T., Gabbatt, A. & Barr, C. (2020). Nearly 1,000 instances of police brutality recorded in US anti-racism protests. *The Guardian*. October 29. https://bit.ly/3IipByG

CHAPTER 4

I'm A Black PhD, and I Still Have to Fight!

Antione D. Tomlin

Introduction

As a Black male educator, I find myself constantly fighting for equity and inclusion. While this constant fight is exhausting, I often wonder, if not me, then who? I am sure I am not the only person of color who feels this way; however, working in predominantly white spaces and fields only illuminates the need to continue the fight. Allison (2008) claimed, "When a Black professor begins teaching at a PWI, he or she must often combat long-standing stereotypes and prejudices held by members of the dominant community, as many whites, and other groups alike, continue to view Blacks stereotypically" (p. 642). When I think about my experiences as a Black male educator, I have never been afforded the opportunity just to be or enjoy my professional endeavor. I have always had to be one step ahead, at least better than the rest if not outstanding in every respect, from fear of being judged by white colleagues or even fired. It is important to note that I do not speak on behalf of all people of color with the experiences shared in this chapter. Yet, I will share my lived experiences of fighting the pandemic of racism. Additionally, I will provide strategies for faculty, both Black and non-Black as well as administration, with hopes that they will become better equipped to lean into making higher education more equitable, inclusive, and peaceful.

A Brief Background

My name is Antione D. Tomlin, and I am a native of Baltimore, Maryland. I was born and raised in Baltimore City, and attended Baltimore City Public Schools. Growing up in Baltimore, I heard many things like "Black men do not make it out of the hood," and "if you graduate from high school, you beat 'the statistic'." There were not many motivating factors to encourage me to stay in school. However, I knew I did not want to end up incarcerated or dead, like many of the familiar faces I remember from my neighborhood. That pushed me to stay in school, even when I did not want to. I was the first person to graduate from high school in my family. While this was a significant feat for my family, I knew it would not be enough to take me from the hood. For me, college seemed like the only option.

After graduating from high school, I attended Stevenson University and earned my Bachelor of Science in Psychology. After graduating, I worked full-time and taught as an adjunct faculty member at some of the colleges in Maryland, while earning my Master of Arts degree in Higher Education Administration, with a focus on Student Affairs, from Morgan State University. After getting my master's degree, I took time to focus on work and what was next. This was when I had the opportunity to teach developmental English. I noticed that many of my students were Black and Brown folks, and this made me want to help even more, as I recognize the power and need for mentoring students (Tomlin & Brad, 2021). I love teaching, and I love that I can show students who look like me that anything is possible with the right resources, grit, and determination. I am currently a tenure-track professor, and hope to achieve tenure soon, continuing to be a voice for my students of color without fear of being silenced or being asked to tone it down. However, this has not always been my experience.

There is literature that discusses Black faculty's experience of racism and stereotyping and the negative impact it has on their professional and personal well-being (Smallwood, 2007). My experience with the impact of racism and stereotyping as a Black faculty member is no different from what Smallwood discovered. I have noticed and realized that many of the assumptions, barriers, and challenges I encounter stem from negative stereotypes formed about people who look like me, that is, people of color. Some of the assumptions, barriers, and challenges I have experienced are not new or unique to my Blackness. In fact, Black faculty have been dealing with many of these assumptions, barriers, and challenges for decades. For example, I still deal with non-Black colleagues who doubt my abilities (Banks, 1984; Johnsrud & Sadao, 1998) and non-Black colleagues who make racist jokes or comments based on social stereotypes (Johnsrud & Des Jarlais, 1994; McKay, 1997; Turner & Myers, 2000) and their limited experience of working with Black colleagues. While it is unfortunate that these are a few of the experiences I have had to endure as a Black faculty member, there is a lot that can be learned by Black and non-Black faculty and administration. Kimberly Griffin and colleagues suggested that delving into how a racialized campus environment "as represented by perceptions and experiences with racism, affects black faculty is an important component of recruiting, retaining, and supporting black faculty members throughout their careers" (Griffin et al., 2011: 496). The aim of the next few sections is to share my experiences of being a Black male in a racialized profession that values whiteness. Through sharing, I hope, as Griffin et al. described, to aid in recruiting, retaining, and supporting Black faculty.

Narratives of The Past

Campus Culture

As a Black male educator working at predominantly white institutions (PWIs), I continue to have challenges around race and inequality (Griffin et al., 2011). These challenges, which include often being one of the only Black faculty, are frustrating and, for other Black faculty, can lead to early departure from an institution or academia altogether (Jayakumar et al., 2009; Trower & Chait, 2002). While I am not always the only Black man in a space, I am often one of very few, and find myself backed into a corner by white structures, systems, or colleagues. Dave Louis and colleagues posit, "The American Academy has historically been a 'white space'. These spaces are perpetuated by not only the building blocks of European university systems, but also colonial ideals that have been fostered for centuries creating university campuses which have enrolled predominantly white populations" (Louis et al. 2017: 7). As a Black faculty person, this shaping of higher education has left me feeling like an outsider or visitor.

Shaw (2014) speaks of a system of power and a structure in higher education that does not consider the needs of non-white people, describing higher education as being "dominated by white male faculty and adminis-tration" (p. 270). Consequently, it feels like I am usually unable to express my concerns about any given topic because of another colleague's reac-tions, attitude, or beliefs. It is claimed that higher education is becoming more diverse; however, it continues to be a white space that is controlled by white power and white belief systems (Louis et al., 2017). Furthermore, within these spaces "black people are typically absent, not expected, or marginalized when present. In turn, blacks ... typically approach [those] space[s] with care" (Anderson, 2015: 10). I truly feel that I must yield my natural expressions, reactions, thoughts, and comments for fear of retali-ation. In this way, it does feel like I have to approach my predominantly white profession and space with care.

One of my most vivid memories comes from when I first started working in education at a four-year institution in Baltimore, Maryland. I did not feel very welcomed to the institution, and everyone always seemed to think I was a student. It got to the point where one of the Deans would ask me weekly if I was lost, who I was looking for, and why I was in an employee-designated office on campus. I forgot to mention that I wore my nametag daily. I constantly had to introduce myself to people I had met just the week before for eight months non-stop; I referred to this phenomenon as "the student curse." I arrived at this name as I was always being referred to as a student. It really began to take a toll on me. One day I was sitting in my office, alone, just completing some documents. Someone knocked on my door; I looked up and said hello. The person looked at me in confusion and said, "I am sorry, I was looking for Mr. Tomlin." I quickly jumped up to say, "Nice to meet you, what can I do for you?" It was not enough that I was in my office alone, sitting at my desk completing paperwork. I guess the student curse was still haunting me. Lori Patton and Christopher Catching have noted that "African Americans and faculty of color in general often experience racial profiling, are presumed to be 'out of place' in the academy, and are subjected to assumptions regarding *whether* and *where* they belong" (Patton & Catching, 2009: 714). For me, it was assumptions like the student curse that would add up over time and take a toll on me. I could not focus on the job at hand because I constantly had to convince colleagues that I belonged in the physical space and higher education at large.

In the Classroom

My next experience helped me be grateful for who I have become and remain humble about my achievements and praise. It was the start of a spring semester. I printed my syllabi, checked my room location, and made sure I did not have any lunch stuck in my teeth. I am a firm believer that first impressions mean a lot. This was only my second semester teaching as an adjunct at one of the community colleges in Maryland. I left my office early enough to get to class twenty minutes before the start. As I walked down the hall to my class, I passed many students excited about their first day of college. I smiled and nodded to say hello, as I love the beginning of the semester; it is nice to see so many motivated scholars ready to take on the world. However, I digress: I walked past all my students outside my class to go in and get settled. As I entered the room to see how things were set up, a white woman halted me and asked, "Excuse me, what are you doing? Where are you supposed to be?" As I pulled out my folder, the thirty copies of my syllabi fell out onto the counter. I told her that I did not have my course location sheet, but I confirmed the room before I left. She got a glimpse of my syllabi, and said, "Oh, you are looking for Academic Development 101, let me call the department chair." I replied, "Yes, let's call *DC*, please." She waved, signaling for me to follow her to a small office in the back as if I were a butler.

All of this unfolded as my students watched; they had entered the room as I did minutes before. Talk about first impressions! I had already been battling with all the stereotypes before. In my mind, everything that could possibly go wrong did. My worst nightmare had come to life. This was my students' first impression of me. I walked to the back as she called the department chair. I attempted to explain the situation, but she gave me no chance to speak, interrupting and cutting me off at every opportunity. When the woman got on the phone, I said, "Could you tell *DC* that her instructor is here as well?" The woman relayed the message. After a few short words with the department chair, the woman looked at me and said, with a very agitated, and quite frankly, rude tone, "Could you tell the instructor to come in here?" Before I could state that I thought it was evident that *I* was the instructor, all of those stereotypes of inadequacy, incompetence, and self-doubt came briefly to mind, and to this day I am still troubled by this experience. I never received an apology, nor was I looking for one, but internally I was looking for answers to all of my "what" and "why" questions. "What about that exchange made me seem like a student? Why was this happening to me? What was I going to do next? Why was I really in education?"

I held my class in an open space on campus until we could get the room reservations corrected. My class was more than understanding of the situation that had just occurred; nonetheless, I felt that this was an unfortunate way of meeting students at the start of a semester. I am all for building rapport and getting to know my students to meet their needs better and help them succeed; however, this situation was definitely a major glitch in building that initial relationship with my students. I felt incompetent and embarrassed at the front of the classroom. I never reported the incident, and I never saw that instructor again. However, this was an experience that still creeps into the back of my mind on occasion. Whenever this happens, I remind myself that I belong in education. The event was a stepping-stone and motivator that drives my determination and willingness to help other Black faculty. On reflection, I do not know why I decided not to report it, but am aware, unfortunately, that

I did not have any support or help to be coached through this traumatic experience, which, as a new faculty member, made me feel alone. If I had had more guidance and support, maybe I would have felt confident enough to have been able to bring this disturbing and humiliating interaction to the administration's attention. However, I thought I had no voice or power, and because of this, I was *not OK* in this situation.

I firmly believe that being African American had a major impact on how the incident played out in front of my students. My being a younger colleague may have been a factor as well. Still, regardless of my race, age, or background, I should have been shown a commensurate level of respect as a professional academic, but I was not. This is what I would like non-Black colleagues to ponder: what role does race, age, or background play in the assumptions, challenges, and stereotypes that non-Black colleagues make about faculty of color? Being a Black male educator is exhausting because I must deal with these situations all the time. Can you imagine having the stress of being a tenure-track professor and the stress of dealing with all the assumptions, judgments, and stereotypes bestowed upon you? To my non-Black colleagues, no, I am not ok. However, you get to decide how you want to help. Boutte & Jackson (2014) have claimed that silence on racism issues for non-Black colleagues is not an option. Moreover, if you decide that this is not your fight, I will note that you chose silence instead of alliance. So, deciding to do nothing or to "stay out of it" is a choice that is not only advised against, but also clearly declines alliance. As a Black faculty member, the least I deserve as a colleague is an equitable and peaceful space.

The Full-Time Faculty Struggle

Before becoming full-time faculty, I was scared even to apply for a position. Even though I had the credentials, I talked myself out of many jobs because I had developed imposter syndrome. I also knew that the majority of higher education is made up of white professionals. I draw attention to this detail because it occurred to me that since I was already having trouble with my non-Black colleagues as an adjunct, there was little reason to believe they would give me a fair chance of becoming full-time. As an adjunct, I found that I had to balance my teaching, college involvement, and commitment to students while also being expected to serve in diversity efforts because I was one of the few Black faculty, as is often the case in US higher education (see Griffin, Bennett & Harris, 2013). I say this to note, being one of the few Black male faculty members can certainly take an emotional, mental, and physical toll of exhaustion (Alexander & Moore, 2008) and for me, it did. I found time to talk to a non-Black ally and colleague about my stress and hesitation in applying for the full-time position. He not only supported me every step of the way, as he was already full-time, he also checked in and provided me with resources to strengthen my application. It is because of this relationship and support that I applied for the position.

As I reflect on my experiences as an adjunct and as full-time faculty, the expectations still exist. As Donnetrice Allison noted, "what Black faculty face is that they are so often overcommitted. Black professors are expected to sit on far more committees than their white colleagues because they tend to be the only face of color available to add the appearance of diversity to the group" (Allison, 2008: 644). From my experience, I had to learn how to manage others' expectations and say no when I needed to. In my current role as full-time, tenure track faculty, I am the only Black male in my division, and one of a few Black faculty in general. While it still has the potential to become overwhelming, I do feel that most of my non-Black colleagues are very supportive. One of the things that has been instrumental in my journey has been having a Black male assistant dean. Without his guidance, care, mentorship, and support, I would not be the faculty member that I am today. Additionally, when it came time for me to apply to be converted to the tenure-track, I was not going to do it. At my institution, tenure is a very competitive process, and not everyone is awarded a track. I came up with every excuse to talk myself out of applying, although it was something that I truly wanted. Additionally, there was no telling when I would have another opportunity to apply, given the competitive nature of the process and the limited number of openings available. However, during the semester I was to apply, none of that mattered. I decided not to apply because I was afraid I was not good enough, and let's face it, in an all-white division, I was sure I was not going to be valued for my gifts and talents. These negative thoughts and self-doubts dictated and clouded my judgment with deciding to apply for the tenure track.

The bottom line is, I was *not OK.* I did not feel that I would be seen and valued for who I was. My assistant dean got word that I would not apply and gave me a very stern talk. He made it very clear that if I did not give my intent to apply, he would find a way to submit my name anyway. That conversation not only changed my career trajectory, but also changed my life. I did go on to apply and earn the tenure-track position, and it would not have been possible without the tough love, support, and encouragement of my Black male assistant dean. Another tip for administration is that Black faculty need to see administrators who look like them. If it had not been for my Black assistant dean, I would have made a major career mistake and would not have understood the detrimental implications of that decision until years later. Black administrators matter, not just to check a box or say you have color in leadership. They matter because faculty of color may have no one else with a similar lived experience to support and help them navigate their professional spaces. I know that I can learn from my colleagues, and I appreciate and value this about where I currently work. Additionally, my relationship with my colleagues of color and assistant dean has created a special place for me to feel that I belong. In those relationships, I can feel that not only do I belong in the profession, but that I can also be OK.

How I Navigate, Survive, and Thrive – The Fight

Remembering that I am not alone helps me to keep going. It is easy to get burned out and beaten up by all the structures allowed to persist in this world and the educational system. However, I had to learn that trying to save the world was too big a task. I had to learn how to involve myself with more manageable missions that would have a major impact. In this way, I can still save the world, but also protect myself from burnout. Here are a few things I learned and implemented to help Black faculty navigate their experiences in academia.

I Cannot and WILL Not Speak for All People of Color

One thing that has helped me thrive as a Black male faculty is to remember that I am the expert of my experience only. This means, as a Black male, I possess just one continued lived experience and perspective of being Black in academia. Therefore, I could never be the expert on all things that relate to Black males. Additionally, if I pretend to have all the answers, then my non-Black colleagues may not deepen their learning through experience. Boutte and Jackson (2014) noted, "If white allies always defer to faculty of color, they may miss this important realization. Even faculty of color who profess to address equity issues may have different interpretations. In short, white allies must develop a deep understanding of the issues and dynamics involved to take discerning, informed actions" (p. 639). With this, I vowed never to be pushed into a space that requires me to represent all people of color because I am not qualified to do so. I am qualified to represent my experience as a Black person, and that experience should not be generalized to all individuals who look like me. Plainly put, it insults me when I am sought after only because of my race, and my experience of race that individuals want me to share. It is insulting because it feels like all my earned and obtained qualifications, credentials, degrees, and professional experiences are devalued, lessened, and ignored when asked to share because I am Black, and not because of my expertise. Another tip for all administrators, policymakers, and diversity, equity, and inclusion (DEI) champions, no matter whether Black or non-Black, is to stop asking Black folks to do things simply because they are Black.

Protect My Time

In the spirit of not burning out, I had to learn how to say "No!" Protecting my time meant saying no every chance I had. I had to get comfortable saying "no" without feeling bad about it, regardless of what I was declining. In my experience, faculty of color are not outstanding at saying "no," so if that is you, you are the faculty of color that is not good at saying "no." Practice with me now. I am serious, go on, say it, no! Again, no! Keep going, no, no, no, no, no, no! As a Black faculty member, I noticed that I was being asked to do much more than some of my white colleagues because of my unique (Black) experience, sitting on diversity committees, providing stern talks to students of color, etc. I realized I was becoming the "Go-To Black Man," as I call it in my research on Black male teachers (Tomlin, 2021). That is the Black guy that non-Black colleagues run to for issues around diversity or students of color. So, not only did I make my demand that I should not be asked to speak for all Black people clear, I also became good at saying "no" when the request did not align with my core values, personal interests, and schedule. I learned that I do not have to feel bad for declining an opportunity, and I did not have to apologize for protecting my time, space, energy, and sanity. I had learned quickly that "no" is a complete sentence that does not require further explanation. Protecting my time in this way also meant protecting my peace.

Call Non-Black Colleagues In, Not Out

Being one of the only Black male faculty in certain spaces allowed me to reflect on my experiences greatly. As a Black faculty, I must voice how I would like to be treated with colleagues, and in many of my experiences, this was more so with non-Black colleagues. I found that being intentional and direct in designing relationships with non-Black colleagues helped me to ask for what I need to feel supported and respected. With co-creating and designing relationships, my colleagues and I set expectations for what our working relationship and environment would and should look like for everyone to feel supported in success. As a result of these strategically designed expectations, we built a rapport that would allow for more genuine learning interactions and experiences. We did not have to make up assumptions of what an experience was like for the other because we could just ask. In thinking about Tomlin, Colbert & Spivey's (2021) idea of calling students in and not out, I believe we must call non-Black colleagues in, as opposed to calling them out. Additionally, when there are moments that lead to adverse reactions, feelings, or emotions, we can voice those concerns and figure out what is next. We often speak about intent versus impact. While we assume good intentions, regardless of the intent, sometimes the impact is hurtful and damaging, so we deal with the impact. This could be as simple as someone saying something offensive. I can quickly say "ouch!" and inform my colleague that something he/she said was offensive. Then, we can talk about it. After dealing with the impact, we view these moments as opportunities to learn and grow. In my experiences, I have learned, it is not about just telling a non-Black colleague what they did wrong and that they should have known better. That does not create a learning moment or space for me to share what impacted me. In this way, we never move from hurt and damage to acceptance and accountability. To move towards acceptance and accountability, the lines of communication must be open. That is heavily dependent on calling my non-Black colleagues in to have a positive intentions-based conversation, not out to be judged or made to feel low. To call colleagues in, it starts with a simple impact conversation where you share how you were impacted by their actions.

Tips on How to Join the Fight

Often, as a Black male, I do not feel I have support. The world has already formed an opinion about my capabilities and trajectory based on my skin color. Before I even open my mouth, many who do not look like me judge me. Therefore, it is vital for non-Black faculty and administrators to know about my lived experience to assist in the fight better. Now that a part of my story is public, I ask both of the aforementioned to join the fight to help me one day live and work in a more equitable and peaceful environment. This is my challenge: Now that you know some of the things I encounter, do better in joining the fight so that I can also be OK within our field. Currently, I am not OK because I have to work ten times harder than many of my non-Black colleagues. Moreover, I am exhausted, but I do not get the opportunity to rest, so please join the fight so that I do not have to go at it alone. Below are some suggestions for how non-Black faculty and administrators can help.

Recommendations for Non-Black Faculty

Co-create and Design a Healthy Relationship with Faculty of Color

I am a firm believer that doing and saying nothing is a choice. Therefore, I challenge non-Black colleagues to get involved because it is your business. Ask faculty of color what they need to feel supported and valued. Brown (2018) has noted that departments should create mentoring programs geared toward supporting minority faculty. A program like this could create the environment for non-Black faculty to start reaching out. Non-Black faculty must let faculty of color know that they want to support them. Do not assume that you know what is best or what faculty of color need or want; simply ask. I encourage non-Black colleagues to be intentional and direct with their approach and acknowledge that they do not know everything and are willing to learn as much as possible. Take that mindset and keep it. Be ready to go out and find additional ways to be a support system. As faculty of color, we are the experts on our own experiences. However, it is not our job to teach non-Black colleagues everything they "need" to know. Build a relationship with us, while also seeking other ways to learn how to support. Lastly, please do not put the burden on faculty of color to educate you. Look for different ways to become more educated.

Stop Apologizing!

When I make a mistake, professionally or personally, I have learned to acknowledge the error, take accountability, and move on. I encourage my non-Black colleagues to do the same. You cannot change what is already done, but you can change how you navigate and operate moving forward. Take accountability for what happened and move on. I say stop apologizing because, believe it or not, it is exhausting to keep hearing that. When non-Black colleagues apologize for the same things numerous times, I feel obligated to appease them. Does that sound weird? I know it does, and that is exactly what has happened. When non-Black colleagues repeatedly apologize, I want to say something to make them feel better. However, it is not my place to make others feel better about something they did that negatively impacted me. If you said something to offend me, hurt my feelings, or have feelings around racism, take accountability for what happened by acknowledging that you understand you had a negative impact and why. Sit in your discomfort, and learn from what happened to move on. Do not overwhelm me with the task of making you feel better when I am trying to process my own emotions, thoughts, and feelings.

Change the Norm

I find that many times, I do not have the space to feel, process, and move on. I feel trapped because I do not get the space (physically and mentally) to be angry about what is going on without fear of being judged for my natural, and most genuine, reaction or response. Miller et al. (2021) raises the idea of Black faculty and fit. That is, Black faculty are challenged with "navigating the tension between authenticity and the need for professional norm adherence in order to demonstrate assimilation" (p. 355). Additionally, Miller et al. shared that these norms can be professional or more culturally specific, such as critique of hair, expression, or diction and tone, which are created to view Black faculty in a negative light. These culturally specific judgment markers have led me to feel that I could not be my most authentic self. In turn, I have bottled up my emotions and figured out what to do with them because I did not feel they would be received or accepted in majority-white spaces, such as higher education. I challenge non-Black faculty to identify the professional and cultural norms that may exist. In identifying, addressing, and removing those professional and cultural norms that may not fit well with Black faculty, you create a space for Black faculty to be more authentic and vulnerable without fear of judgment or retaliation.

Show Up for Me

When necessary, I expect my non-Black colleagues to stand up and speak out against injustice and discrimination. Boutte & Jackson (2014) concluded, "White allies will have to become astute at noticing ongoing microaggressions against people of color and not excuse them as coincidental or idiosyncratic to a particular person's style or personality. If it looks and feels like racism, then most likely it is" (p. 633). No matter how big or small, I want my non-Black colleagues to be comfortable standing up for what is right and equitable in all situations. When decisions, policies, and processes have the potential to impact me negatively because of my race, I want to feel confident that my non-Black colleagues will do the right thing. Yes, I am encouraging the motto "if it looks and feels like racism, then it is." The only way to change an unjust system is to fix the problems by acknowledging rather than excusing them. Non-Black colleagues standing up and speaking out is one small effort that creates a major impact. So, administrators give non-Black colleagues the space to notice injustice and talk about it without fear of retaliation. If we say, as higher education professionals, that we want to change, give everyone the space to notice and identify what needs to be changed. Change is uncomfortable, but we have to be uncomfortable as a profession to make space for everyone to move toward a state of comfort, equity, and peace. Stop excusing racism.

Reframe Your Perspective

A commitment to diversity, equity, inclusion, and anti-racism is my life's work. I am not saying that this work and fight for equity and peace has to become the life's work of non-Black colleagues. However, I am saying that I encourage everyone to think of this work as ongoing and never fully finished. In Boutte and Jackson's words, "in order for real transformation to occur, all involved have to be prepared to struggle. White allies cannot just layer 'diversity' on top of what they are doing. Addressing issues of equity requires deep structural changes – not touristy tinkering." (2014: 639). When implementing this level of change, there is no end date or timeline for this work, but rather a way of being and of conducting the work. Thus, for colleagues who think a workshop, a timeframe, or a certificate can fix things, I offer you an opportunity to rethink and reframe your perspective. Becoming an ally, undertaking related professional development courses, and obtaining diversity certificates are great first steps. I encourage non-Black colleagues to think about how these concepts and ways of being more equity-minded and inclusive can be ingrained into your everyday work to create deeper structural changes that will in turn create peace for faculty of color. Additionally, I challenge non-Black colleagues to take an oath of commitment to long-term engagement, learning, and support of faculty of color.

Recommendations for Administration

Provide A Contact/Resource

When Black faculty have situations that may warrant administration's attention, they should be very clear about their options for reporting or receiving support. While this sounds elementary, in my previously shared experience, I did not know who to contact. It is known that "Black faculty members have to establish their credentials as faculty and present themselves as 'professionals' in an environment which often does not cast or value them in this high-status role. They have to fight to defend their professionalism and competency" (Toliver, Moore & Redcross, 2015: 35). With all that Black faculty have to face, they must have additional support and contacts available when needed. Administration should be sure that faculty of color, full-time and adjunct, have places they can go to feel safe and supported when incidents occur. Additionally, faculty should know exactly how to access this resource when needed.

Recruit More Black Administration

Recruiting and hiring Black faculty is important. Recruiting and hiring more Black administrators is equally as essential. It is no secret that hiring committees are often composed of small numbers of faculty and administration on committees, "leaving room for biases and discriminatory practices to creep in" (Dupree & Boykin, 2021: 15). These practices can lead to fewer Black administrators being hired. Therefore, hiring practices must be reviewed in order to maintain fair and equitable searches. Black administrators can bring another equitable voice to the decision-making table, especially regarding policies and procedures that have the potential to impact Black faculty. Black faculty might also have no Black mentor in leadership and, as a result, may not be able to envision themselves aspiring for leadership. Having no one who looks like them in administration can also jeopardize the upward mobility of Black faculty (Dupree & Boykins, 2021). Black faculty need to see administrators who look like them.

Let Black Faculty Say No!

If we expect Black faculty to say "yes" to every request, in addition to all of their other teaching and faculty obligations, they will get burnt out. Administration should not only be agreeable, but also encouraging Black faculty to say "no" and practice self-care. When Black faculty say "no", it's not without reason. Administration needs to listen. While there has been scholarship around coping mechanisms and strategies for Black faculty (Zambrana et al., 2021), administration has to provide the space and autonomy for Black faculty to say no, without being convinced otherwise or made to feel bad about it. Let Black faculty say "no" when they need to.

Conclusion

Unfortunately, as a Black male educator, I will always have to think about how others will receive my Blackness and skin color. I will always have to deal with the negative stereotypes people hold about my brown skin. I am very aware that I do not have the luxury of going into society or educational settings and not worrying about how I show up in a space. As a Black man, I must be conscious of where I go, what I say, and how I complete daily activities. Non-Black colleagues typically do not have to worry about how their skin or physical appearance might make others feel when they enter or hold a space in the same way that I do. It is exhausting having to worry about how others will receive you consistently. However, this is something that many Black people deal with daily. Moreover, Black educators deal with this, on top of all the other obligations of the profession.

I hope that non-Black faculty, administrators, policymakers, and DEI champions will take something away from the experiences and recommended strategies that I have provided in this chapter. I will reiterate that this chapter does not, nor does it attempt to, speak for, or generalize, the experiences of all Black faculty. These are my individual lived experiences, representing my perspective of being a Black male faculty member in a predominantly white space. While many of my experiences tell me I am *not OK*, having support, allies, and non-Black colleagues committed to joining the fight helps me *be OK* as a Black male faculty member.

REFERENCES

Alexander R. & Moore S. E. (2008). The benefits, challenges, and strategies of African American faculty teaching at predominantly white institutions. *Journal of African American Studies*, 12(1), 4–18. doi: 10.1007/s12111-007-9028-z

Allison, D. C. (2008). Free to be me? Black professors, white institutions. *Journal of Black Studies*, 38(4), 641–62.

Anderson, E. (2015). The white space. *Sociology of Race and Ethnicity*, 1(1), 10–21.

Banks, W. M. (1984). Afro-American scholars in the university: Roles and conflicts. *American Behavioral Scientist*, 27(3), 325–38.

Boutte, G. S. & Jackson, T. O. (2014). Advice to white allies: Insights from faculty of color. *Race, Ethnicity and Education*, 17(5), 623–42.

Brown, Z. (2018). Experiences of black faculty members within agricultural education departments at predominantly white institutions. Thesis. Iowa State University. https://bit.ly/31pv7iq

Dupree, C. H. & Boykin, C. M. (2021). Racial inequality in academia: Systemic origins, modern challenges, and policy recommendations. *Policy Insights from the Behavioral and Brain Sciences*, 8(1), 11–18.

Griffin, K. A., Bennett, J. C. & Harris, J. (2013). Marginalizing merit? Gender differences in black faculty D/discourses on tenure, advancement, and professional success. *Review of Higher Education*, 36(4), 489–512.

Griffin, K. A., Pifer, M. J., Humphrey, J. R. & Hazelwood, A. M. (2011). (Re)Defining departure: Exploring black professors' experiences with and responses to racism and racial climate. *American Journal of Education*, 117(4), 495–526.

Jayakumar, U., Howard, T., Allen, W. & Han., J. (2009) Racial Privilege in the professoriate: An exploration of campus climate, retention, and satisfaction. *The Journal of Higher Education*, 80(5), 538–63.

Johnsrud, L. K. & Des Jarlais, C. D. (1994) Barriers to tenure for women and minorities. *Review of Higher Education*, 17(4), 335–53.

Johnsrud, L. K. & Sadao, K. C. (1998) The common experience of "otherness": Ethnic and racial minority faculty. *Review of Higher Education*, 21(4), 315–42.

Louis, D., Thompson, K., Smith, P., Williams, H. M. A. & Watson, J. (2017). Afro-Caribbean Immigrant Faculty Experiences in the American Academy: Voices of an Invisible Black Population. *The Urban Review*, 49(4), doi: 10.1007/s11256-017-0414-0

McKay, N. Y. (1997) A troubled peace: Black women in the halls of the white academy. In Benjamin, L. (ed.), *Black Women in the Academy: Promises and perils*. Miami: University Press of Florida.

Miller, T. L., Wesley, C. L., Bell, M. P. & Avery, D. R. (2021). Hold the torch: Shining a light on the lives of black management faculty. *Journal of Management*, 47(2), 351–67. doi: 10.1177/0149206320968621

Patton, L. D. & Catching, C. (2009). "Teaching while black": Narratives of African American student affairs faculty. *International Journal of Qualitative Studies in Education*, 22(6), 713–28.

Shaw, P. W. H. (2014). New treasures with the old: Addressing culture and gender imperialism in high level theological education. *Evangelical Review of Theology*, 38(3), 265–79.

Smallwood, S. (2007) Noose discovered on office door of black professor at Columbia U. *The Chronicle of Higher Education*. October 9. https://bit.ly/3EuB63s

Toliver, S. D., Moore, P. J. & Redcross, N. (2015). Intra-racial dynamics of black faculty and black students: Barriers to success in the academy in predominantly white institutions. *European Scientific Journal*, 1. https://eujournal.org/index.php/esj/article/view/5068

Tomlin, A. D. (2021). When they see us: Narratives of black male teachers. Dissertation. University of Maryland. https://bit.ly/3EIzpPs

Tomlin, A. D. & Brad, J. C. (2021). A foundational guide for mentoring students. *Interfolio*. https://bit.ly/3GdKp8D

Tomlin, A. D., Colbert, G. L. & Spivey, J. (2021). Thriving despite the challenges: Tips for HBCU students and faculty. *Interfolio*. https://bit.ly/3dm8mho

Trower, C. A. & Chait, R. P. (2002) Faculty diversity: Too little for too long. *Harvard Magazine*, March–April, 33–7.

Turner, C. S. V. & Myers Jr, S. L. (2000) Faculty of Color in Academe: Bittersweet success. Boston: Allyn and Bacon.

Zambrana, R. E., Valdez, R. B., Pittman, C. T., Bartko, T., Weber, L. & Parra-Medina, D. (2021). Workplace stress and discrimination effects on the physical and depressive symptoms of underrepresented minority faculty. *Stress and Health*, 37(1), 175–85. doi: 10.1002/smi.2983

CHAPTER 5

Surviving Higher Learning: Microinvalidations of Black Junior Faculty in Higher Education

Derrick Robinson, Tempestt R. Adams, Brian K. Williams, and Nakeshia N. Williams

If existing in higher education as Black junior faculty is difficult, arriving there by the doctoral journey is even more of a challenge. Nationally, only 1.8 percent of the US population holds an earned doctorate (United States Census Bureau, 2021). What this tells us is that those who have earned a doctoral degree are members of a rare group. Drilling down this understanding to explore the Black earned doctorate, reveals a disproportional discrepancy. The National Science Foundation's 2019 Survey of Earned Doctorates report suggests that, of the 55,195 doctorates earned in 2017, 3,058 were earned by Black doctoral students (National Science Foundation, 2019). Thus, while Black people constituted 13.4 percent of the US population in 2017 (United States Census Bureau, 2019), less than half of that proportion of doctorates, 5.5 percent, were earned by Black students (National Science Foundation, 2019). For perspective, while white populations were 76.3 percent of the US population (United States Census Bureau, 2019), they accounted for more than half of the proportion of earned doctorates, 52 percent, that year (National Science Foundation, 2019). While white populations were not over-represented in earned doctorates, we are observing a severe under-representation of Black earned doctorates with respect to their proportion of the total US population. As an earned doctorate is the recognized standard for entry into a tenure-track faculty position, the conditions for Black junior faculty to become underrepresented in institutions of higher education have been set.

The purpose of this chapter is to explore the reflections, stories, and experiences of Black tenure-track faculty as they find their voice and identity in the academy. According to the 2018 Condition of Education report, 6 percent of full-time faculty at degree-granting post-secondary institutions are currently Black faculty (McFarland et al., 2018). While underrepresented in higher education, we see, through the National

Science Foundation Survey of Earned doctorates, a 16.8 percent increase in Black earned doctorates over the ten-year period 2009–2019 (National Science Foundation, 2019). In exploring their perceptions and experiences, we seek to learn how this underrepresented, but growing, group perceives the development of their professional identity in Institutions of Higher Education (IHEs). We compare their stories with identified variables found in the literature on faculty socialization in higher education: (a) finding and developing support (Cole, McGowan & Zerquera, 2017; Gillespie et al. 2005), (b) doctoral socialization (Cole, McGowan & Zerquera, 2017; Kniess, Benjamin & Boettcher, 2017), and (c) institutional normativity (Garrison-Wade et al., 2012; Thandi-Sule, 2014). We seek to address three questions: How do Black junior faculty perceive their support and belongingness in institutions of higher education; what factors are perceived as challenges for Black junior faculty in higher education; and what are the enculturation experiences of Black junior faculty on higher education campuses?

Theoretical or Conceptual Framework

In the analysis of higher education culture and climate, it is important that we examine the impact of *enculturation*. Cultural anthropologists describe enculturation as a process by which culture, or beliefs, values, and understandings of acceptable behaviors, is transmitted to individuals who enter an established environment (Lumen Learning, n.d.). For higher education faculty, this study is developed upon a framework of *faculty enculturation*. Faculty enculturation of Black junior faculty rests upon the integration of three conceptual perspectives: (a) *resiliency*, (b) *Afrocentric thought*, and (c) *faculty socialization and fit*.

Although the work of resiliency, as posited by Prince-Embury (2011), is primarily associated with adolescent development and learning, its principles, *sense of mastery*, *sense of relatedness*, and *emotional reactivity*, can parallel the process of junior faculty. As it is problematic to assess Black faculty by a Eurocentric lens, we employ Afrocentric thought and its components, *the right to be*, *maintaining the integrity of community*, and *sense of connectedness*, to speak to the ideal motivations found in literature on Black faculty in higher education. Finally, we employ faculty socialization and fit to speak to the challenges of *interpersonal*, *performance*, and *structural fit* needed to navigate the culture of higher education (Bilyalov, 2018; Richards & Templin, 2019; Thandi-Sule, 2014). The integration of these concepts creates three themes by which faculty enculturation, as a lens, is applied to this work on Black junior faculty in higher education: (a) *individual task efficacy*, (b) *collegial cohesion*, and (c) *institutional alignment*.

In considering individual task efficacy, we integrate sub-concepts of sense of mastery (Prince-Embury, 2011), performance fit, as professional socialization, performance proficiency, and discarding norms (Bilyalov, 2018; Richards & Templin, 2019; Thandi-Sule, 2014), and the "right to be" (Johnson, 2001). Here, we contend that by positioning Black junior faculty as experts and assets to the academy, they can find spaces where they can harmoniously acculturate themselves as faculty on their campuses. Collegial cohesion refers to the interpersonal relationships that Black junior faculty develop, internal and external to campus, that sustains them in their development as professors. Through the lens of collegial cohesion, we integrate the sense of relatedness (Prince-Embury, 2011), interpersonal fit, as acculturation, people, and enacting norms (Bilyalov, 2018; Richards & Templin, 2019; Thandi-Sule, 2014), and spirituality or sense of connectedness (Johnson, 2001). Finally, faculty enculturation considers institutional alignment, framed as ease or tension that Black junior faculty encounter in the enculturation process. Institutional alignment is centered upon emotional reactivity (Prince-Embury, 2011), structural fit, as organizational goals and values, politics, and transforming norms (Bilyalov, 2018; Thandi-Sule, 2014), and maintaining the integrity of community (Johnson, 2001).

Review of Related Literature

Literature on Black junior faculty suggests three key areas in which they occupy space and agency within higher education: (a) finding and developing support, (b) doctoral socialization, and (c) institutional normativity. These themes found in the literature will be aligned and integrated and supported with the framework of this study.

Finding and Developing Support

Literature suggests that major challenges for Black junior faculty are levels of vulnerability and anxiety about being on the tenure-track, feelings of being uninformed, and needing the support of senior faculty to provide direct and race-specific support (Cole, McGowan & Zerquera, 2017; Gillespie et al., 2005; Hirschkorn, 2010; Trower, 2009). Cole, McGowan & Zerquera (2017) supports this assertion in noting that, for Black junior faculty, advice from senior Black faculty is viewed as a source of *navigational capital*. Black junior faculty, particularly in their first year, find themselves needing to negotiate their research, teaching, and service identity with institutional goals and expectations. Grappling with legitimizing research agendas that are race-specific (Bonner II et al., 2014), teaching expectations and evaluations (Garrison-Wade et al., 2012; Smith, 2009), and service expectation and validation (Bonner II et al., 2014; Garrison-Wade et al., 2012), Black junior faculty note finding themselves and their agendas in conflict with colleagues and students (Cole, McGowan & Zerquera, 2017). The absence of senior faculty support then places the responsibility of finding such support on the shoulders of Black junior faculty.

Institutions can take on efforts to provide more support to junior faculty, for which Black junior faculty can proactively select. Gillespie et al. (2005) suggest that initiatives such as *research circles*, affinity groups designed to help junior faculty, extend and refine their research writing to provide junior faculty with a supportive research community. Institutions, according to Gillespie et al. (2005), can provide such resources to reduce the anxiety, isolation, and ambiguity associated with higher education institutions. For Black junior faculty, creating their own such communities, when such campus-wide communities are absent or hidden, requires developing networks through doctoral program connections or social media platforms. Where doctoral program support is part of the grooming process, social media platforms in the form of Facebook groups or Twitter provide a national external network where ideas, encouragement, and resources can be shared (Cole, McGowan & Zerquera, 2017). Such resources provide daily affirmations that can lead to future opportunities for research projects.

The isolation and ambiguity of being on the tenure-track are compounded when considering the constant reminder of the delicate and personal nature of tenure and promotion. Where Hisrchkorn (2010) notes the subtle threats to *not make waves* for fear that someone will later be on your tenure committee, Bonner II et al. (2014) suggest that "African-American faculty spend more time on activities that do not promote their professional socialization, which lessens their chances for attaining tenure and promotion" (p. 42). According to Trower (2009), there is a unique level of uncertainty and skepticism existing among Black junior faculty, who are encouraged to believe that a tenure process is performance-based. These assertions suggest that the research, teaching, and service that Black junior faculty do as part of their personal agenda, conflict with their institutional goals.

Doctoral Socialization

Black junior faculty tend to be non-traditional doctoral degree students. According to Offerman (2011), this population is generally part-time, ethnically diverse, mostly women, over 30 years old, married with children or dependent parents, working full-time, and self-funded. This suggests that, in addition to transitioning to the academy as junior faculty, there is also transitioning from a practitioner mindset, where deadlines, timelines, and expectations are the norm, to a faculty mindset, where these realities are much more vague and poorly defined (Kniess, Benjamin & Boettcher, 2017; Tierney, 1997). Consequently, there is little opportunity to develop the socialization patterns that would be helpful in transitioning into the academy. However, Cole, McGowan & Zerquera (2017) note Black junior faculty received the bulk of their grooming from the doctoral experience. Further, they note that this process required suspending their personal lives in favor of institutional success and advancement. Pressure to publish and present prior to entering the academy, while self-funding through full-time employment, for example, required finding mentors to emulate (Cole, McGowan & Zerquera, 2017; McGaskey, 2015). This *self-generated network*, a patchwork of mentorship, required going to conferences to meet the researchers that they often use in their work, connecting to social media groups, and learning from *second-hand mentors*, mentors of peers, about how to navigate the academy, search for jobs, and develop scholarship. As Black doctoral students were less likely to hold research assistantships, the challenge to compete for entry into the academy is particularly challenging (McGaskey, 2015).

While literature on doctoral socialization is present for general doctoral students entering the academy, literature for Black potential junior faculty is scant. Austin (2002), speaking for general doctoral students, suggests ongoing processes of apprenticeships, observations, and interactions with faculty to aid in the social transition to higher education. Where Cole, McGowan & Zerquera (2017) and Bonner II et al. (2014) find that Black junior faculty avoid stressors by putting their personal life and values on the periphery of educational aspirations, Austin (2002) suggests that doctoral socialization is enhanced with greater family and friend interactions and acceptance. Austin (2002) suggests a five-part approach to improving the socialization process: (a) more attention to mentoring, advising, and feedback, (b) structured opportunities to observe, meet, and talk with peers, (c) diverse, developmentally oriented teaching opportunities, (d) information and guidance on faculty responsibilities, and (e) regular and guided reflection with advanced faculty. Integrating Austin's (2002) recommendations through an Afrocentric lens (Johnson, 2001), literature could support the recommendation for intentional pairing and mentoring experiences with Black senior faculty to further their "right to be" and maintain the integrity of the Black faculty community.

Institutional Normativity

The presence of Black faculty in the academy can be regarded as in conflict with institutional norms. As role congruity theory asserts that higher status is assigned to leaders who fit the imagery of a leader in the minds of the viewers (Triana, Richard & Yücel, 2017), it is not surprising that Thompson, Bonner II, & Lewis (2016) note instances where Black faculty were mistaken for custodial staff. Images of the academy, and its actors, are part of institutional normativity. Where the presence of Black people as faculty violates normative imagery and causes status incongruence, role congruency helps drive the viewer back to institutional normativity to increase their comfort. Black junior faculty often find their research, teaching, and service in conflict with the norms, validations, and expectations of their respective institutions. These assertions are supported by research that suggests that Black junior faculty, in particular, must contend with determining how and whether to enact, discard, or transform institutional norms in a way that allows the non-dominant group experience to survive in dominant white spaces (Cole, McGowan & Zerquera, 2017; Garrison-Wade et al., 2012; Thandi-Sule, 2014). The research of Thandi-Sule (2014) implies that institutional norms vary in importance to the reproduction of institutional practices. Thus, while some norms are optional or malleable, others are core to institutional existence. In enacting norms of the institution, such as participation in the tenure and promotion process, Black junior faculty knowingly participate in the unavoidable process of reproducing institutional norms (Thandi-Sule, 2014).

Black junior faculty often find themselves in the position of needing to discard some institutional norms. Using Cole, McGowan & Zerquera (2017) and Thandi-Sule (2014) as guidance, we see discarding and transforming norms as creating and/or accepting structures that speak directly to the cultural needs of Black junior faculty. The devaluing of Black faculty scholarly agendas, particularly research that is race-specific and race-affirming, places the academic integrity of the researcher at odds with the institution that holds tenure and promotion (Thandi-Sule, 2014). It is at these moments that the informal networks supported by the research of

Cole, McGowan & Zerquera (2017), McGaskey (2015), and Thandi-Sule (2014) help support discarding norms viewed as trivial. When these norms cannot be integrated or transformed within the institution, Black junior faculty will find agency and relief in disregarding norms that conflict with their integrity. Transforming institutional norms, as posited by Thandi-Sule (2014), is often done post-tenure when Black faculty have a strong enough voice to alter discourse on merit and inequity, through committee involvement, and alter pedagogical practices, through mentorship. Acknowledging that Black junior faculty are still engaged in not making waves (Hirschkorn, 2010), mentorship and support from Black senior faculty can ease the grooming processes (Bonner II et al., 2014; Cole, McGowan & Zerquera, 2017; Trower, 2009).

Methodology

This chapter employs a qualitative approach informed by a design integrated with narrative and ethnographic principles to form a fictional narrative ethnography. In use of this technique of qualitative research, our goal was to discover the various stories, experiences, and perspectives of adjusting to life as tenure-track faculty and constructing one fictional retelling of that experience. This approach is supported by Nardi (2016) and Ollerenshaw & Creswell (2002), which suggest that the themes, present applications, and future implications of narrative recounts can be re-constructed into a *new story* for the audience. Further, through fictional narrative ethnography, we can integrate participant experiences into a composite experience that tells an enriched story of the tenure-track experience of populations that are often voiceless (Smyth & McInerney, 2013).

Data Collection

Data for this study was collected through semi-structured interviews of 10 Black junior faculty at IHEs. This method of data collection is supported by Creswell (2013) and Glesne (2011) in gathering the stories and experiences of study participants in narrative ethnography. The protocol for interviews is based upon the central research questions of the study and the three themes that support the conceptual framework. Through peer debriefing, we developed a ten-question interview instrument. Questions prompted participants to provide stories and experiences that encapsulate task efficacy, collegiality, and institutional goals and values. Participants were asked, for example, to "share an experience that convinced you that you could share vulnerability with a colleague."

Instrumentation

Instrumentation for the interview protocol began with codes derived from our research questions, literature themes, and framework themes. We developed and coded thirty questions. These questions were put into a survey form where three peer debriefers anonymously ranked questions from zero (bad question) to three (excellent question). The average score for all questions was 2.58. We chose the top ten questions, the scores for which ranged from 2.67 to 3.0. These questions were placed in a protocol and organized by research question, literature theme(s), and theoretical framework theme(s). Our peer-debriefing team consisted of Black junior faculty not included in the study.

Data Analysis

Interview data was analyzed using thematic analysis informed by a hierarchical, *in vivo* coding process. We utilized significant statements of the participants and coded them into elements, or key phrases. We then grouped the elements into key meaning units, creating another level of codes, and clustered the meaning units into themes, the highest level of coding. For the stories and experiences collected in the study, we organized them into a storyline that would guide the fictional story. The storyline was used, in conjunction with the themes, to create a patterned understanding of a fictional Black junior faculty member in high education.

Participants

Our study had ten Black tenure-track faculty as participants. We used a criterion sampling procedure. Inclusion in the study meant participants had to: (a) identify as Black/African American, (b) be a junior (tenure-track) faculty in an institution of higher education; and (c) have at least one year of teaching experience in higher education. While our study focused primarily on Black junior faculty on predominantly white campuses, we had one participant who started his tenure-track at a predominantly white institution (PWI), but moved to a historically Black college and university (HBCU) after two years.

Findings

Findings from this study reveal emerging themes: (a) *dual battles*, (b) *microinvalidations*, (c) *doctoral socialization*, and (d) *protected spaces*. Participants indicated that they often felt that they were fighting two battles simultaneously to justify their worthiness, one with students and the other with collegial or institutional norms. Participants indicated that their work, research, and presence were relegated to the status of uninvited guests in higher education and that these feelings of microinvalidations complicate their navigation of higher education. Participants shared mixed experiences on the doctoral socialization processes. Where some participants felt that their doctoral experience prepared them for life as junior faculty, many felt that there were missed opportunities to prepare them for all aspects of faculty life. Finally, participants felt that there were limited opportunities on campus where they could be themselves and relate with students of color outside the faculty–student dynamic.

The Making of the Re-Story

The story that follows represents a composite narrative of participant experiences told through two characters: (a) Dr. Maurice Phipps, full professor and mentor; and (b) Dr. Malik Williams, first year junior faculty and mentee. Significant statements of the participants were integrated in the quoted dialogue between the two professors during their mentoring meeting. The dialogue of the two represented patterns found within the findings of the participants, which align with an ethnographic focus (Creswell, 2013).

Setting

Our story takes place in the Spring of 2020 at Panera Bread, an artisan bread restaurant that groups of people frequent. This is the first formal meeting of the two since their initial meeting at the College of Education's welcome back breakfast. Dr. Phipps is an Endowed Professor of Urban School Leadership at Central Columbus University (CCU), located in the Southeast region of the United States. Dr. Malik Williams is a new junior faculty member in the Counseling and Psychology Department of Central Columbus University. Malik recently earned his PhD from Taney State University, under the guidance of Dr. Armstrong C. Luck, Endowed Professor of Educational Research and Director of the Center for Urban

Research. Dr. Luck and Dr. Phipps are colleagues who began their journey in higher education together.

Just to Get By – The Story

Dr. Phipps arrived at the Panera slightly after 1 pm, after meeting with other advisees. Although he was late, Dr. Phipps still arrived before Malik. Moments later, Malik entered the restaurant. Malik looked disheveled and exhausted, far from what he was when he entered CCU, and when Dr. Phipps first met him. His clean-cut face was now a gray-peppered beard. His eyes had the look of a lack of consistent sleep and he was at least twenty-five pounds heavier. Something was clearly off with Dr. Williams. The feeling of guilt crept into Dr. Phipps mind. They should have talked a while ago. The two greeted and stood in line to order their respective food. Malik formally greeted Dr. Phipps as "Dr. Phipps," to which he was advised that it was fine just to use "Maurice." Looking defeated and embarrassed, he apologized and added, "I just had a student the other day email me and say, 'Malik, I was just talking to Dr. Eaton', Malik's white colleague in the department. Dr. Williams continued, "I was immediately taken aback. What about Dr. Eaton made him Dr. Eaton and what about me made it comfortable to be addressed as Malik?" Dr. Phipps laughed and told him about Role Congruity theory and how he does not fit the student's ideal image of a college professor (Triana, Richard & Yücel, 2017). Dr. Phipps ended by asking, "So brother, how are you?" To which Dr. Williams replied, "I'm getting by." They finished their orders and moved to an open table.

Although Dr. Phipps had heard a few things around campus about Dr. Williams, he thought it best to get Malik's assessment of the first semester. Dr. Phipps opened, "[So], how was your experience in higher education compared to your ideas of how the experience would be?" Looking down, Dr. Williams, shaking and raising his head stated:

> Exactly what I thought . . . I watched [Dr. Luck], an endowed professor and scholar and the way they treated him at Taney State . . . and it was never that they called him n****r or anything, that would be too ridiculous. They would question him. He was an endowed professor, but they would question everything he did.

Already familiar with that experience of his friend and colleague, Dr. Phipps nodded in agreement. Malik continued, "Now, did I think that I was gonna have the police called on me? I didn't know it would be this hostile. I mean, in what world do Black people exist where there's no hostility?" Dr. Phipps inquired further about the police situation. Malik sighed and explained, "Several colleagues got together and filed a false police report against me. Uh, the argument was that I threatened to harm someone." Although the report was proven false, Malik would explain further what was in the report when Dr. Phipps asked him, "Do you sometimes feel like you're being kind of surveilled?" Dr. Williams nodded yes and added:

> Not only do I feel it, I do know that I am being surveilled. The police report revealed that at one point, something was produced, a document was produced. Right. Uh, and it had every time I had made a mistake in it, like by date and time. Some of it was, oh, "he slightly raised his voice at a meeting."

As Dr. Williams explained these slights, he began to talk about the weird existence of being both surveilled, but invisible at the same time. Dr. Phipps then asked, "Tell me about the other times you felt microaggressions from colleagues?" Dr. Williams quickly returned, "not micro, they were macro!" Sitting up, Dr. Williams shared an experience of being publicly mistaken for another Black colleague:

> I was walking away [out of the Dean's office] and somebody kept calling, "Jamal, Jamal." I kept walking. I hear them calling "Jamal!" I don't see Jamal. I'm looking around, they were like, "Jamal." I turned around, I was like, "I am not Jamal." And in my mind I'm like, "we don't all look alike" and then she immediately was like, "oh, his hair was like that yesterday." First of all, no it wasn't, because I have locks and he does not, right.

An awkward laugh was exchanged. Dr. Phipps shared a story from his second year in the academy. He stated, "Armstrong [Dr. Luck] and I would joke because we would be mistaken for each other everywhere we went. I was at the airport and a white man walked up to me and said he really liked my interview on TV." Dr. Phipps gave a bewildered look and continued, "I called Armstrong and asked, 'Were you just on TV?' He said 'yes' and I said, 'How would I know.'" The adage of Black people all looking alike appeared to be alive and well in the academy. Shaking his head, Dr. Williams added, "I feel like, in some instances, higher education drops the ball. Knowing how hard people of color have to work to actually get into the [academy], that they would already have systems in place to support us." Their food arrived, they said a quick prayer and began to eat. Dr. Phipps continued the conversation, "So, do you have opportunities to connect with students of color?" They laughed, and then Dr. Williams explained the mixed feelings that he gets from students. He explained:

> [I have one class where] all of my students are Black so, uh . . . I have plenty of opportunities to connect with students of color, uh, but I created most of them myself. I conduct Saturday write-ins and students show up and we write. We work, uh, but inside of all that, we also check in with each other. And, uh, it's like a family within a family. It started off with mostly my advisees, but then other people said, I want in, I want into this system!

Dr. Williams's facial expression lightened up and he smiled as he explained that story. However, immediately after sharing the story of that group of students, he also provided another experience. Dr. Williams added, "[my other class] . . . students had a different expectation of me. And so, I thought that I was pouring as much as I could into them. But at the end of the semester, my marks were very, very, very low." He continued, "I allowed them to give input into what we were doing in classes. I felt as though I was going above and beyond. [But] I had responses like, 'There's just something about [his] teaching style that I don't agree with." Dr. Williams then went on to tell Dr. Phipps about an incident that had just happened that morning, when a group of white students seemingly joined to question the content that he was teaching. Dr. Williams, while qualified to teach the course, does teach one course, Introduction to Counseling, which is outside his degree concentration, but more aligned with his professional background of twenty-two years prior to entering higher education. He added, "[there was] a lot of pushback [today] where people ask[ed] questions like, 'Well why, and how do you know?' . . . it makes me feel like their hostility stems from them not trusting my credentials." Recognizing that experience, Dr. Phipps opened up and shared a personal story from his first year at CCU:

> During my first semester here, one of my colleagues tried to get me fired. He actually hand wrote my student evaluations and had them submit it. The students later admitted that. I mean, they were racially charged. They [students] explicitly stated that he was trying to get me fired.

Hearing this, Dr. Williams posited, "Sometimes, I feel like, man, where am I? Dr. Luck did a great job preparing me for the hustle and bustle of this. But there are aspects you just gotta be . . . you just gotta get by."

Slightly changing the subject, Dr. Phipps asked, "Speaking of getting by, tell me about your networks on and off campus?" Dr. Williams responded, "So, my networks were built through my PhD program. [It's] a lot of the professors, the professors who graduated a few years before me or, um, even people who are still in the program." Nodding his head in approval, Dr. Phipps replied "Good." Dr. Williams continued, "I would [also] say social media, a lot of those networks like Race Mentoring on Facebook or First Gen. Doc. Students on Twitter." With further approval, Dr. Phipps added, "[When I first came to CCU] I was fortunate enough to have two or three Black professors that I would have conversations with on a weekly, if not a daily basis." Dr. Phipps continued:

[We ask] about each other personally . . . as far as emotional well-being, as far as mental well-being. A lot of the networks that I have outside of the university [had] to do with opportunities like a book chapter, article, or, um, "would you like to present at this conference?"

Dr. Williams, listening attentively, asked, "What about you, are there places on campus where you can go and feel connected to people who have similar interests to yours?" With a slight laugh, Dr. Phipps reared back and said:

You know, my favorite place on campus where I can get away and talk to people are the people that are of service staff on campus. So, um, custodians, cafeteria staff . . . they don't have the same professional interest, but it's like you have a safe place for me and somewhere where I feel at ease. But other than that, other places on campus, no.

The conversation continued well after they finished eating. Dr. Phipps could feel that Dr. Williams was evading the major question, research productivity. Dr. Williams was touted for his research and writing capability, well before entering CCU. However, no talk of research had come up thus far. So, Dr. Phipps pressed forward, "So, do you think there is pressure on you to publish here? How is the research coming along?" The question seemed to hit Dr. Williams as a surprise. It took a few minutes for him to formulate a response. Finally, Dr. Williams looked up and explained, "I'm in this work because I'm passionate, I care about it, and I don't want to feel like I'm put in a box as far as what I can write about or where I need to submit." He continued, "[I] almost feel like I have to kind of become fake in a way. I would have to modify the work just to meet that one checkmark." Dr. Phipps inquired why he would feel this way.

Dr. Williams has written some dynamic works on race and bias in data analysis, but had begun to fear that he would be framed as one-dimensional. Dr. Williams replied, "It's siloed me and put me in a position where students saw me as the guy who talks about race, forgetting that I'm the guy who talks about the law, about policy." He continued:

I actually had a conversation with someone the other day and they said, uh . . . but what about, what about um, this topic we can write about? I told them it's a really good topic and I would love to write about it. However, you know, if I write on that topic, I may appear all over the place and that I'm not focused enough . . . so I can't really write about it. Even though I'm passionate about that topic and I like it, I don't want my tenure packet to say that I'm focused on five or six different topics and I do not get tenure because I'm not focused enough.

Having heard the same thing, Dr. Phipps nodded in agreement. Dr. Williams turned the question onto Dr. Phipps and asked if he ever felt constrained on his way to tenure. Dr. Phipps recalled a similar situation:

> I was in a course one time and we didn't talk about race at all. And the students were so disappointed. Like, well, 'Do you not talk about race anymore?' No. I still talk about race, but at the end of the day, this is not what this course is about. And, for me, it was about my sanity. Here, I'm the only person teaching about race. Then how do I find a space of comfort?

Dr. Phipps also shared his disappointment in his Black peers, that "[even] other black faculty members, they didn't feel comfortable teaching about race because you get lower evaluations." He concluded, "it's ongoing, I don't want to say battle, but I'm going [to say] battle for lack of a better word, to move up in the ranks and to be successful."

As the two continued to talk, Dr. Williams's phone calendar sent him a reminder. He was now running late for an advising session. As he apologized and informed Dr. Phipps, Dr. Phipps posed a final question: "Tell me about a norm within the university that represents a conflict with you?" Preparing his backpack and standing up, Dr. Williams replied simply, "Passive aggression." He continued, "You can't be straightforward with people. [People] have to beat around the bush. [Things could be] more mapped out. Um, the expectations should be more concrete." As Dr. Phipps stood, Dr. Williams returned the question and Dr. Phipps recalled, "Perfection." He continued to reflect, then added:

> Not only do people want me to be successful, I feel like they want me to be almost perfect and it's not a healthy world to live in. Constantly worrying, did I get into a high enough journal or was this work free of any error? It's not just perfection. It's everyday excellence where other people get a day off. They get to not do things. I have to be here all the time doing something great. If I'm missing for a day, it seems to make it all the way to the provost.

They smiled, and as they exchanged hugs, they promised to be more intentional in meeting. While few problems were resolved, Dr. Williams walked away knowing that he had been heard.

Discussion and Conclusion

This story depicts a dilemma for Black junior faculty. While they stand to benefit greatly from the mentorship of senior Black faculty, the cycle of navigational stress, time, and safe spaces often allows time to pass by without notice. We see two characters who, while well intended, have not met for an entire semester. This observation can be improved through the work of Cole, McGowan & Zerquera (2017) and Trower (2009), who both posit that the interaction and support of superiors helps to reduce uncertainty and provide *navigational capital*. Austin's (2002) recommendation of structural mentorships and apprenticeships, with an Afrocentric lens (Johnson, 2001), may provide an institutional incentive to address this observation.

Black junior faculty also contend with role incongruity. Our findings affirm the work of Thompson, Bonner II & Lewis (2016) and Triana, Richard & Yücel (2017), which asserts that institutional actors, staff, and students, often negate Black faculty through identifying them as anything but a professor and speaking to them in informal tones, such as *Malik* rather than Dr. Williams. Such microinvalidations also appear in the findings, in which Black faculty credentials and research agendas are brought into question. Indeed, Black junior faculty fight wars on two fronts. First, as indicated in Dr. Williams's and Dr. Phipps's encounters with white students and Smith's (2009) assessment, Black junior faculty face micro-aggressions from students in class and through student evaluations. In the second battle, as evidenced in the police report of Dr. Williams, and the peer-written evaluation of Dr. Phipps, Black junior faculty are also in conflict with their white counterparts in the academy. These assertions of dual battles are supported in the findings of Cole, McGowan & Zerquera (2017), which notes that Black junior faculty find themselves in tense relationships with colleagues and students.

The findings also indicate that Black junior faculty desire to make efforts to connect with Black students on campus. Dr. Williams's single bright spot in the academy has been through working with Black students and engaging them in Saturday write-ins. While this appears as a great act of service, relationship development, and grooming to potential junior faculty (Cole, McGowan & Zerquera, 2017; McGaskey, 2015), research also notes that these are the kinds of acts that are not counted as service and, as a consequence, lessens movement toward tenure (Bonner II et al., 2014). Thandi-Sule (2014) asserts that including Black voices in conceptualizing and legitimizing research, teaching, and service of Black faculty is an institutional norm that needs transformation. The work of Cole, McGowan & Zerquera (2017), McGaskey (2015), and Williams et al. (2018) support the findings that Black junior faculty find community through self-generated networks that are rarely assisted by their institutions. Our findings indicate that custodial staff, social media groups, and doctoral programs serve as sources of community for Black junior faculty.

With vague expectations (Kniess, Benjamin & Boettcher, 2017; Tierney, 1997; Trower, 2009) and pressure to survive delicately to tenure (Hirschkorn, 2010), Black junior faculty find themselves under stress to be perfect. Through the words of Dr. Phipps, our findings continually reveal the loneliness and stress of Black exceptionality. Research supports the view that Black junior faculty enter the academy under pressure not to make mistakes (Bonner II et al., 2014), place family and personal values on the periphery (Cole, McGowan & Zerquera, 2017), and "publish, publish, publish" (Bonner II et al., 2014: 31). Our findings added to this understanding in Dr. Williams's reluctance to write on topics that he was passionate about for fear that it may make him look unfocused in his tenure files. Dr. Phipps's analysis of being pigeonholed as "the race guy" also indicates another challenge for Black junior faculty with a race, culture, or equity-focused agenda. While some Black junior faculty fear that their research agenda will be devalued by having a focus on racial issues, other Black faculty find themselves marginalized as only able to be "the race person." As the work of Thandi-Sule (2014) supports discarding reproductive norms that place the university at odds with Black research agendas, our findings note the stress of "becoming fake" to meet the perceived criteria for tenure.

The Way Forward – Recommendations

This study calls three stakeholders to action: (a) university administration, (b) university doctoral professors, and (c) Black senior faculty. For university administration, our findings suggest intentional monitoring and support of the socialization process for Black junior faculty. Providing equity for Black junior faculty may mean providing some advantages to ensure that they do not feel like *uninvited guests* at their institution. We recommend that administration, especially those in offices dedicated to diversity and inclusion, re-imagine research, teaching, and service with respect to Black junior faculty. Knowing that Black faculty face battles with publishing on passion topics, teaching evaluations, and service activities, leadership can work to be more inclusive and protective of Black junior faculty. Administration should also work to provide protected spaces for Black faculty to network and de-stress. Finally, we recommend that administration welcome and support Black junior faculty external networks by finding overlapping spaces include speakers from their networks, multi-institutional grant projects, and collective research circles.

University doctoral professors also share a responsibility to Black junior faculty. For Black doctoral students who aspire to the professoriate, sharing your current and past experiences in higher education can help to shape expectations and possibilities for future Black junior faculty. Additionally, university doctoral professors are recommended to help Black junior faculty generate networks in higher education. This is often best done through sharing your networks with them and extending opportunities for aspiring Black faculty to join research projects and conferences. For Black senior faculty, we recommend formal and informal mentoring. Where Black senior faculty may not always have the time to mentor directly, opening your spaces (for example, homes and social events) to Black junior faculty increases a sense of relatedness. As our findings consistently indicated Black senior faculty have limited time available, sharing networks is recommended as a less time-consuming form of mentorship.

REFERENCES

Austin, A. (2002). Preparing the next generation of faculty. *The Journal of Higher Education*, 73(1), 94–122. https://doi.org/10.1080/00221546.2002.11777132

Bilyalov, D. (2018). Organizational socialization and job satisfaction of faculty at Nazarbayev university in Kazakhstan. *European Education*, 50(3), 229–48. https://doi.org/10.1080/10564934.2017.1401436

Bonner II, F. A., marbley, a. f., Tuitt, F., Robinson, P. A., Banda, R. M. & Hughes, R. L. (eds.) (2014). *Black faculty in the Academy: Narratives for negotiating identity and achieving career success*. New York: Routledge. https://doi.org/10.4324/9781315852164

Cole, E. R., McGowan, B. L. & Zerquera, D. D. (2017). First-year faculty of color: Narratives about entering the academy. *Equity & Excellence in Education*, 50(1), 1–12. https://doi.org/10.1080/10665684.2016.1262300

Creswell, J. W. (2013). *Qualitative Inquiry and Research Design: Choosing among five approaches*. 3rd ed. Thousand Oaks, CA: Sage.

Garrison-Wade, D. F., Diggs, G. A., Estrada, D. & Galindo, R. (2012). Lift every voice and sing: Faculty of color face the challenges of the tenure track. *The Urban Review*, 44(1), 90–112. doi: 10.1007/s11256-011-0182-1

Gillespie, D., Dolsak, N., Kochis, B., Krabill, R. Lerum, K., Peterson, A. & Thomas, E. (2005). Research circles: Supporting the scholarship of junior faculty. *Innovative Higher Education*, 30, 149–62. https://doi.org/10.1007/s1 0755-005-6300-9

Glesne, C. (2011). *Becoming qualitative researchers: An introduction*. 4th ed. Boston: Pearson.

Hirschkorn, M. (2010). How vulnerable am I? An experiential discussion of tenure rhetoric for new faculty. *The Journal of Educational Thought*, 44(1), 41–54.

Johnson, V. D. (2001). The Nguzo Saba as a foundation for African American college student development theory. *Journal of Black Studies*, 31(4), 406–22. https://doi.org/10.1177/002193470103100402

Kniess, D., Benjamin, M. & Boettcher, M. (2017). Negotiating faculty identity in the transition from student affairs practitioner to tenure-track faculty. *College Student Affairs Journal*, 35(1), 13–24. https://doi.org/10.1353/csj.2017.0002

Lumen Learning (n.d.). 'Enculturation'. *Cultural Anthropology*, chapter 2: Culture. https://bit.ly/31HJpdS

McFarland, J., Hussar, B., Wang, X., Zhang, J., Wang, K., Rathbun, A., Barmer, A., Forrest Cataldi, E. & Bullock Mann, F. (2018). *The Condition of Education 2018*. Washington, DC: US Department of Education, National Center for Education Statistics (NCES). https://nces.ed.gov/pubsearch/pubs info.asp?pubid=2018144

McGaskey, F. G. (2015). Facilitating the creation of knowledge: An investigation of the factors that influence the research productivity of black doctoral students at predominantly white institutions. *Journal of Negro Education*, 84(2), 187–201. https://doi.org/10.7709/jnegroeducation.84.2.0187

Nardi, E. (2016). Where form and substance meet: Using the narrative approach of *re-storying* to generate research findings and community rapprochement in (university) mathematics education. *Educational Studies in Mathematics*, 92(3), 361–77. https://doi.org/10.1007/s10649-015-9643-x

National Science Foundation (2019). Doctoral recipients by ethnicity, race, and citizenship status: 2009–2019. Survey of Earned Doctorates. Table 19. Washington, DC: National Center for Science and Engineering Statistics. https://ncses.nsf.gov/pubs/nsf21308/table/19

Offerman, M. (2011). Profile of the nontraditional doctoral degree student. *New Directions for Adult & Continuing Education*, 2011(129), 21–30. https://doi.org /10.1002/ace.397

Ollerenshaw, J. A. & Creswell, J. W. (2002). Narrative research: A comparison of two restorying data analysis approaches. *Qualitative Inquiry*, 8(3), 329–47 https://doi.org/10.1177/10778004008003008

Prince-Embury, S. (2011). Assessing personal resiliency in the context of school settings: Using the resiliency scales for children and adolescents. *Psychology in the Schools*, 48(7), 672–85. https://doi.org/10.1002/pits.20581

Richards, K. A. R. & Templin, T. J. (2019). Chapter 3: Recruitment and retention in PETE: Foundations in occupational socialization theory. *Journal of Teaching in Physical Education*, 38(1), 14–21.

Smith, B. P. (2009). Student ratings of teacher effectiveness for faculty groups based on gender and race. *Education*, 129(4), 615–24.

Smyth, J. & McInerney, P. (2013). Whose side are you on? Advocacy ethnography: some methodological aspects of narrative portraits of disadvantaged young people, in socially critical research. *International Journal of Qualitative Studies in Education*, 26(1), 1–20. https://doi.org/10.1080/09518398.2011.604649

Thandi-Sule, V. (2014). Enact, discard, and transform: A critical race feminist perspective on professional socialization among tenured Black female faculty. *International Journal of Qualitative Studies in Education*, 27(4), 432–53. https://doi.org/10.1080/09518398.2013.780315

Thompson, G.L., Bonner II, F. A., Lewis, C. W. (2016). *Reaching the Mountaintop of the Academy: Personal narratives, advice, and strategies from black distinguished and endowed professors*. Charlotte, NC.: Information Age Publishing.

Tierney, W. G. (1997). Organizational socialization in higher education. *The Journal of Higher Education*, 68(1), 1–16. https://doi.org/10.2307/2959934

Triana, M. D. C., Richard, O. C. & Yücel, İ. (2017). Status incongruence and supervisor gender as moderators of the transformational leadership to subordinate affective organizational commitment relationship. *Personnel Psychology*, 70(2), 429–67. https://doi.org/10.1111/peps.12154

Trower, C. A. (2009). Toward a greater understanding of the tenure track for minorities. *Change: The Magazine of Higher Learning*, 41(5) 38–47. https://doi.org/10.3200/CHNG.41.5.38-45

United States Census Bureau (2019). Quick facts: United States population estimates [July 2019]. https://www.census.gov/quickfacts/fact/table/US/PST045219

(2021). Educational attainment in the United States: 2020. United States Census Bureau. Current Population Survey. https://bit.ly/3zdsw7p

Williams, M. S., Burnett, T. J. B., Carroll, T. K., & Harris, C. J. (2018). Mentoring, managing, and helping: A critical race analysis of socialization in doctoral education. *Journal of College Student Retention: Research, Theory & Practice*, 20(2), 253–78. https://doi.org/10.1177/1521025116657834

CHAPTER 6

How Race Impacts Teaching Returning Adult Students

Antija M. Allen

Introduction

When applying for teaching positions, educators are often asked to provide a philosophy of teaching. This statement commonly outlines their teaching methods and what influences those methods. Educators will often point out theorists who they align themselves with, some will mention learning styles, and others will credit being inspired by their favorite teachers. What is rarely mentioned in these statements is race, whether it be the race of the professor or the race of the students. According to King & Lawler (2003), it is essential to understand how social and cultural contexts influence education. In a research study exploring whether educators of returning adult students changed their teaching approaches to meet their students' needs, an unexpected finding emerged (Allen, 2018). Faculty reported that race had a direct impact on how they interact with their students. This was an unprompted yet vital finding in a study where more than half of the participants were people of color (nine identified as Black and one as Hispanic). Although there are quite a few studies that examine a faculty of color's experience when teaching at a predominantly white institution (PWI) (for example, Eagan & Garvey, 2015), this researcher could not find any that focused specifically on educators of returning adult students. Therefore, this chapter will add to adult learning literature by exhibiting the perspectives of Black faculty who educate returning adult students. The author will further explore how and why some Black faculty individualize their teaching approaches (delivery, communication style, and content) based on the race or ethnicity of their students.

Returning Adult Students

A **returning adult student** is an adult student aged 25 or over who is either reentering undergraduate education after being away for a period of time or starting college for the first time. These students are also referred to as adult learners, mature students, reentry students, and nontraditional students. There has been a significant increase in the number of adults returning to school (or entering for the first time), even larger than the number of traditional students. There has been a decline, however, in the proportion of younger people attaining an undergraduate degree. A growing number of returning adult students are pursuing postsecondary credentials to further their career and earning possibilities (Collom, Biddix & Svoboda, 2021). According to Carney-Crompton & Tan (2002), over the past decade, the number of students entering postsecondary institutions immediately following high school has progressively decreased, while the registration of nontraditional students has substantially increased. Singh, Matthees & Odetunde (2021) note that non-traditional students have one or more characteristics suggestive of adult duties such as working full time. They do not rely on others for financial support, have dependents other than a spouse, and care for children as single parents. Their academic journeys often result in dropping out of higher education to take care of immediate needs.

Robert J. Hansen, the chief executive of the University Professional and Continuing Education Association, estimates that 700 four-year campuses offer continuing education programs for older students (25 and over) to earn a bachelor's degree (Zipkin, 2014).

According to Ritt (2008), adult students have barriers that can make it very difficult to return to college. These barriers can be *personal, professional,* or *institutional.* Some examples of *personal* barriers are family commitments, lack of childcare, or general fear of returning to school. A *professional* barrier would be relevant to adult students who are employed. An example is not receiving any form of tuition reimbursement from their employer, which can cause them to bear the financial burden alone. An *institutional* barrier deals more with the actual college or university than the student himself. An example of an institutional barrier is the high cost of education (that is, the rising costs of tuition and fees). On a daily basis, educators of adults are expected to acknowledge these openly, and other barriers, and work with adult students to provide options and alternatives.

Kenner & Weinerman (2011) stated that there are three main groups of students that make up adult learners returning to school: (a) workers who had lost their jobs because of the recession of 2008 and who required developmental coursework to refresh their entry level collegiate skills, (b) veterans returning from Afghanistan and Iraq who had delayed their education to serve in the armed forces, and, (c) adults who had just completed their General Educational Development (GED) tests and were moving on to higher education classes. Experts in the field have also found that returning adult students include career changers, those who have previously deferred college, and those who want to be role models for younger family members (Zipkin, 2014).

In a study conducted by the present author, participants perceived adult students as tenacious – being more committed to their education, more focused, and harder working in their classes. One participant stated that the older learners he had in class are more persistent, more tenacious, and more dedicated because if they were not, they would not have come back to school. Participants also talked about adult students' abilities to multitask, to juggle their many life roles in addition to their student role. They also perceived that while adult learners are typically prepared to devote themselves to study, specific study skills and confidence in the classroom might be lacking, and thus a final subtheme emerged related to the duality of adult learners' preparedness. (Allen, 2018: 79)

Research Approach

Allen (2018) studied the teaching approaches of seventeen behavioral science (psychology, sociology, and anthropology) faculty members from various satellite campuses throughout the United States as well as faculty who reported that they taught returning adult students at a community college. Ten faculty members were from the satellite campuses of four-year institutions, while seven taught at a community college. The faculty members were all educators of returning adult students who were either pursuing a bachelor's degree in behavioral sciences or an associate degree. Data was collected via qualitative research methods.

Semi-structured interviews were the main research method utilized. The information that was obtained from these seventeen in-depth individual interviews formed the basis for the overall findings of this study. Each interview was digitally recorded and transcribed. Once transcribed, all digital recordings were deleted, and all identifiable information was removed. In this way, all interview transcripts were confidential.

The analysis of data was guided by the study's conceptual framework. The coding categories were created and refined on an ongoing basis throughout the course of the study.

In the Classroom

Having such a diverse group of participants was valuable in that it allowed for voices to emerge and share experiences about how their race, gender, and upbringing has had a direct impact on how they interact with their students. Two participants conveyed how their race influenced their ability to adapt to the needs of their returning adult students.

Sandra explained her background as an African-American student in a predominantly white institution. And when educating returning adult students who are in a similar situation, she finds that she can relate to them, which influences the way she teaches:

> I've been in this field for over 30 years and honestly because the majority of the students in the classes were African American in a predominantly white institution, so I could relate to them because I went to a predominantly white institution as an undergrad and came up in an era which you know and I think it's probably still true to this day, I knew I had to really kind of do, let's say, do double the work for people to know that I did know what I was talking about cause I went to undergrad in the '70s. That really guides the way I teach. (Sandra: Black, female, community college)

Mary also explained how being Black influenced the way she interacted with her students. Like Sandra, she finds that she can relate to her students, specifically those from vulnerable populations. Unlike Sandra, she expressed how not only her race, but also her gender, professional experience, background in education, and upbringing have helped her adapt to the needs of her returning adult students:

> I think that my ability to teach students is a combination of having lived in the environment in which I've had to teach. I've had to navigate it as somebody of a vulnerable population, both as a female and as a Black person. And, outside of that, being involved with leadership and having to communicate the needs of the students, so there's a consciousness that kind of arose through time, and practice, and experience. And my undergrad is in early childhood education, pre-K to three, and then reading, pre-K-3, and then special education. And then, the other part of that is the way that I was raised. I watched my mother and my grandmother really take time to hear people, and to understand who they were interacting with before they acted. When I'm in a class – it's not, oh, well this is what I did last year, so this is what I'm gon' do this year. (Mary: Black, female, 4-year institution)

The above examples show how race can have a positive influence on a Black faculty member's teaching approach. However, there is another side to this. One's race can place unspoken and unwritten restrictions on a Black faculty member's behavior. Oftentimes when working at a PWI, I will have students say things like "Why don't you just let us out early, my other professor never keeps us here until 9 p.m." (when attending a three-hour evening class) or anything related to bending rules, and the joking response I give is that I am not tenured – a response that soon may no longer be true. I do not tell them the real reason I do not attempt to bend rules, which is that I know that it would not be met with the same reaction. I can almost guarantee that, if caught, there would be consequences. To provide a non-academic example, on January 6, 2021, a date that many of us will never forget, hundreds of Trump supporters stormed the US capitol leaving several injured and some dead. A statement that was echoed not only by Black people, but by many from various racial backgrounds, was that it would have never been allowed to get that far if the terrorists had been Black. And, to give proof, a photograph of the National Guard standing on the steps of the Lincoln Memorial has been circulated. The photo was taken June 2, 2020, during a peaceful Black Lives Matter protest. A group of terrorists storm a US capitol, killing police officers and threatening the life of the Vice President and other politicians inside, and the national guard was nowhere in sight, but a peaceful protest of those saying "our lives matter too, so stop killing us" was met with several armed guards in uniform equipped with tear gas. The message cannot be any clearer. We as Black people are not operating under the same rules as our white counterparts.

Enforcing Class Policies

Unwritten restrictions are one aspect of the Black faculty experience that guides our teaching approach. Something connected to this aspect is being tasked with enforcing what are often basic policies and procedures. In recent years, I have found myself saying these are not only my rules: everyone in my discipline is required to do the same thing. The unfortunate and unfair part of this is that we all could very well be enforcing these rules, but how a student will respond to me is very different from how they will respond to my white colleagues. For example, when I say, via email, the syllabus states that students cannot submit an assignment late, I can be met with a rude and angry reply. Even the request, or rather demand, to submit an assignment late has a tone of disrespect. In a study conducted by Haynes et al. (2020), the researcher-participants (all Black faculty at PWIs) found they had similar experiences where students attempted to undermine their authority. They discussed how students questioned decisions regarding grading, late work, course design, and classroom etiquette. One researcher-participant, Jasmine, recalled a specific interaction where she received an email from a white woman student seeking feedback on an assignment before submission, who also perceived Jasmine to be particularly young. Jasmine responded saying she "did not have the capacity to review an assignment twenty-four hours prior to the deadline," to which the student replied, "That's the craziest thing I've ever heard." The student then forwarded the email thread to Jasmine's faculty colleague – another white woman who was not involved in the course – and asked her whether Jasmine's response was valid. This student's effort to "fact-check" Jasmine's pedagogical decisions was not an isolated event.

Whitfield-Harris et al. (2017) studied nurse faculty employed in predominantly white schools of nursing (PWSON) who self-identified as Black or African American and most of the participants (n = 14) expressed similar experiences with students, such as feeling disrespected, feeling uncomfortable, or their teaching styles being questioned. Students queried grades and challenged them with the deans. All but one of the deans (n = 14) did not change students' grades; however, one dean changed a grade on an assignment without first speaking with the participant. One participant felt that students disrespected her to make her change their grades. She felt bullied, "They challenged me to act inappropriately; they challenged my integrity; my ability to be honest and fair across the system. They never displayed this behavior with white faculty" (Whitfield-Harris et al., 2017: 610–11).

The start of the COVID-19 pandemic created a new set of policies and a new set of challenges for Black faculty. Although many of us had the privilege of working from home and teaching online, several faculty who, because of the nature of their courses or decisions made by their institutions, had to continue to teach face to face. Now, in addition to the usual policies and procedures that Black faculty were being challenged on, they also had the added responsibility of ensuring that students were wearing masks and social distancing during class time. It is no secret that mask wearing quickly became a politicized topic. One example of this occurred at a bakery in a market in New York City. A white woman with children walked into a bakery without wearing a mask. A Black bakery worker politely asked her to put a mask on and she refused, which was when he then declined to serve her. She in turn responded by using a number of expletives including calling the worker the n-word. The security guard got involved and threatened to call the police because the customer was being uncooperative. One account says the police did not respond to any calls from the market while another states that the woman left before the police arrived. This customer was a self-proclaimed Trump supporter who believed the coronavirus was a hoax and therefore saw being required to wear a mask as a political matter (Chung, 2021).

Imagine a Black male faculty member asking a white female returning adult student to wear her mask when she feels strongly that it is her constitutional right not to wear one. This, in some cases, may be putting that faculty member in danger. Over the past year we have seen numerous instances of people being harmed who were simply trying to enforce a policy that has become commonplace in most establishments. The faculty member will have to approach the unmasked student and ask them to put their mask back on before potentially having to escalate it to contacting campus security or police perhaps to remove the student for not wearing a mask. At some institutions that enforce mask wearing, they see refusal to wear a mask as having an impact on the safety and well-being of the other students. For some, this may be just another tedious duty, but for Black Indigenous People of Color (BIPOC) faculty like Jasmine, for example, this could be a burden that could cause her stress and possible harm. She may need to think about how she can request that a student wear their mask in a gentle way that could in no way be perceived as confrontational in order to get the student to comply.

Code-Switching

When interacting with adult students, Black male faculty in particular have expressed how they have to be mindful of how they are perceived by their students, especially white females. A Black faculty member in teacher education shared that his classes are almost exclusively white females. He is very aware of the negative stereotypes that exist about Black men and how, sadly, they persist in the classroom setting. Therefore, he mentioned that when teaching he softens the tone of his voice so as not to seem intimidating or aggressive. He smiles more than usual to show that he is approachable and friendly, but despite all of this still finds himself the victim of racism. He explained how, while walking around the classroom, he noticed that his female students, almost without thought or pause, would quickly move their purses. If they kept their purses on the floor where he would have to walk, then moving them out the way would make perfect sense, but they were not. They were on their desks or tables next to them, but apparently too close to their Black male professor's hands. It's almost laughable. If he were to grab their purse, how far would he really take it? Why would a professor risk everything to steal a purse and whatever is in it? The questions defying logic in this situation are almost endless. This points to another issue, that of lack of representation, not just in higher education but also throughout a student's educational journey. Students need to see and interact with Black educators more often.

Proving Competence

One of the major issues that Black faculty face is having to operate in a space where those you are there to educate do not consider you – on the basis of race, and in some cases gender – as a credible voice. This undoubtedly arises in end of course evaluations, which will be discussed in the next section, but is also evident in the interactions that take place between students and their Black professors. There is an assumption that Black faculty have only been hired to diversify the faculty rather than because they are qualified for the position.

White faculty operate from a posture of privilege, and whether it be among colleagues, students, during job interviews, or everyday academic interactions, minority faculty carry the additional burden of addressing insinuations of inferiority and incompetence (Mendez & Mendez, 2018: 180). One example is the use of a professor's title when they are addressed. Some Black faculty have reported that students do not call them "Doctor," but address them by their first names instead – although the same students address white faculty as "Doctor" (Whitfield-Harris et al., 2017). I have not held the title of Doctor for very long, but I quickly realized that students were continuously calling me by my first name, even though I introduced myself as "Doctor Allen" and referred to myself as such. To eliminate this option for students, I removed my first name from my syllabus and email signature. Doctor is a title that has been earned and expresses a level of expertise and competence that should be recognized by students.

In a study conducted by Bridget Turner Kelly and colleagues, in which they explored what they referred to as "opportunity hire programs," researchers spoke with nineteen Black faculty about their experiences at a PWI. Participants reported being recruited heavily, then having to prove they were qualified to be faculty, and then having no institutional support in place to retain them. One participant stated during her first year of teaching at a PWI, she was thrown off by a student not believing what she said was factual:

> I have had – one of my first encounters – this was – it was horrible, 'cause it caught me off guard. I was writing something on the board, and I said to

a student, "I sent a list of facts to some students." And this older white woman, nontraditional student in the class – and I looked really young. She said, "Well, I don't know about that. I'd have to check up on that." And I was writing on the board, and before I could stop myself, I turned around and said, "Well, I do." (Rachel) (Kelly, Gayles & Williams, 2017: 312)

Assumptions of competence and teaching ability may influence the relationship between a student and faculty member (Mendez & Mendez, 2018). One participant in the Whitfield-Harris et al. study (2017) stated, "When they [students] wanted an answer, they wouldn't ask me, they went to white faculty, although it was my area of expertise." Others revealed, "They [students] insinuated that I bought my degree and was not credible enough" to teach them; "They [students] verified information [class lectures] with white colleagues" (Whitfield-Harris et al., 2017: 610).

In Mendez & Mendez (2018), the researchers found that students maintain positive assumptions toward white faculty when given instructor options, either by profile picture or in name according to the format that one would see in a university schedule. The study specifically focused on the preconceptions that students may harbor for faculty on the basis of race and gender before they have even set foot in the classroom. Student respondents in the photograph section of the survey had a strong, statistically significant preference for white faculty compared to minority faculty, and this preference became stronger when limiting the responses to white students only. Using the framework of Critical Race Theory (CRT), overall student selection of white faculty by picture alone indicates assumptions of competence that is granted.

End of Course Evaluations

"Intimidating," "inaccessible," "unprepared," "disorganized," "unapproach-able," and "pompous." These are the code words that are often used by students to describe Black faculty on course evaluations (Whitfield-Harris et al., 2017). One participant from this author's research study who identified as a Black female, spoke about the racism she endured when educating white returning adult students. She in no way believed that all her white students were racist, but when speaking of the results of her course evaluations from one class, she noted that two men definitely were.

She could not allow negative comments to hold too much weight because there was an understanding that those she identified as racist would more than likely provide her with lower scores and negative comments as a result. This participant indicated that she was fine as long as the racist was not outright disrespectful or physically aggressive toward her. The researcher did not probe further into this, but a question that could have been asked – and should be asked in future research – is, "How do faculty of color learn to adapt to the presence of returning adult students who are racist toward them?" Turner, González & Wong (2011) explored whether anything had changed since the landmark 2003 *Gratz* v. *Bollinger* and *Grutter* v. *Bollinger* Supreme Court rulings on affirmative action in student admissions. When conducting research with predominantly white research universities, they found that very little had changed for women faculty of color. Faculty described experiences of marginalization, subtle discrimination, racism and institutional racism, gender-bias and institutional sexism, and difficulties with students who do not expect to be taught by women of color.

According to Smith & Hawkins (2011), there is a relatively small amount of quantitative data from researchers who have explored the effects of race or ethnicity and student evaluations in higher education. Five studies were found that included faculty race or ethnicity, but, only one of those included Black faculty (Smith & Hawkins, 2011: 151). With this in mind, I was thrilled to find some recent studies that discuss evaluations. Murray et al. (2020) analyzed the website *RateMyProfessors.com*, which is a site where students can apply ratings to and make comments about teachers, whose names and courses are displayed. They found that men tended to be rated higher than women when it came to teaching quality and white faculty were rated higher than any other race.

Porter et al. (2020) added another element that has not yet been addressed in this chapter, which is Black faculty who hold a contingent status, that is, who are adjunct or short-term contract employees. They explained that the intersection of race (racism), gender (sexism), and academic appointment (positional status) is always at play for them as researcher-participants in the classroom. They stated that they experience an intersectional subordination that both nuances and characterizes conflict with students and colleagues because of their identities as Black women with contingent status. They believe that their classroom choices directly impact their appointment status and therefore they must constantly think about how they engage students, how they show up in the classroom, how much academic freedom they have (or do not have) to talk about and assign readings that center race and/or critical perspectives, whether their classroom decisions and engagements will show up in their teaching evaluations, and what impact all of the above will have on whether their contracts are renewed.

Evaluations hold weight not only with contract renewals for contingent faculty, but also with tenure and promotion decisions. An account from a study participant in Parsons et al. (2018) provides a heart-wrenching, yet all too common, depiction of how the teaching approach of a Black faculty member in a PWI can be changed in an attempt to prevent poor evaluations and gain tenure. Dee self-identified as an African-American female. She was an associate professor in science education, and this was her very first job in academia:

> My very first year was a very rocky year at first. I had extremely poor evaluations. I was asking them [the students] to write coherent paragraphs on different assignments, and they told me it was not a writing class, it was a science class. The other thing they resented was I tried to bring in a cultural understanding piece, and they tore up my evaluations, saying "she's trying to make us learn this culturally relevant stuff, this is ... science methods courses." And what I did was I tried to bring in some of Geneva Gay's stuff, some of Delpit's stuff, ... So I wanted them to understand the cultural issues that they could probably face in an urban school, and I had them actually read one piece by McIntosh that ... they called me racist. I said "well, this is a little white lady that wrote this; I didn't write it, an African American didn't write it – she's a white lady saying this." So, I just gave up after two years because my evaluations were horrible . . .. And I got called to the carpet, and I had to go in and sit with my chair, and we had a face-to-face about my evaluations. Wasn't nothing pretty ... After I met with the chair, he came in and observed me again, and actually said ... he thought my classroom culture was just fine ... we have what's called the faculty devel-opment center, I had them come in and give me some tips, and I went to a couple of workshops. So I tried to show that I was doing all the things they thought I should be doing, at least making some attempt to improve my teaching. But I understood the two main things I did was to not even ask them to write and not talk about culture. That really turned it around ... From that point on I started getting excellent, excellent, excellent. [The] only thing I did different from my perspective was to not ask the students to do two of the things I really felt they needed to know how to do. I just didn't do it, after two years of trying to get them to see ... trying to get them to understand that teachers write ... and you won't teach all white kids. It wasn't going anywhere, so my husband said, "Turn the evaluations around, I mean, if you don't do it you won't get tenure." So, to be honest I had to go against my own beliefs in terms of being at least an acceptable writer and the importance of having students understand the importance of their cultural beliefs and how it impacts how they teach. I did not do those things the next two years. Evaluations turned around. (Parsons et al., 2018: 383–4)

Thus far, the examples provided have mainly been from Black female faculty, but Black male faculty also experience discrimination in their evaluations. In Haynes et al. (2020), one participant, Steve, who identified as a queer Black man, discussed how he was well liked by his students, or seemed to be, until he brought content related to race and privilege into the course:

> Each week, the research of Scholars of Color and White scholars who studied issues of diversity, power, privilege, and racism in higher education were featured, but the contents of the articles were rarely discussed. Instead, we focused on research design, methodology, and theory. However, if an article featured critical race theory, then of course I had to provide context about what that theory is about. I did the same with Bourdieu and his conceptualization of cultural and social capital. (Haynes et al., 2020: 714)

Steve was surprised when reading his end-of-term teaching evaluations. Students accused him of "teaching a diversity course." They characterized him as "ego-driven," and used their course evaluations to describe what they experienced as a contentious "power dynamic" in his classroom. Steve felt like some students were penalizing him for introducing them to literature and concepts that challenged whiteness. He wrote:

> White supremacy is a peculiar thing. It rears its ugly head in the most interesting manners. These students complimented me the entire semester and appeared engaged but waited until evaluation time to discuss their disdain for me and my class due to my having them confront and challenge racism, power, and privilege in the research process. (Haynes et al., 2020: 714)

What we are seeing is a pattern of Black faculty who in a sense have lost their academic freedom because they know the power of evaluations. The 1940 *Statement of Principles on Academic Freedom and Tenure* affirms, "teachers are entitled to freedom in the classroom in discussing their subject" (American Association of University Professors, n.d.). In the cases of both Steve and Dee, they are utilizing diverse material, but technically because the course materials are relevant, they should be covered by academic freedom. Unfortunately, because they are Black faculty, any mention of racism, privilege, or diversity is automatically seen as agenda pushing rather than culturally responsive or inclusive teaching.

Recommended Strategies

Each strategy listed below relates back to the obstacles and challenges faced by Black faculty that have been outlined in this chapter. These strategies could assure Black faculty that they are at an institution that values them, respects their expertise, and wants to protect them. Although this chapter has been specifically geared toward educators of returning adult students, the following recommendations would be beneficial for all Black faculty, students, and the institution overall:

Make a conscious effort to hire Black faculty, but have support in place for them (for example, institutional policies, mental wellness programs, mentors, sponsors, and inclusive practices).

Data from a case study conducted by Kelly, Gayles & Williams (2017) showed there was a decrease in the number of tenured Black faculty over a twenty-year period revealing that once Black faculty left, new Black faculty were not coming in to take their place. The authors stated that this displayed not only the importance of the recruitment of Black faculty, but also the building of an environment that is welcoming and appreciative of what Black faculty contribute to the campus. Ensuring that Black faculty can cultivate mentors and sponsors within their program, department, and university is a part of what it means to create an environment in which faculty can thrive.

Hire a Chief Diversity Officer, a Director of Diversity, Equity, and Inclusion, or a Director of Faculty Diversity and Retention.

This is not a position that should be lumped in with an existing role, since the responsibilities are too great, and the need is much too high. This chapter and this book as a whole show that this is a major issue that, if not taken seriously, will result in Black faculty continuing to leave academia, with the consequent loss for students as well as the institution overall.

Make a college-wide commitment to culturally-responsive pedagogy.

A culturally responsive curriculum recognizes the importance of cultural diversity in learning (Maluleka, 2020). This aids both in faculty utilizing diverse materials without fear and in creating an inclusive campus environment because the views of students from various circumstances, cultures and backgrounds are recognized. This should be mandatory for all courses starting with first-year experience (that is, college experience).

Incorporate diversity, equity, and inclusion (DEI) training (that is, cultural competency programs) led by diverse staff into new student and new faculty orientations (or an existing new faculty academy).

The outcomes of strong cultural competency programs can include an increased sense of efficacy among faculty that results in student persistence and success, and an increased sense of satisfaction with educational opportunities and services among faculty, staff, and students. These programs must be complemented by other diversity-related initiatives, for example, existing courses or curricula that emphasize cultural understanding, inclusive hiring practices, the presence of a diversity officer, the opening of a diversity or cultural center, and the hosting of campus-wide cultural events. In addition, at the start of the training the President of the institution should provide a statement of commitment to DEI that can be conducted virtually or in person during the training. This combination is more effective at changing attitudes, cognitions, and behaviors because it communicates a genuine organizational commitment to and support for diversity (Kruse, Rakha & Calderone, 2018).

Ensure that Black faculty know that they have academic freedom.
Outline exactly what that means at your institution, and show your commitment to supporting faculty as they utilize that freedom.

Put policies in place that guarantee consequences for student to professor discrimination and/or bullying, and enforce them.
If students see that their actions have consequences, this could make instances of discrimination less likely.

Eliminate end of course evaluations and replace them with forms of evaluation less open to abuse by biased students.
More informal evaluations have been proven to be helpful to professors (Allen, 2018). There are also numerous other ways to determine the effectiveness of a professor, for example, informal student feedback, peer teaching evaluations, clearly outlined course outcomes, and teaching activities and assessments (Haynes et al., 2020).

White colleagues should not respond to emails from students of Black faculty but simply remind them they are not their professor and therefore not at liberty to comment on matters that do not involve them.
If your institution does not have a policy regarding communication between professors and students, then one should be added.

REFERENCES

Allen, A. M. (2018). Exploring the teaching approaches utilized by educators of returning adult students on satellite campuses and community college campuses: To what extent do faculty change their teaching approaches to meet the needs of the adult learner? Dissertation. Columbia University. https://doi.org/10.7916/D83X9Q3Q

American Association of University Professors (AAUP). (n.d.). 1940 Statement of principles on academic freedom and tenure. https://www.aaup.org/AAUP/co mm/rep/A/class.htm

Carney-Crompton, S. & Tan, J. (2002). Support systems, psychological functioning, and academic performance of nontraditional female students. *Adult Education Quarterly*, 52(2), 140–54. doi:10.1177/074171360205200205

Chung, J. (2021). Video shows unmasked woman's racist rant against black worker at LES bakery. *Gothamist*. March 24. https://bit.ly/31KPVRE

Collom, G. D., Biddix, J. P., & Svoboda, B. L. (2021). "I'm not letting nothing stop me this time": Transitions among adult learners using the Tennessee reconnect grant. *Community College Review*, 49(4), 413–34. https://doi.org/10 .1177/00915521211026679

Eagan Jr, M. K., and J. C. Garvey. 2015. Stressing out: Connecting race, gender, and stress with faculty productivity. *The Journal of Higher Education*, 86(6), 923–51.

Haynes, C., Taylor, L., Mobley Jr, S. D. & Haywood, J. (2020). Existing and resisting: The pedagogical realities of black, critical men and women faculty. *The Journal of Higher Education*, 91(5), 698–721. https://doi.org/10.1080/00221 546.2020.1731263

Kelly, B. T., Gayles, J. G. & Williams, C. D. (2017). Recruitment without retention: A critical case of black faculty unrest. *Journal of Negro Education*, 86(3), 305–17.

Kenner, C. & Weinerman, J. (2011). Adult learning theory: Applications to non-traditional college students. *Journal of College Reading and Learning*, 41(2), 87–96. doi:10.1080/10790195.2011.10850344

King, K. P. & Lawler, P. A. (eds.) (2003). *New Perspectives on Designing and Implementing Professional Development of Teachers of Adults*. San Francisco, CA: Jossey-Bass.

Kruse, S. D., Rakha, S. & Calderone, S. 2018. Developing cultural competency in higher education: An agenda for practice. *Teaching in Higher Education*, 23(6), 733–50.

Maluleka, K. J. (2020). Humanising higher education through a culturally responsive curriculum. *South African Journal of Higher Education*, 34(6), 137–49. https://doi.org/10.20853/34-6-3764

Mendez, J. M. & Mendez, J. P. (2018). What's in a name … or a face? Student perceptions of faculty race. *Journal of Political Science Education*, 14(2), 177–96. https://doi.org/10.1080/15512169.2017.1389282

Murray, D., Boothby, C., Zhao, H., Minik, V., Bérubé, N., Larivière, V. & Sugimoto, C. R. (2020). Exploring the personal and professional factors associated with student evaluations of tenure-track faculty. *PLoS ONE*, 15(6), e0233515. https://doi.org/10.1371/journal.pone.0233515

National Center for Education Statistics (NCES). (2017). Characteristics of post-secondary faculty. *The Condition of Education 2017*. Washington, DC: US Department of Education. https://nces.ed.gov/pubsearch/pubsinfo.asp? pubid=2017144

Parsons, E. R. C., Bulls, D. L., Freeman, T. B., Butler, M. B. & Atwater, M. M. (2018). General experiences + race + racism = work lives of black faculty in postsecondary science education. *Cultural Studies of Science Education*, 13, 371–94. https://doi.org/10.1007/s11422-016-9774-0

Porter, C. J., Moore, C. M., Boss, G. J., Davis, T. J. & Louis, D. A. (2020). To be black women and contingent faculty: Four scholarly personal narratives. *The Journal of Higher Education*, 91(5), 674–97. https://doi.org/10.1080/00221546 .2019.1700478

Ritt, E. (2008). Redefining tradition: Adult learners and higher education. *Adult Learning*, 19(1–2), 12–16. doi:10.1177/104515950801900103

Singh, J., Matthees, B. & Odetunde, A. (2021), Leaning online education during COVID-19 pandemic – attitudes and perceptions of non-traditional adult learners, *Quality Assurance in Education*, 29(4), 408–21. doi: 10.1108/QAE-12-2020-0147

Smith, B. P. & Hawkins, B. (2011). Examining student evaluations of black college faculty: Does race matter? *The Journal of Negro Education*, 80(2), 149–62. https://www.jstor.org/stable/41341117

Turner, C. S. V., González, J. C. & Wong, K. (2011). Faculty women of color: The critical nexus of race and gender. *Journal of Diversity in Higher Education*, 4(4), 199–211. doi: 10.1037/a0024630

Whitfield-Harris, L., Lockhart, J. S., Zoucha, R. & Alexander, R. (2017). The lived experience of black nurse faculty in predominantly white schools of nursing. *Journal of Transcultural Nursing*, 28(6), 608–15. https://doi.org/10 .1177/1043659617699064

Zipkin, A. (2014). Many adults falling short of degrees. *New York Times*, March 18. Section F, 7.

PART II

Promoting Mental Wellness

CHAPTER 7

Promoting Mental Wellness among Black Faculty: Strategies for Coping

Narketta Sparkman-Key and Shuntay Z. Tarver

> Caring for myself is not self-indulgence, it is self-preservation, and that is an act of political warfare.
>
> Audre Lorde

Introduction

There is not a break from the onslaught of racial injustices that Black faculty experience within the academy that affords grace to focus on their mental wellness. Rather, being Black in higher education requires the engagement in what Audre Lorde defines as the political warfare of caring for ourselves as an act of self-preservation (Lorde, 1988). Black faculty must reckon with the reality that institutions of higher education are based upon white supremacy that benefits from the labor, thrives on the exclusion, and echoes the dehumanization of Black people. Consequently, navigating systemic inequalities requires Black faculty to engage in the strategic and simultaneous tasks of discerning what is happening to us, and actively employing numerous coping strategies that will allow us to thrive in hostile and unwelcoming contexts (Alexander & Moore, 2008; Bonner et al., 2014; Spates et al., 2020). This chapter explores this conundrum by discussing how Black faculty experiences cause mental strain, and the various coping strategies utilized to achieve mental well-being.

Black faculty embody a great deal of resilience to navigate systemic inequality successfully (Davis, Chaney & BeLue, 2020; Louis et al., 2016). Such resiliency is essential amidst pervasive institutional barriers that not only distract from professional success, but also undermine it through individual actions, systemic policies, and institutional practices. For Black faculty, becoming an expert in their field and securing a coveted position in the academy does not automatically result in institutions welcoming and valuing their presence and empirical contributions (Alexander & Moore, 2008; Louis et al., 2016). Consequently, the phrase 'publish or perish', often reflects a deeper, and more troubling, reality for Black faculty, who must find coping strategies that will prevent them from mentally, emotionally, and physically perishing within the ivory tower, irrespective of the number of publications one has on the road to tenure. Black faculty are often challenged by racial exclusion, psychological torment, and institutional inequities that manifest as persistent mental, spiritual, and emotional attacks, or microaggressions that occur throughout one's tenure (Decuir-Gunby et al., 2019; Griffin et al., 2011; Settles, Buchanan & Dotson, 2019; Thomas & Hollenshead, 2001). Nonetheless, Black faculty continue to protect their mental well-being amidst the challenges experienced within higher education. The purpose of this chapter is to examine how Black faculty promote mental well-being through the utilization of various coping strategies. Beginning with an explanation of Black faculty experiences in the academy, authors discuss how adverse experiences within higher education contribute to the mental strain of Black faculty. Next, we present strategies that Black faculty engage in to cope with the hostile climate of the academy. Finally, we conclude with the assertion that the resilience of Black faculty within the academy illustrates that they belong in the ivory tower, despite the multitude of messages and experiences that suggest otherwise.

Black Faculty Experiences

Black faculty experiences within the academy are less than favorable. It has been well documented that the presence of Black faculty has consistently been met with institutional inequities, racial microaggressions, and systemic marginalization (Alexander & Moore, 2008; Thomas & Hollenshead, 2001). However, with the increasing exposure of racial inequities within the larger society, more attention has been paid to these experiences within the last few years. Black scholars have begun openly sharing more of their experiences beyond traditional academic outlets, such as journal articles and conference presentations, in active resistance to the illusion that the presence of Black faculty in higher education is reflective of systemic inclusion. Alternatively, social media has been adapted in numerous ways to unveil existing racial disparities within the academy. For example, a Twitter-originating movement titled, "Black in the Ivory," erupted on social media in solidarity with global outrage over the murder of George Floyd, an unarmed Black man, by Minnesota Police officer Derek Chauvin. The tweets inspired Black academics across the United States to recount their experiential encounters with anti-Black racism within the academy. One scholar tweeted, "today a colleague mistook me for our janitor . . . the only thing we have in common is that we're both Black women." In another tweet a scholar stated, "I've experienced many different types of racisms but the type where white people make you do all the work and then erase you is new to me." This movement shed light on the experiences, treatment, barriers, and overall inequity within academia toward Black faculty. Social media has made it far easier to express these experiences to a wider audience. Despite this recent trend, Black faculty experiences, critiquing systemic oppression within the academy, have been empirically articulated for decades because of persistent racial discrimination and adverse treatment in higher education.

The experiences of Black faculty within higher education are plagued with overburdening due to service demands, barriers to promotion, individual racial microaggressions, and systemic discrimination embedded in institutional policy and practices. Such experiences threaten the advancement of Black faculty within higher education. Faculty of color are often heavily recruited, then subjected to cultures in which they must prove they are qualified, with no institutional support to retain them (Kelly, Gayles & Williams, 2017). According to Stanley (2006), "The wounds of covert and overt racism, sexism, xenophobia, and homophobia run deep for many faculty of color. Discrimination cuts across many areas of the academy such as teaching, research, service, and overall experiences with the campus community" (p. 705). This results in institutions rendering faculty of color simultaneously *hypervisible* in problematic ways, yet adversely *invisible* at the same time (Settles, Buchanan & Dotson, 2019). For example, as Settles and colleagues have asserted: Faculty of color, as an underrepresented group that lacks power within the academy, may be *hypervisible* due to their race and other markers that distinguish them from dominant group members. At the same time, their marginalized group status may render them invisible in terms of their personal identities, personhood, or work performance. As a result, achievements warranting recognition may be largely unnoticed, whereas mistakes and missteps, whether real or merely perceived by dominant group members, may be amplified, and receive heightened scrutiny (Settles, Buchanan & Dotson, 2019: 63).

Such hypervisibility renders any perceived deviation of Black faculty from implicit standards of behavior to be overemphasized and pathologically interpreted. At the same time, significant contributions made by Black faculty are often overlooked or misattributed to someone other than Black faculty. The experiences of faculty of color within academia are convoluted with tokenism and exclusion, while the nuanced injustices characterizing their experiences are often ignored (Griffin et al., 2011; Louis et al., 2016).

Faculty of color experience issues related to teaching, from students, including problematic attitudes and behaviors, questioning of their authority and credibility in class, and resistance to the incorporation of diversity perspectives in course content (Stanley, 2006). Often, teaching evaluation scores are lower for Black faculty in comparison to their white colleagues, and negative comments from students are used to challenge the advancement of faculty of color (Smith & Hawkins, 2011). In fact, these evaluations are often cited in annual reviews and promotion materials, with little to no consideration to how they may represent biased perspectives that skew the performance of Black faculty.

Black faculty experiences are also characterized by marginal or inadequate mentorship within the academy. Lack of mentorship has an impact on faculty of color's knowledge of the culture, ability to develop collegial relationships, and overall value within their institution. The experiences of many Black faculty reflect issues with an institution's lack of formalized processes of mentorship, resulting in adverse mentorship experiences. While many institutions of higher education successfully engage in mentorship of white faculty, Black faculty experiences often reflect institutional barriers that restrict professional advancement. In such instances, faculty sponsored mentorship assignments result in exploitation, microaggressions, and limited professional opportunities. In addition, institutionally assigned mentors may possess adverse beliefs of Black faculty. Problematic beliefs include perceptions such as the "fail or succeed entirely" mentality – the belief of success being achieved without mentoring, belief in a "one size fits all" type of mentoring, and the idea that if someone needs mentoring something about that individual must be lacking (Stanley, 2006).

Within the academy, faculty of color are often invisible to their colleagues and must prove, or over-prove, their presence or worth (Stanley, 2006). This reality is directly influenced by how faculty of color are hired by institutions, and existing biases toward institutional hiring processes. Negative views of affirmative action and opportunity hires have led to the erosion of Black faculty credibility, challenges in the tenure process, and microaggressions (Kelly, Gayles & Williams, 2017). As a result, lack of collegiality by disgruntled colleagues may become a barrier to success, despite the belief that collegiality is automatically an aspect of being a faculty member. Black faculty may be perceived in terms of attributes and stereotypes related to their gender, race, ethnicity, nationality, sexual identity, religion, culture, and socioeconomic status (Stanley, 2006). Their identity within the academy, thus influenced by how others view them, often leads to discriminatory practices (Griffin et al., 2011). In such instances, colleagues see Black first and a professor second (Griffin et al., 2011). The lack of control over how they are viewed within the academy has a negative impact on the success of Black faculty (Alexander & Moore, 2008).

Research has found that faculty of color experience microaggressions frequently in their professional life (Louis et al., 2016). In fact, many noted daily experiences ranging from snide remarks, condescending comments presented as jokes, mixed messages in job performance, racialized comments, assumptions that race would be the deciding factor in tenure, and surreptitious action (Griffin et al., 2011; Louis et al., 2016). In addition, racism shows up in the form of microaggressions for many Black faculty, resulting in feelings of powerlessness and high levels of stress (Louis et al., 2016). Such instances exacerbate the ill effects of Black faculty being overburdened with service responsibilities and ignored in promotion processes (Stanley, 2006). Service, such as the mentoring of students of color, recruitment and retention activities, community support, and educating white faculty, administrators, staff, and students on issues of diversity, are rarely counted toward tenure and promotion, yet faculty of color are often saddled with these added responsibilities (Settles, Buchanan & Dotson, 2019; Stanley, 2006).

Racism is a constant thread within the experiences of faculty of color. Both individual and institutional racism plague the journey and success of faculty of color within the academy (Griffin et al., 2011; Stanley, 2006). Racist practices and policies disadvantage faculty of color based on their racial group and nationality (Bhopal, 2016; Griffin et al., 2011; Stanley, 2006). Black faculty have also described institutional resistance and failure to increase the number of Black faculty on campuses as racism (Griffin et al., 2011). This leads to marginalization, isolation, and feelings of not belonging within their departments or among colleagues (Griffin et al., 2011). Black faculty are often the only people of color in their departments, colleges, and/or universities. Lack of representation has a direct impact on the experience's Black faculty encounter within the institution (Alexander & Moore, 2008; Bhopal, 2016). Numerical underrepresentation leads to tokenism and being treated as though the individual epitomizes their entire race (Alexander & Moore, 2008). Institutional racism is also visible in tenure processes when Black faculty's engagement in race-related work is not seen as scholarly (Alexander & Moore, 2008; Griffin et al., 2011). Lack of institutional support to retain faculty of color is prevalent across institutions in which groups designed to support multicultural faculty lack proper financial support, are not advisory, and have no reporting mechanism to university leadership (Kelly, Gayles & Williams, 2017).

Collectively, there is a significant cost that Black faculty pay for enduring complex and multifaceted challenges within academia. Persistent experiences with individual and institutional racism adversely contribute to the mental strain of Black faculty. To examine how this occurs, the following section discusses the influence of hostile academic contexts on the mental health of Black faculty.

The Impact of Hostile Contexts on Black Faculty's Mental Health

Continuous encounters of racism within the workplace affect the physical and mental well-being of employees (Memon et al., 2016). Everyday events such as threats, being treated with less respect, or being thought of as having lower intelligence due to race, constitute chronic racism (Woods-Jaegar et al., 2021). It is known that racism can lead to physical and mental health challenges such as chronic and acute forms of stress (Novacek et al., 2020). In Black individuals, stress caused by racism manifests as hypertension, depression, anxiety, psychological distress, and low self-esteem (Woods-Jaeger et al., 2021). Chronic racism characterizes the experiences of many Black faculty within higher education. Research on the actual mental health impact of Black faculty experiences in the academy is limited, which could be due to a lack of reporting. However, researchers have found that the inability to recognize symptoms of mental illness, rejection of mental health related symptoms, and fear of stigmatization lead to a lack of reporting (Arday, 2020). Alternatively, the ability of Black faculty to navigate hostile environments is essential to their survival within higher education. Thus, limited research on the mental well-being of Black faculty may also reflect their ability to mask the influence of toxic contexts on their mental strain through utilization of maladaptive coping strategies (DeCuir-Gunby et al., 2019). In addition, within academia, the physical and mental well-being of Black faculty remains an afterthought. There is a lack of concern and focus on the impact of racism, as well as a lack of resources provided to support Black faculty. Race-related crisis exacerbates feelings of anxiousness, isolation, and marginalization (Palmer & Ward,

2007). Yet, Black faculty are often requested to lead diversity efforts on campuses with no acknowledgment of how societal events impact them as Black individuals.

Black faculty within higher education have consistently experienced extremely high levels of stress, powerlessness, isolation, marginalization, discriminatory practices, and overt and covert racism within academia (Salazar, 2009; Settles, Buchanan & Dotson, 2019). Elevated levels of stress often impact job performance among Black faculty (Louis et al., 2016). Daily experiences of microaggressions from colleagues and students in the professional lives of Black faculty have an impact on well-being. For example, researchers found that after an encounter with microaggressions, Black faculty reported not feeling calm and feeling angry, with a smaller percentage feeling depressed and anxious (Robinson, 2014). Consistent exposure to microaggression influences the mental well-being among Black faculty (Louis et al., 2016). Furthermore, Black faculty are often stigmatized and rejected, causing them to disengage with their environment out of fear of mistreatment, leading to further isolation. Feeling like an outsider within social networks, along with tokenism, exacerbates stress among Black faculty (Louis et al., 2016). Lack of social networks results in compounded feelings of marginalization and residing on the periphery of social circles, which negatively affects mental well-being (Arday, 2020). Isolation also has a negative influence on spiritual well-being. Spiritual well-being is defined as "a high level of hope and commitment in relation to a well-defined worldview or belief system that provides a sense of meaning and purpose to existence, in general, and offers an ethical path to personal fulfillment" (Heintzman & Mannell, 2003: 207). In addition, "social isolation affects one's spirituality or sense of connectedness to others and is characteristic of a cold campus climate that disconnects [Black] faculty from their colleagues" (Alexander & Moore, 2008: 6). Tokenism has been associated with psychological trauma (Alexander & Moore, 2008). Psychological trauma is the experience of an event that was too overwhelming for a person to manage and results in symptoms that adversely impact the well-being of the individual. These symptoms may include recollections of the trauma, reactivity to response reminders, negative beliefs about self and others, inability to feel close to others, being easily startled, dissociation, emotional numbness, and inability to remember aspects of the trauma (Franklin, Boyd-Franklin & Kelly, 2006).

Black faculty report the need always to be alert, guarding their actions and responses to disprove inaccurate perceptions (Louis et al., 2016). Perpetual self-monitoring leads to decreased autonomy and self-determination

(Alexander & Moore, 2008). Decreased self-determination can impact performance and lead to more stress among Black faculty. In addition, symptoms of anxiety can manifest, with the need to consistently self-monitor and perfect acceptable views and behaviors.

Imposter syndrome also presents challenges to mental well-being among Black faculty, and is highly, but not exclusively, experienced by Black women faculty (Trotman, 2009). It occurs often among high-achieving Black women within academia, where people with institutional power and authority simultaneously overburden them with work while questioning their authority. Symptoms of imposter syndrome include intellectual self-doubt, accompanied by anxiety and often depression. Trotman states, "the subtle and not-so-subtle attacks on the African-American woman as a student, a professor, or an administrator in US institutions of higher education can seem relentless" (2009: 78). Consequently, Black faculty consistently work to disprove the stereotype of their incompetence throughout their career by taking on the stress of proving their merit, even when that merit is apparent (Meyers, 2002).

Collectively, racism has a significantly adverse impact on the mental health of Black faculty. Despite limited research, empirical studies have uncovered stress, psychological trauma, anxiety, depression, and imposter syndrome as challenges to the mental well-being of Black faculty. However, Black faculty are resilient and often succeed within the academy. Their ability to cope with limited support and resources is a testament of their amazing strength and tenacity. The following section explores various coping strategies that drive the resilience of Black Faculty.

Coping Strategies

The resilience of Black faculty within the academy is evidenced by their ability not only to succeed, but also to thrive amidst systemic inequalities. This resilience is only possible through the utilization of a host of coping strategies that buffer the adverse influence of discrimination, racial exclusion, and microaggressions on the mental health of Black faculty. Research indicates that Black faculty engage in both maladaptive and productive coping strategies to be resilient (DeCuir-Gunby et al., 2019). However, while maladaptive strategies are less than ideal to engage in, it is important to note them to avoid the consequences of coping with institutional hardships by creating personal ones. Alternatively, productive coping strategies are actions and behaviors that not only allow Black faculty to endure adverse experiences, but also allow them to thrive in hostile environments (DeCuir-Gunby et al., 2019). Collectively, each of the coping strategies detailed below contribute to the tenacity, determination, and drive it takes to be successful in the academy without perishing.

Maladaptive Coping Strategies

Maladaptive coping strategies are defined as, "negative or unhealthy approaches that may increase stress [despite the] attempts to mentally, emotionally, and physically remove stressors" (DeCuir-Gunby et al., 2019: 3). At the time of engagement, it may or may not be apparent that the coping strategy being utilized is maladaptive because the focus becomes surviving the microaggressions, discriminatory issues, or systemic barriers that one is experiencing. Maladaptive strategies include, but are not limited to, overworking, feeling suppression, and avoidance (DeCuir-Gunby et al., 2019).

Overworking

Many Black faculty have experienced being taught that you must work twice as hard to get ahead, or that you must be twice as good to be accepted (Salazar, 2009; DeCuir-Gunby et al., 2019). However, there are adverse consequences that come from putting pressure on yourself that results in overworking. Although it is common to work extended hours in the academy, overworking becomes problematic when it is done in response to institutional issues, such as having one's reputation questioned, attempting to meet excessive demands, and working to meet changing or informal expectations (DeCuir-Gunby et al., 2019). Overworking produces heightened levels of stress and can have adverse mental and physical ramifications on the body, such as exacerbated stress-related disorders like depression, anxiety, hypertension, and diabetes (Woods-Jaegar et al., 2021). Unfortunately, overworking rarely lifts the institutional barriers that exist for Black faculty. However, many choose to cope by striving to fulfill the unrealistic institutional expectations.

Feeling Suppression and Avoidance

At times, Black faculty attempt to deal with hostile situations in the academy by suppressing their feelings and avoiding contexts that will introduce microaggressions (Griffin et al., 2011; Decuir-Gunby et al., 2020). Black faculty who cope with hostile situations with avoidance of potential traumatic experiences, may be at greater risk of being (re)traumatized by the very inequalities they seek to alleviate (DeCuir-Gunby et al., 2019). Despite the tempered professionalism that Black faculty exhibit, interactions led by feelings of suppression and avoidance are often interpreted as being disengaged or non-collegial. These coping methods exacerbate internal frustrations and may inadvertently create a more contentious context for Black faculty.

Productive Coping Strategies

Productive coping strategies position Black faculty to thrive and excel in the academy amidst hostile contexts (DeCuir-Gunby et al., 2019). Such strategies require a great deal of tenacity and resistance in navigating institutional policies and practices in ways that protect, affirm, and enhance their productivity. There are many productive coping strategies that Black faculty engage in to succeed within higher education, including forgiveness, intentional self-care, expanded networking, and creating culturally specific professional spaces.

Forgiveness

Black faculty often cope with institutional inequalities by forgiving the offenses of administrators, colleagues, and students who perpetuate dis-criminatory behaviors. Such forgiveness does not denote or reflect the acceptance of problematic behaviors and does not require Black faculty to ignore offenses. Rather, forgiveness requires acknowledgment of one's own humanity and the justified feelings of anger, deception, resentment, and fear that follow experiences of institutional inequities. It also requires an internal evaluation of one's feelings, and how holding on to negative feelings can hinder future interactions. However, it does not mean that Black faculty accept or permit adverse behaviors to go unaddressed. Alternatively, an initial first step toward forgiveness is often confronting the perpetrator of racial injustice in an authentic way. Furthermore, forgiveness is a realization that holding on to detrimental feelings, irre-spective of how justified they may be, will have far more adverse personal consequences, such as stress, resentment, anger, and bitterness. Such negative feelings will prevent future professional interactions. Thus, for-giveness requires Black faculty to release damaging feelings personally held toward perpetrators of microaggressions, injustices, and other offenses, in liberating ways. This is a necessary coping strategy because, in many cases, offenders who carry out institutional inequities, racial exclusions, and microaggressions, are often colleagues that Black faculty will have to interact with on an ongoing basis. As a result, many Black faculty find forgiveness an essential coping strategy for thriving within the academy.

Intentional Self-Care

As stated at the opening of this chapter, "self-care is an act of resistance," and intentionally engaging in self-care "is self-preservation" in the academy (Lorde, 1988: 132). Self-care strategies include working out, maintaining a healthy diet, engaging in therapy, praying, journaling, meditating, and a host of other ways that relieve and/or prevent adverse levels of stress. Intentional self-care is validating and requires consistent engagement practices that remind Black faculty that they matter and are valuable contributors to the academy. It is essential to be intentional about one's self-care practices, because the academy makes little to no room for building up and affirming the esteem of Black faculty. The positive impact of engaging in self-care is well documented (Barnett et al., 2007) and intentional self-care is a critical component to the success of Black faculty within higher education (Nicol & Yee, 2017).

Expanded Networking

Successful Black faculty have well-established networks beyond their institutional departments and universities (Alexander & Moore, 2008; Salazar, 2009). Expanded networking includes both traditional and non-traditional connections for advancing within higher education. Traditional networking may include connecting with colleagues at conferences who have similar research interests, maintaining collegial relationships with post-doctoral students, and connecting across one's institutional department or college. Non-traditional opportunities are those that may not be institutionally supported but are vital to the success of Black faculty. Creating networks, such as community connections and connecting with other Black professional organizations, is critical to the success of Black faculty within the academy. Collectively, an expanded network provides support, encouragement, and strategies for navigating institutional injustices. They may also offer additional employment options if institutional climates become toxic (Griffin et al., 2011).

Creating Culturally Specific Professional Spaces

When Black faculty have had difficulty accessing traditional sources of academic advancement, they have coped by creating culturally specific professional spaces (Dyce & Williams, 2015). This includes the establishment of journals with targeted interests, developing conferences with specific topics and expanded networking opportunities, establishing sections and interest groups within existing professional organizations, and establishing organizations that support Black faculty's resistance to white supremacist practices and ideologies. The creation of culturally specific professional spaces has proven to be an effective coping strategy that supports the advancement of Black faculty within higher education.

Implications for Institutions of Higher Education

Engaging in Culturally Relevant Retention Efforts

Many institutions of higher education have responded to the racialized climate of the academy by focusing on recruitment efforts. However, recruiting Black faculty into toxic environments only enhances the institutions' inability to present diverse representation within the academy. Alternatively, engaging in culturally relevant retention efforts requires institutional efforts to focus on institutional inclusion of Black faculty. Such inclusion efforts include, but are not limited to, mentoring Black faculty to assume existing and forthcoming leadership roles; removing intuitional expectations that overburden Black faculty with service; training all faculty on methods of cultural inclusion in ways that improve the institutional climate; holding white faculty and students accountable for racial microaggressions, discrimination, and engaging in oppressive actions; including the institutional work of Black faculty in processes of tenure and promotion; and recognizing the inherent worth, dignity, and contributions of Black faculty in ways that do not exploit them for institutional gain. In addition, retention of Black faculty should include providing equitable salary compensation and academic start-up packages. Culturally relevant retention efforts require critical and consistent evaluation of institutional policies and practices, and attention to how such practices influence the experiences of Black faculty.

Utilize Institutional Funding to Support Expanded Networking

Black faculty experiences are nuanced with social isolation, lack of collegiality and a lack of support in the promotion of mental wellness (Alexander & Moore, 2008; Bhopal, 2016; Kelly, Gayles & Williams, 2017). Institutions must promote mental wellness through the funding of expanded networks that provide a sense of community, mentorship, and resources that support Black faculty. These networks, both inside and outside the institution, should have a focus on combating the negative experiences of Black faculty by being a resource and support network. Institutional affinity groups often lack the funding really needed to provide programming and resources to support the needs of Black faculty and aid their retention. Institutions must make it a priority to fund internal networks, while also providing funding to give Black faculty the opportunity to identify their own external networks that will be an asset in their academic journey.

Conclusion

This chapter has illustrated the resilience of Black faculty in the academy, despite the persistence of institutional barriers, racial exclusion, discriminatory practices, and a host of other experiences that make the academy a hostile context. Black faculty have demonstrated their resilience by engaging in both maladaptive and productive coping strategies that enable them to excel in hostile situations. Black faculty's ability to maintain their sanity and cope in ways that protect their mental health is illustrative of their belongingness in academic spaces. Through contributions to their respective fields of study and the creation of culturally specific professional spaces, Black faculty exert significant influence within higher education. Thus, at the core of promoting the mental wellness of Black faculty within the academy is the inherent belief and acknowledgment that Black faculty belong in the academy. To thrive, it is imperative that Black faculty draw from a wide range of coping strategies to remind themselves, and those around them, that caring for oneself through promoting mental well-being is both self-preservation and an act of academic warfare.

REFERENCES

Alexander Jr, R. & Moore, S. E. (2008). The benefits, challenges, and strategies of African American faculty teaching at predominantly white institutions. *Journal of African American Studies*, 12, 4–18.

Arday, J. (2020). No one can see me cry: Understanding mental health issues for black and minority ethnic staff in higher education. *Higher Education*. https://doi.org/10.1007/s10734-020-00636-w

Barnett, J. E., Baker, E. K., Elman, N. S. & Schoener, G. R. (2007). In pursuit of wellness: The self-care imperative. *Professional Psychology: Research and Practice*, 38(6), 603–12. https://doi.org/10.1037/0735-7028.38.6.603

Bhopal, K. (2016). *The Experiences of Black and Minority Ethnic Academics: A comparative study of the unequal academy*. London and New York: Routledge.

Bonner II, F. A., marbley, a. f., Tuitt, F., Robinson, P. A., Banda, R. M. & Hughes, R. L. (eds.) (2014). *Black Faculty in the Academy: Narratives for negotiating identity and achieving career success*. New York: Routledge. https://doi.org/10.4324/9781315852164

Davis, D. J., Chaney, C. & BeLue, R. (2020) Why "We can't breathe" during COVID-19. *Journal of Comparative Family Studies*, 51(3–4), 417–28. https://doi .org/10.3138/jcfs.51.3-4.015

DeCuir-Gunby, J. T., Johnson, O. T., Edwards, C. W., McCoy, W. N. & White, A. M. (2019). African American professionals in higher education: Experiencing and coping with racial microaggressions. *Race Ethnicity and Education*, 23(4), 492–508. https://doi.org/10.1080/13613324.2019.1579706

Dyce, C. M. & Williams, T. M. (eds.) (2015). *D.I.V.A. Diaries: The road to the Ph.D. and stories of black women who have endured.* New York: Peter Lang.

Franklin, A. J., Boyd-Franklin, N. & Kelly, S. (2006) Racism and invisibility, *Journal of Emotional Abuse*, 6 (2–3), 9–30. doi: 10.1300/J135v06n02_02

Griffin, K. A., Pifer, M. J., Humphrey, J. R. & Hazelwood, A. M. (2011). (Re) Defining Departure: Exploring black professors' experiences with and responses to racism and racial climate. *American Journal of Education*, 117(4), 495–526.

Heintzman, P. & Mannell, R. C. (2003). Spiritual functions of leisure and spiritual well-being: Coping with time pressure. *Leisure Sciences*, 25(2–3), 207–30.

Kelly, B. T., Gayles, J. G. & Williams, C. D. (2017). Recruitment without retention: A critical case of black faculty unrest. *The Journal of Negro Education*, 86(3), 305–17.

Lorde, A. (1988). *A Burst of Light: Essays.* Ithaca, NY: Firebrand Books.

Louis, D. A., Rawls, G. J., Jackson-Smith, D., Chambers, G. A., Phillips, L. L. & Louis, S. L. (2016). Listening to our voices: Experiences of black faculty at predominantly white research universities with microaggression. *Journal of Black Studies*, 47(5), 454–74. doi:10.1177/0021934716632983

Memon, A., Taylor, K., Mohebati, L. M., Sundin, J., Cooper, M., Scanlon, T., de Visser, R. (2016). Perceived barriers to accessing mental health services among black and minority ethnic (BME) communities: A qualitative study in Southeast England. *British Medical Journal Open*, 6(11), e012337. doi: 10.1136/ bmjopen-2016-012337

Meyers, A. B. (2002). Developing nonthreating expertise: Thoughts on consultation training from the perspective of a new faculty member. *Journal of Educational and Psychological Consultation*, 12(1–2), 55–67.

Nicol, D. J. & Yee, J. A. (2017). "Reclaiming our time": Women of color faculty and radical self-care in the academy. *Feminist Teacher*, 27(2–3), 133–56.

Novacek, D. M., Hampton-Anderson, J. N., Ebor, M. T., Loeb, T. B. & Wyatt, G. E. (2020). Mental health ramifications of the COVID-19 pandemic for black Americans: Clinical and research recommendations. *Psychological Trauma: Theory, Research, Practice, and Policy*, 12(5), 449–51. https://doi.org/10 .1037/tra0000796

Palmer, D. & Ward, K. (2007). "Lost": Listening to the voices and mental health needs of forced migrants in London. *Medicine, Conflict and Survival*, 23(3), 198–212. doi: 10.1080/13623690701417345

Robinson, O. V. (2014). Characteristics of racism and the health consequences experienced by black nursing faculty. *The ABNF Journal: Official Journal of the Association of Black Nursing Faculty in Higher Education*, 25(4), 110–15.

Salazar, C. F. (2009). Strategies to survive and thrive in academia: The collective voices of counseling faculty of color. *International Journal for the Advancement of Counselling.* 31, 181–98. https://doi.org/10.1007/s10447-009-9077-1

Settles, I. H., Buchanan, N. T. & Dotson, K. (2019). Scrutinized but not recognized: (In)visibility and hypervisibility experiences of faculty of color. *Journal of Vocational Behavior*, 113, 62–74. https://doi.org/10.1016/j.jvb.2018.06.003

Smith, B. P. & Hawkins, B. (2011). Examining student evaluations of black college faculty: Does race matter? *The Journal of Negro Education*, 80(2), 149–62. http://www.jstor.org/stable/41341117

Spates, K., Evans, N. M., Watts, B. C., Abubakar, N. & James, T. (2020). Keeping ourselves sane: A qualitative exploration of black women's coping strategies for gendered racism. *Sex Roles*, 82, 513–24. https://doi.org/10.1007/s1 1199-019-01077-1

Stanley, C. (2006). Coloring the academic landscape: Faculty of color breaking the silence in predominantly white colleges and universities. *American Educational Research Journal*, 43(4), 701–36. https://www.jstor.org/stable/4121775

Thomas, G. D. & Hollenshead, C. (2001). Resisting from the margins: The coping strategies of Black women and other women of color faculty members at a research university. *The Journal of Negro Education*, 70(3), 166–75. https://doi.org/10.2307/3211208

Trotman, F. K. (2009). The imposter phenomenon among African American women in U.S. institutions of higher education: Implications for counseling. In Walz, G. R., Bleuer, J. C. & Yep, R. K. (eds.), *Compelling Counseling Interventions: Vistas 2009*. Alexandria, VA: American Counseling Association, 77–87.

Woods-Jaegar, B., Briggs, E. C., Gaylord-Harden, N., Cho, B. & Lemon, E. (2021). Translating cultural assets research into action to mitigate adverse childhood experience-related health disparities among African American youth. *American Psychologist*, 76(2), 326–36. https://doi.org/10.1037/amp0000779

CHAPTER 8

Preserving the Mental Health of Black and Brown Professors in Academia

Anica Camela Mulzac

Professors are human. This statement may not seem revolutionary, but the intense demands and pressures of academic life often obscure its simple truth. For many Black and Brown professors, their herculean efforts to excel in academia, despite the limitations imposed by chronic interpersonal and institutional racism, can result in their humanity being overlooked. The unrelenting exigency of teaching, researching, publishing, administrating, and mentoring, all the while building and maintaining vibrant personal lives, can amass enormous strain on the health and well-being of these professionals. In their research on the promotion and tenure (P&T) process and its impact on the health of Black faculty who pursue this track, Arnold, Crawford & Khalifa (2016) not only found the psychological cost to be high, but also its deleterious effects to be far reaching. One Black female professor described the negative impact of work and life stressors on her health by stating:

> Since I have been a faculty member, I have gained at least 40–50 pounds . . . During my seven years, I have had fertility issues, and an increased number of things I am allergic to. I have always had migraines and stomach issues, but these have gotten worse in the last few years. I have been under a doctor's care for depression and anxiety. (Arnold, Crawford & Khalifa, 2016: 910)

In recent years, the demand for psychological and counseling services by students on college and university campuses nationwide has increased exponentially (Binkley & Fenn, 2019), prompting many in academia to prioritize student well-being, in addition to their learning. However, the same level of attention has not always been given to the mental health of the professors who teach them, and even less to those of color (Alves, Oliveira & Paro, 2019; Nguyen, 2020; Souza et al., 2020). Though once thought to be a low-risk population for suicidality and other psychological conditions due to their education level and socioeconomic status (Flaherty, 2017), professors have become increasingly vocal about the hardships they face. In a published essay, famed chemical biologist and professor, Hilal Lashuel, openly discussed his heart attack and the negative consequences of an unhealthy academic work schedule (Lashuel, 2020; Nguyen, 2020). While Lashuel's transparency was revered and served as a wake-up call for many in academia to reassess their work–life balance, high consternation and caution remain among professors about how they may be viewed if they followed suit. Lashuel gave voice to this fear when he stated:

> In reality we, like our students, frequently experience stress, fear and insecurity, as well as anxiety, depression and burn out. As faculty, many believe that admitting we are stressed or going through a mental health crisis would be a mistake; that if we do, no one will see us the same way, and that it may compromise our relationship with our students, our colleagues, and our superiors. (Lashuel, 2020: The storms of academia section, paragraph 6)

These concerns are not unwarranted as poor responses, such as invalidation and gossip among administrators and peers in the field, can subject a struggling professor to even greater distress, while signaling to others that their needs are not important, and that silence is their only protection (Flaherty, 2017). This may be particularly true for those who are early in their career or do not have the benefit of tenure. For Black and Brown professors, who may already view their placement in academia as a precarious one, greater hesitancy about disclosing their mental struggles may be felt. For, in addition to the negative stigma around mental health in the larger society, such admission may provide yet another pretext for the questioning of their abilities, value, and worthiness for promotion. As a result, the cost of unveiling the pressures, stressors, and limitations they experience may prove too high, and deter many from seeking out needed support.

While the world of academia is a grand one, it is by no means excluded from, or unaffected by, the events and conditions affecting society at large. The onset of the COVID-19 pandemic has necessitated substantial changes to the way institutions operated, requiring professors of all stripes to modify and reinvent the way they teach and work. Feelings of burnout and occupational stress, already experienced by many in the academy (Alves, Oliveira & Paro, 2019; Flaherty, 2020c; Thorsen, 1996), have been exacerbated by conditions brought on by the pandemic such as remote teaching, the homeschooling of children, and virtual meetings (Flaherty, 2020c; Nguyen, 2020). A cross-sectional study conducted during the pandemic, of more than 100 university professors in Brazil, found that almost 50 percent experienced a high degree of anxiety (Souza et al.,

2020). For Black and Brown professors in the United States, the existing toll on their mental health is compounded further still by incidents such as the frequent killings of the unarmed by police (Johnson, 2020), and the physical and verbal attacks on the Asian American Pacific Islander community by those falsely believing them responsible for the spread of the coronavirus (Lu, 2021).

Though by no means exhaustive, the next section of this chapter will provide an overview of key factors undermining the mental health of faculty of color in higher education. Among these are the racial disproportionality within the faculty population, cultural taxation, the ambiguity of the P&T process, and racism. While all the noted stressors may not be exclusive to Black and Brown professors, their cumulative impact likely is, thus warranting attention.

Stressors Influencing the Mental Health of Black and Brown Faculty

Disproportionality in Academia and Cultural Taxation

Research has long documented the tremendous benefits and added value diversity brings to organizations, including institutions of higher learning. Yet, disparities in the hiring, promotion, and retention of faculty of color remain high (Arnold, Crawford & Khalifa, 2016; Burden, Harrison & Hodge, 2005). According to the National Center for Education Statistics (2020), data on the fall 2018 semester revealed that, across the United States, white men and women accounted for over 70 percent of all faculty in degree-granting institutions. For Black and Brown faculty, the isolation and exclusion that is experienced from being one of few can have negative effects on their mental health. Among these are feelings of rejection, low worth, and distress, as well as depressive symptoms. Furthermore, an enduring consequence of being a racial minority in a majority space is the contradictory experiences of hypervisibility and invisibility. The former results in professors of color being easily singled out and overly scrutinized, and the latter stems from an indifference to their efforts. The increased internal and external pressure to prove their worth undoubtedly compounds these adverse effects on their mental health (Arnold, Crawford & Khalifa, 2016; Settles, Buchanan & Dotson, 2019).

The paltry number of Black and Brown faculty in higher education has also meant an increased demand for the few who are present. As the US population has become more racially diverse, so too has the college age population (Brey et al., 2019). Students from marginalized communities seeking advice, counsel, mentorship, or a listening ear, when faced with racism or bias on campus, typically seek out professors of color, who may be seen as better able to relate to them (Dancy II & Brown, 2011). The racial gap between student and faculty populations is poised to worsen should things remain constant, thereby intensifying the load placed on professors of color. The terms "invisible labor" and "cultural taxation" are used to describe the burden Black and Brown professors carry from contributing to their institution's efforts and successes in cultivating diversity, but for which they receive little to no reward. This may manifest in professors of color being asked to participate on numerous committees as representatives of marginalized voices, aid the development and creation of inclusive course curricula, engage with local community groups in need of expertise, mentor junior faculty of color, and support students from racial minority groups, but having these activities discounted or uncompensated (Dancy II & Brown, 2011; Grollman, 2015).

Research has shown that, on college and university campuses, female, and Black and Brown faculty are largely responsible for all initiatives around diversity and inclusion (Dancy II & Brown, 2011; Jimenez et al., 2019). These formal and informal duties shouldered by faculty of color are often done in addition to their teaching and research expectations (Grollman, 2015; Stanley, 2006). This imbalance in workload is vocalized by professors themselves who report feeling tokenized, which amplifies their sense of alienation, and bolsters their decision to depart academia out of self-preservation, often before achieving tenure (Arnold, Crawford & Khalifa, 2016; French et al., 2015, Settles, Buchanan & Dotson, 2019).

Ambiguity in the Promotion and Tenure Process

For many Black and Brown professors, the dream of earning tenure is not always realized, in part due to the ambiguity of the P&T process (Turner, González & Wood, 2008; Settles, Buchanan & Dotson, 2019). While excellence in teaching, service, and research is expected from all who apply, the shifting standard on what is deemed "excellent" can leave professors of color in the lurch. Despite being sought after and tasked with various service projects, these acts by Black and Brown professors can be relegated as inconsequential when seeking P&T. Regarding research, the emphasis on publications in prestigious journals that center around quantitative methods tend to favor white faculty, as faculty of color are more likely to utilize qualitative measures. Faculty of color are also more likely to study topics centered on matters affecting marginalized communities, such as race and racism. However, their scholarship and expertise can be devalued, dismissed, or seen as subjective by white colleagues and administrators involved in the P&T process (Arnold, Crawford & Khalifa, 2016; Dancy II & Brown, 2011; French et al., 2015; Stanley, 2006; Turner et al., 2008).

One aspect of the P&T process that is particularly disadvantageous for faculty of color is the overreliance on Student Evaluation of Teaching (SET) to assess professors' effectiveness and quality of teaching. While these measures are used as a means of including student feedback in key decisions such as merit pay, and the promotion of professors, they have frequently shown a bias against women and faculty of color. The comments left by students of these professors generally take on a harsh tone and are riddled with personal attacks (Stanley, 2006; Uttl, White & Gonzalez, 2017). Furthermore, despite anecdotal reports of the value of employing SETs in the P&T process, research has shown that they hold little or no validity in accurately assessing instructor performance or student learning (Uttl, White & Gonzalez, 2017). The continued inclusion of these measures in the estimation of Black and Brown professors' qualification for P&T can make their bids more arduous, and the toll on their mental health even greater.

Often lacking access to the mentorship and support available to white peers, many professors of color are left on their own to decipher the written and unwritten rules of successfully applying for P&T (Settles, Buchanan & Dotson, 2019; Turner, González & Wood, 2008). However, despite their best efforts and high achievement in their respective fields, success is not guaranteed. Two prominent professors at the University of Virginia experienced this firsthand when their bids for tenure were rejected, despite stellar achievements (Flaherty, 2020a). Paul Harris, one of the professors who ultimately won his tenure following a public outcry and an appeal (Flaherty, 2020b), described his experience in academia by stating, "African Americans, in general, have always had to work twice as hard to get the same amount of credit. A Ph.D. does not change that" (Flaherty, 2020a, Paul Harris section, para. 21). For Black and Brown professors like Dr. Harris, the energy and work required to continually defend, explain, and prove themselves is physically and psychologically taxing.

Racism

Experiences of racism and discrimination on college and university campuses are not limited to students of color, but are shared by racially marginalized faculty (Burden, Harrison & Hodge, 2005). Professor Tyrone Hayes gave a public account of his experiences of overt and covert racism in top tier academic institutions in which his presence as a Black male was questioned, his contributions to the university restricted, and his voice muted by exclusion, dismissal, and devaluation (Rothfels Lab, 2020). Unsurprisingly, the perpetuation of racism is not limited to the colleagues and administrators of Black and Brown faculty, but can also be found among the students they are tasked with educating. Many have given accounts of having their scholarship and position of authority outright challenged by white students who believed them unqualified (Arnold, Crawford & Khalifa, 2016; Stanley, 2006). One Black male professor reflected on his experiences of racism, stating, "African-American professors are confronted with institutional racism on a daily basis. Some of my students have challenged my credentials in and outside of the classroom" (Stanley, 2006: 721). Black and Brown professors often must contend with the assumption of some that their appointments and placements in academia resulted from affirmative action bids rather than their true intelligence and merit (Stanley, 2006). This air of suspicion around their employment can undermine any sense of belonging and inclusion professors of color hope to experience on their campuses.

The sting of racism has enduring effects that persist long after the offending incident has ended. Research has consistently shown the profound negative psychological and physical impact of racial microaggressions and discrimination on their targets (Anderson, 2020; Powell, 2019; Sue et al., 2019). These effects can take the form of health conditions including diabetes, obesity, and hypertension, as well as anxiety, depression, and suicidality. Exposure to even subtle forms of racism has proven to undermine work performance and increase the stress of racial minorities. The mere labor required in ascertaining whether a slight was racially motivated or not is equally as taxing (Settles, Buchanan & Dotson, 2019; Sue et al., 2019). Compromises to professors' mental health may also manifest in Racial Battle Fatigue (RBF), a condition characterized by negative emotional and physical symptoms resulting from repeatedly being the target of racism (Arnold, Crawford & Khalifa, 2016). For Black female professors, there appears to be a double bind of racism and misogyny, which can exponentially increase the mental weight they carry and heighten the demand to prove themselves equal (Arnold, Crawford & Khalifa, 2016; Stanley, 2006).

Faculty of color report that vocalizing their concerns and racial experiences can be met with deaf ears and indifference, rather than empathy and support (Arnold, Crawford & Khalifa, 2016; Settles, Buchanan & Dotson, 2019). Responses such as these are sure to maintain the status quo, and thwart any efforts to create substantial movement toward multiculturalism. Additionally, the failure of institutions of higher education to heed the cries of their faculty of color will do little to bolster the recruitment and retention rates of this important group.

Recommendations for Change

In this section, recommendations will be offered to aid with fostering the health and success of Black and Brown faculty. However, it is paramount to first highlight the importance of recognizing and framing the disparities and hardships outlined above from an institutional lens, rather than solely an interpersonal one. While interpersonal expressions of prejudice and discrimination may be more readily seen, the covert nature of structural racism typically results in it being more insidious and enduring. Failure to adopt a structural approach will likely end in finite shifts toward change that may (temporarily) improve the experiences of a few, without addressing the larger elements that first made those shifts necessary. Additionally, hyper-focusing on the individual could imply that the person of color, and not the existing social system, is the true problem in need of remediation.

To illustrate the value of an institutional frame better, consider the following scenario: Your department has five classrooms, listed A through E. Everyone who has used classroom A is aware that the computer system is unreliable, as it is known to automatically reboot, unprompted, while in use, creating many a delay in class presentations and even the loss of valuable data. Your new hire has been assigned to work in classroom A this semester, and to support them with this well-known stressor, you encourage the hire to reserve a laptop and mobile projector from the IT department, which can be used in lieu of the built-in computer system. Aware of the miscommunication commonly experienced when your department makes a request to IT, you take the extra step of assisting the hire in completing the order forms and following up to ensure that the equipment has been delivered on the scheduled days. While these efforts are laudable and greatly improve the teaching experience of the new hire, much of the work centered on managing the inconvenience, rather than addressing its cause. In other words, the matter was addressed from an individualized frame, not a systemic one.

Now, consider how efforts may shift if the issue observed in classroom A expanded to all the classrooms in your department. While securing mobile devices may be consequential in the moment, such a remedy would in no way be sustainable over the course of an entire academic year if quality of teaching is to remain high. In addition to the above, you may seek to inform everyone in your department of this sweeping issue, invite them to alert you of any other technical difficulties observed, and you may take deliberate steps to have the entire computer system inspected and upgraded department-wide. While such intervention may be inconvenient, and even costly, tremendous benefit would result from investment in the changes needed to foster a functional and thriving academic department. Recognition that the computer system issue was not unique to classroom A prompted a level of engagement and investment that was not initially seen. In a similar manner, when matters of racism, prejudice, and bias are not viewed as isolated incidents unique to a few professors of color, but rather a systemic issue that undermines the health and performance of your entire institution, greater commitment is given to remedying it, and substantial change is experienced.

Considering the importance of identifying both interpersonal and systemic interventions for addressing the mental health needs of Black and Brown faculty, the recommendations offered are directed toward professors and administrators respectively, given their distinct roles, powers, and responsibilities within an institution.

For Black and Brown Professors

Identify, Validate, and Advocate

The pressure and determination to prove oneself, and overcome the barriers erected to undermine advancement, can discourage self-reflection and care. However, the quest for growth and achievement becomes a Sisyphean feat if those gains cannot be maintained. Sustainability on the ladder of success rests on continued attentiveness to one's mental health and overall well-being. Thus, professors are encouraged to frequently pause and identify the emotions and sensations they are experiencing without judgment or qualification. Whether it is five minutes, or an hour, this simple act can grant professors keen insight into their internal states, and how they are being impacted by the world around them. Rather than minimize or dismiss these observations, consideration of them as valid and worthy of recognition sets the stage for advocacy and change where needed. Namely, through increased self-awareness professors would be better positioned to communicate effectively with, and make appropriate requests of, important others when addressing their difficulties.

Consider Professor Z, who is in his tenth year of teaching, and has recently observed feelings of dread, irritability, and sadness, as well as a slight headache at the beginning of each work week for the last month. Although the feelings typically dissipate over the course of a day, they return each Monday morning without fail. Upon closer reflection, Professor Z recognized that his week starts with a two-hour meeting for the operations committee, a forum he dislikes and believes his weekly attendance unnecessary given the limited scope of the material covered. However, he agreed to the department chair's request that he temporarily fill in for his colleague who will return from sabbatical in three weeks. By first acknowledging his emotional state, and then drawing the valid connection between his internal experiences and the events of his work week, Professor Z was able to speak with the committee chair who agreed that it was not essential for him to attend every session. Through this small act of advocacy, Professor Z was able to reduce his level of engagement with the committee, thereby lowering the emotional toll experienced. Similarly, professors who attend to their emotional and physical responses, related to the demands placed on them, may use the information garnered to guide their actions for self-care.

On the point of advocacy, it is beneficial to note that it need not be a conflictual or combative endeavor. Rather, one grounded in both reason and respect for self and others. By asking for what is needed to maintain quality performance, Black and Brown professors inevitably alert administrators to any barriers they face, help set realistic expectations for their performance, and secure resources essential for the effective completion of tasks, all of which set them up for success. Examples of appropriate requests professors may make include setting a limit on the number of committees they join while fulfilling teaching, service, and research obligations; defining their nonworking hours and establishing boundaries around them; requesting compensation (monetary or otherwise) for activities completed that benefit the institution but are not part of their job description; inquiring about funds needed for professional development or books and other class-related materials; and securing flexibility in the work schedule to allow for balance and rest, for example, remote or hybrid classes, delayed starts, dedicated lunch hours, and time off.

Build Community
As noted earlier, due to the dearth of faculty of color in academia, many Black and Brown professors experience isolation and loneliness, which can contribute to depression and anxiety. Thus, the cultivation of a safe and healthy community of people, with whom they have shared experiences,

values, and goals, may prove vital for the preservation of their mental health. By connecting with and investing in relationships with others on and off-campus, professors curate a support network that arms them with advocates, resources, and knowledge they may not have otherwise. Some of these communities may already be accessible through institution-based affinity groups and Employee Resource Groups (ERGs) for staff and faculty, which center around key aspects of identity such as race, sexual orientation, and gender.

For many people of color working in predominantly white spaces, the labor of code-switching and continually dispelling myths and stereotypes about their intelligence, capabilities, and general worthiness can be exhausting. Thus, the existence of safe spaces where they can freely present in their bodies without explanation, vent their frustrations, indulge in their culture, and connect with others in their communities is invaluable. These spaces may further provide the normalization of experiences that professors of color have in academia, and through which they may receive advice, validation, and empathy from knowing peers (Burden, Harrison & Hodge, 2005; Sotto-Santiago, Tuitt & Saelua, 2019). To develop such spaces, professors may seek out connections and relationships with Black and Brown faculty in their department, those in other departments at their institution, as well as faculty of color at other colleges and universities they encounter in various places (for example, professional events, conferences). Professors may further build community through a more personalized connection with a trusted colleague in the form of a mentor–mentee relationship. Research has shown that engagement in a mentor–mentee relationship can be beneficial for the growth and advancement of Black and Brown faculty (Burden, Harrison & Hodge, 2005; Dancy II & Brown, 2011; Stanley, 2006). By having a mentor who is both in a position of power, and knowledgeable of the politics and nuances of higher education, professors of color may have access to a "decoder" of sorts, one offering insights and guidance needed for navigating the nebulous sphere of academia.

Lastly, the communities built need not only be professional in nature. Personal and private relationships with loved ones, and close friends may also provide safety and acceptance not found in other spaces. While it may be tempting to deprioritize these relationships for the sake of professional achievement, deliberate investment in them can provide the affirmation, grounding, and sense of self that Black and Brown professors need to stand up to the goliaths they battle. Additionally, involvement in spiritual communities, such as those found in a local church, synagogue, or mosque, can bolster the resiliency and faith needed to cope with life and work stressors.

Engage in Services
Individuals who pursue careers in academia are typically high achievers, earning their degrees and positions through grit and determination. However, mental health challenges may not be easily overcome by mere effort, potentially leaving many to perceive their struggles as evidence of a personal failing or character flaw. Furthermore, the negative stigma that lingers generally and within racial minority communities about mental conditions may heighten this false perception (Armstrong, 2019; McClean Harvard Medical School Affiliate, 2021). Through engagement in confidential therapeutic services with a licensed therapist, Black and Brown professors may openly process their thoughts and feelings without fear of exposure, retaliation, or demotion. Therapy may further provide the space needed to deepen insight into their functioning, challenge negative self-talk, as well as garner healthy and effective strategies for coping. Increased public dialogue in the last decade about the importance of mental health, and the passage of the Affordable Care Act, has resulted in expanded insurance coverage for mental health treatment (Baumgartner, Aboulafia & McIntosh, 2020). Thus, inquiring about in and out of network insurance benefits, as well as the perks of employee assistance programs, may aid professors of color in establishing quality care at an affordable cost.

Due to the bidirectional connection between mental and physical health, attention to one's physical well-being is also critical for preserving mental health. By making time for regular exercise, consuming nutritious foods, and getting quality sleep, Black and Brown professors may nurture a lifestyle that allows them to thrive. Participation in local gyms, and utilization of health promoting technologies (for example, mindfulness and meditation apps, sleep tracking apps) are examples of the small ways professors may pursue these goals. Additionally, creating and attending appointments with physicians for annual checkups and follow-up visits may further enable professors to make informed decisions regarding their health and treatment.

For Administrators

Increase Racial Diversity
The hypervisibility and invisibility that come from being one of few has been shown to impact the mental health of Black and Brown professors negatively (Settles, Buchanan & Dotson, 2019). As a result, the preservation of mental health among this group requires an increase in their presence on college and university campuses. The racial disparity among faculty in higher education will not amend without deliberate effort and attention. Administrators tasked with recruiting, hiring, and retaining professors need to first view

the presence of Black and Brown faculty as essential to the quality, growth, and enhancement of their institutions. The rapidly increasing racial diversity within the student body and general population demands swift and immediate action if these groups are to be well served in academia (Burden, Harrison & Hodge, 2005; Gasman, 2016).

Examination of current hiring processes, including written policies and unwritten practices, to identify potential areas of bias and discrimination is recommended. Engagement in this practice may better enable administrators to address structural barriers negatively affecting employment of part-time and full-time professors of color. These barriers can be replaced with fair and equitable initiatives. Administrators may further seek to expand and develop the candidate pipeline to help source qualified and racially diverse professors to their institutions (Kezar, 2020). Burden, Harrison & Hodge (2005) endorsed the recruitment of "Prospective faculty of color by creating multicultural summer research/teaching fellowship programs designed to allow such faculty to mentor diverse candidates prior to their induction at the institution" (p. 228). When offers are made, administrators are encouraged to onboard multiple professors of color at the same time, a practice that is also known as "cluster hires" (Stanley, 2006). This practice may provide incoming faculty with a built-in cohort of similar peers, allowing for connection and community-building. Lastly, administrators may develop mentoring programs that facilitate the connection of incoming Black and Brown faculty with suitable peers within the institution who may be reliable resources and supports for them (Dancy II & Brown, 2011; Turner, González & Wood, 2008; Stanley, 2006; Sotto-Santiago, Tuitt & Saelua, 2019).

There is often an assumption that diversity and excellence are in opposition, and that to increase one would be to decrease the other. In this assumption lies an inherent dismissal of the intelligence, skill, and knowledge that professors of color possess, in addition to their lived experiences as a racial minority in a majority setting. As college and university administrators seek to diversify their ranks, it is important to recognize and challenge this false dichotomy when it arises. The immense value educators of color bring to their respective institutions has been well documented, and thus attention must be given to addressing their distinct experiences if their presence in the field is to be maintained, and eventually expanded.

Establish Clear Policies and Maintain Transparency

A persistent mental health stressor for Black and Brown faculty is the ambiguity within polices, practices, and procedures of academia, particularly in the P&T process. Faculty of color are disproportionately affected by this lack of clarity and transparency, placing them at greater disadvantage in the quest for securing tenured positions. Administrators are encouraged to establish clear and objective standards to facilitate achievement of these aims. It is equally important that the established standards are expanded to recognize scholarship and excellence in research, service, and teaching matters that largely affect racial minority communities. In doing so, administrators may fully consider the high achievements of Black and Brown faculty, which can be overlooked under the traditional frame of what is deemed noteworthy. The creation of diverse P&T committees that include scholars knowledgeable of applicants' areas of expertise may further aid in this pursuit. Lastly, the provision of clear benchmarks, direct and consistent feedback, and professional development services to Black and Brown faculty on the tenure track is vital for promoting their success (Dancy II & Brown, 2011; Stanley, 2006).

Strive Toward Anti-Racism

The weight of racism, prejudice, and bias largely falls upon the shoulders of the target of such hate. For faculty of color, this burden can be ever present, undermining their ability to thrive within their chosen institutions. While administrators may not be able to eliminate all forms of prejudice and bias from their departments fully, efforts can be made to strive toward an anti-racist framework. By considering how resources are distributed, whose voices and needs are amplified and whose are not, and the influence of privilege on relational dynamics among their staff, administrators may better identify and respond to racial imbalances and blind spots that have long plagued their campuses. Investment in ongoing education and training on initiating and navigating exchanges on race-related matters may further demonstrate the institution's commitment to diversity, while providing its members with effective tools for healthy engagement on the topic.

It is important that administrators talk, as well as listen, giving space to faculty of color to share their experiences honestly, voice concerns, and offer feedback. If an incident of bias occurs, administrators are to respond proactively, resisting the urge to be defensive, dismissive, or reactive. Consider this: Professor Z was the target of racial microaggressions during his tenure on the operations committee and alerted his department chair of the matter. Rather than question the validity of Professor Z's report, his department chair responded by stating:

> Thank you for bringing this to my attention. I am saddened to hear that this was your experience as it is not my wish to have anyone in our department

feel excluded or marginalized. If you can do so now, I would appreciate it if we could talk about this in more detail so that I may better understand your experience and consider appropriate ways we may address it to move forward as a team. If you would rather take some time to privately process, I am happy to schedule a meeting later this week for us to chat.

By recognizing the gravity of the experience and possibility that Professor Z may not be ready to discuss the matter in depth, the department chair has validated, and humanized Professor Z. The expression of lament for what transpired, and an offer to discuss and address the matter, further highlights the safety of the space and conveys the seriousness with which his report was received.

Administrators are further encouraged to acknowledge and directly address events in the larger society, such as killings and attacks on communities of color, by naming those events, creating space for discussion, and considering how faculty and staff of color may be particularly affected. Lastly, the work of dismantling racism, prejudice, and bias within the organization is the responsibility of everyone, not just that of people of color. These elements negatively impact everyone to varying degrees, thus administrators are encouraged to ensure that the bulk of the work does not largely rest upon Black and Brown faculty. Ways administrators may cultivate an inclusive and anti-racist work environment include challenging white faculty to highlight and discuss the role of race in the subjects they teach and research; inviting them to participate on committees and/or attend events that tackle diversity; and partnering with Black and Brown faculty on projects to help increase the visibility of these individuals. Other initiatives include establishing diversity integration in research, teaching, and service as part of the criteria for P&T; highlighting efforts around diversity in annual evaluations; and recognizing the mentoring of students of diverse backgrounds, as well as involvement in community outreach as highly valuable forms of service. Efforts to include Black and Brown faculty on non-diversity-based initiatives may also help with affirming their value to the organization beyond multiculturalism and highlight their contribution as experts in their field.

Foster a Healthy Work Culture
The productivity-driven culture of higher education may detrimentally affect the health of Black and Brown professors who already feel pressured to work twice as hard (Dancy II & Brown, 2011; Thorsen, 1996; Settles, Buchanan & Dotson, 2019) as their white peers. Administrators can challenge unhealthy self-care practices by championing greater work–life balance among faculty. They may communicate esteem for the personal, as

well as the professional, by showing respect for private time and upholding boundaries around nonworking hours. Mental health practices may be promoted by starting or ending meetings with mindfulness and meditation exercises, providing education on the signs of psychological struggles and healthy ways of coping, promoting available mental health resources, and offering mental health days. Department retreats or gifts that encourage self-care and rest (for example, massage gift certificates, gym memberships) may also be valuable. Lastly, publicly giving appropriate recognition and acknowledgment to faculty of color for their successes and achievements may provide them much needed affirmation, fostering an increased sense of belonging and acceptance within the institution.

Conclusion

Everything does not have to be about race, but race is present in everything. Thus, failure to acknowledge the unique stressors of Black and Brown faculty would be detrimental both to the health of these individuals, as well as the institutions in which they work. Professors of color are encouraged to bring their full and authentic selves into the spaces they inhabit by living in accordance with their core values, recognizing their right to belong and thrive in their earned placements, and speaking truth about their needs and experiences. While there is no single panacea to treat all the mental health struggles they may face, it is vitally important that Black and Brown faculty continue to tell their stories. By giving voice to their hardships and experiences they not only shine a light on the inequities that persist, but create opportunity for their validation, affirmation, and healing.

REFERENCES

Alves, P. C., Oliveira, A. D. F. & Paro, H. B. M. D. S. (2019). Quality of life and burnout among faculty members: How much does the field of knowledge matter? *PLos ONE*, 14(3), e0214217. https://doi.org/10.1371/journal.pone.0214217

Anderson, G. (2020). The emotional toll of racism. *Inside Higher Ed*. October 23. https://bit.ly/3dWR6Qq

Armstrong, V. (2019). Stigma regarding mental illness among people of color. *National Council for Mental Wellbeing*. July 8. https://bit.ly/30WBH8Q

Arnold, N. W., Crawford, E. R. & Khalifa, M. (2016) Psychological heuristics and faculty of color: Racial battle fatigue and tenure/promotion. *The Journal of Higher Education*, 87(6), 890–919. https://doi.org/10.1080/00221546.2016.11780891

Baumgartner, J. C., Aboulafia, G. N. & McIntosh, A. (2020). The ACA at 10: How has it impacted mental health care? The Commonwealth Fund. April 3. https://doi.org/10.26099/2ajx-qg59

Binkley, C. & Fenn, L. (2019). Colleges struggle with soaring student demand for counseling. Associated Press. November 19. https://apnews.com/article/25905a5c3d28454ba0d84dcb958fe32c

Brey, C. D., Musu, L., McFarland, J., Wilkinson-Flicker, S., Diliberti, M., Zhang, A., Branstetter, C. & Wang, X. (2019). *Status and Trends in the Education of Racial and Ethnic Groups 2018*. Washington, DC: US Department of Education. https://nces.ed.gov/pubsearch/pubsinfo.asp?pubid=2019038

Burden, J. W., Harrison, L. & Hodge, S. R. (2005). Perceptions of African American faculty in kinesiology-based programs at predominantly white American institutions of higher education. *Research Quarterly for Exercise and Sport*, 78(2), 224–37.

Dancy II, T. E. & Brown, M. C. (2011). The mentoring and induction of educators of color: Addressing the impostor syndrome in academe. *Journal of School Leadership*, 21(4), 607–34. https://doi.org/10.1177/105268461102100405

Flaherty, C. (2017). Aftermath of a professor's suicide. *Inside Higher Ed*. April 21. https://bit.ly/3dUpziA

(2020a). Botched. *Inside Higher Ed*. June 22. https://bit.ly/3EZDUGl

(2020b). UVA reverses tenure denial. *Inside Higher Ed*. July 27. https://bit.ly/3q3TrPb

(2020c). Burning out. *Inside Higher Ed*. September 14. https://bit.ly/3s509Kl

French, B. H., Adair, Z. R., Cokley, K., Lindsey, T. B., Morales, A., Morales, E., Neville, H. A., Wang, K. & Worthington, R. L. (2015). As people of color formerly employed by Mizzou, we demand change. *HuffPost*. November 17. https://bit.ly/3q2PRo6

Gasman, M. (2016). The five things no one will tell you about why colleges don't hire more faculty of color. *The Hechinger Report*. September 20. https://bit.ly/3DLM7gv

Grollman, E. A. (2015). Invisible labor. *Inside Higher Ed*. December 15. https://bit.ly/3m9Ykot

Jimenez, M. F., Laverty, T. M., Bombaci, S. P., Wilkins, K., Bennett, D. E. & Pejchar, L. (2019). Underrepresented faculty play a disproportionate role in advancing diversity and inclusion. *Nature Ecology & Evolution*, 3, 1030–3. https://doi.org/10.1038/s41559-019-0911-5

Johnson, G. (2020). Police killings and black mental health. *Penn Today*. June 23. https://bit.ly/3yu8qFK

Kezar, A. (2020). Undoing years of affirmative action: The growth of non-tenure-track faculty. In Taylor, M., Turk, J. M., Chessman, H. M. & Espinosa, L. L. (eds.) *Race and Ethnicity in Higher Education: 2020 supplement*. Washington, DC: American Council on Education. https://bit.ly/3dWc3L6

Lashuel, H. A. (2020). Mental health in academia: What about faculty? *eLife*, *9*. https://doi.org/10.7554/eLife.54551

Lu, J. (2021). Why pandemics give birth to hate: From bubonic plague to COVID-19. *NPR*. March 26. https://n.pr/3oVIEam

McClean Harvard Medical School Affiliate. (2021). How can we break mental health barriers in communities of color? https://bit.ly/33rxaTv

National Center for Education Statistics (NCES). (2020). *The Condition of Education 2020*. Washington DC: US Department of Education. https://nces.ed.gov/pubsearch/pubsinfo.asp?pubid=2020144

Nguyen, T. (2020). Faculty open up about mental health under the COVID-19 pandemic. *C&EN: Chemical and Engineering News*, 98(19). https://bit.ly/3yugS7M

Powell, A. (2019). Trust, belonging, keys to mental health of students of color. *Harvard Gazette*. September 19. https://bit.ly/3dSKZwb

Rothfelds Lab. (2020, June 4). The Rothfels lab stands against racism everywhere. *Rothfels Lab*. https://bit.ly/3s6ZDsf

Settles, I. H., Buchanan, N. T. & Dotson, K. (2019). Scrutinized but not recognized: (In)visibility and hypervisibility experiences of faculty of color. *Journal of Vocational Behavior*, 113, 62–74. https://doi.org/10.1016/j.jvb.2018.06.003

Sotto-Santiago, S., Tuitt, F. & Saelua, N. (2019). All faculty matter: The continued search for culturally relevant practices in faculty development. *The Journal of Faculty Development*, 33(3), 83–93.

Souza, A. P. D. S., Silva, M. R. M., Silva, A. B. J. D., Lira, P. C. D., Silva, J. M. L. D., Silva, M. L. D., Carmo, T. S. D., Leite, S. C. P., Silva, R K. P., Silva, K. G. D., Filho, P. T., A., Fernandes, M. S. D. S., Barros, W. M. A. & Souza, V. D. O. N. (2020). Anxiety symptoms in university professors during the COVID-19 pandemic. *Health Science Journal*, 14(7), 773. doi: 10.36648/1791-809X.14.7.773

Stanley, C. A. (2006). Coloring the academic landscape: Faculty of color breaking the silence in predominantly white colleges and universities. *American Educational Research Journal*, 43(4), 701–36. https://doi.org/10.3102/0002831204300470

Sue, D. W., Alsaidi, S., Awad, M. N., Glaeser, E., Calle, C. C. & Mendez, N. (2019). Disarming racial microaggressions: Microintervention strategies for targets, white allies, and bystanders. *American Psychologist*, 74(1), 128–42. http://dx.doi.org/10.1037/amp0000296

Thorsen, E. J. (1996). Stress in academe: What bothers professors? *Higher Education*, 31(4), 471–89. https://doi.org/10.1007/BF00137127

Turner, C. S. V., González, J. C. & Wood, J. L. (2008). Faculty of color in academe: What 20 years of literature tells us. *Journal of Diversity in Higher Education*, 1(3), 139–68. https://doi.org/10.1037/a0012837

Uttl, B., White, C. A. & Gonzalez, D. W. (2017) Meta-analysis of faculty's teaching effectiveness: Student evaluation of teaching ratings and student learning are not related. *Studies in Educational Evaluation*, 54, 22–42. https://doi.org/10.1016/j.stueduc.2016.08.007

PART III

Strategies for Inclusion and Retention

CHAPTER 9

Testimonials of Exodus: Self-Emancipation in Higher Education through the Power of Womanism

Jean Swindle and Larissa Malone

Introduction

Longstanding, Black people have identified with biblical stories and related them to their lives (Cone, 1997; Morris, 2004). One of the more popular tales is Moses leading his people from the bondage of slavery to the Promised Land. His resolute cry of "Let my people go!" has been repeated throughout iconic eras in Black history and represents the bold demand of not remaining in oppression. This particular story's re-telling usually underscores the dramatic ending, when Moses holds out a rod to separate the waters, resulting in an exodus to freedom and the drowning of a tyrannical regime. However, what is often left out of the narrative is the role women played in assuring emancipation. For it was two midwives who first defied the Pharaoh's order to kill male-born babies, a mandate that should have resulted in the infant Moses' death. Next, it was his mother who hid him for months from public sight. His sister protected him when he was placed into a basket near the riverbank. A female slave retrieved Moses from this precarious situation, and, finally, it was Pharaoh's daughter who raised him. If it were not for these women, there would have been no emancipation.

Women were key actors in the emancipatory process, presumably relying on their instinct alone during the tension-filled ethnic clash between two nations, as it is documented that they did not talk directly to God. We refer to this as cultural intuition, defined as acknowledging and allowing space for one's actions to be guided by guttural feelings. Cultural intuition is embedded in critical race feminism (Delgado Bernal, 1998; hooks, 1989; Rocha et al., 2016; Walker, 1983), making room for these visceral inclinations. Dillard (2006) explicitly applies the concept to Black women scholars, encouraging us to illuminate "the spirituality that is all too often rendered invisible or insignificant in (white) academe by virtue of

our race, gender, and other identity positions and the 'isms' other embrace"
(Dillard, 2006: paragraph 6).

Positionality

We amplify this notion as we peer into our own experiences for this
writing. I (Jean), the lead author, am a bilingual (English-Spanish) African-
American scholar from the South who embraces her role and responsibility
as a global citizen. I (Larissa) am an Afro-Latina motherscholar, and I am
from the Midwest. While we differ in particulars, we share similar educational experiences. We were both classroom teachers and in K-12 educational leadership within majority white schools. We both attended
graduate programs and accepted tenure-track positions that mirror the
demographics of our practitioner experiences. We both identify as Black
cisgender females with solid roots in spirituality that influence and shape
our professional and personal lives.

Our connection began via a statewide program that focused on supporting and retaining Black and Brown undergraduate pre-service teachers. We
were the only Black faculty in attendance and our participation was beyond
the scope of our regular duties as we both worked exclusively in graduate
studies. We intuitively saw the need and decided to meet it with no direct
benefit. In parallel, we were also experiencing extraordinary isolation and,
at times, hopelessness at our small private institutions. Through our
involvement in orchestrating this temporary escape for our students, we
realized that we needed to do the same for ourselves in the long term. How
to participate in *self-emancipation* – that is, set ourselves free, especially
from legal, social, or political restrictions (Merriam-Webster, n.d.) –
became a regular part of our conversations and, eventually, a mutual
goal. We document our experiences here to provide cathartic healing of
our minds, bodies, and spirits, help other Black female professors who find
themselves in similar situations, and identify areas of opportunity for
institutions to attend to the needs of Black women faculty.

Theoretical Framework

Our shared vantage at the intersection of race, gender, and spirituality
motivated us to use the social theory of womanism (Hudson-Weems,
2020; Maparyan, 2012; Ogunyemi, 1985; Walker, 1983). While each of
these scholars provides different framings of womanism that are sometimes
contradictory, there are several points of convergence. We have chosen to

highlight the components that are most relevant to our positionality. Womanism centers upon race, differentiating itself from gender-centered feminism, and approaches lived experiences pertaining to culture (Hudson-Weems, 2020; Maparyan, 2012; Walker, 1983). Maparyan (2012) describes womanism as a worldview "that Black women have had a special role to play in its propagation and promulgation" (p. 7). It is established in spirituality, yet not limited to the constructs, limitations, or exclusivity of any particular religion (Maparyan, 2012). We also draw from Ogunyemi (1985), who expanded the breadth of womanism into political and economic landscapes.

We are particularly drawn to how womanism emphasizes "healing the wounds of oppression, restoring communities, and bringing order and balance to the world" (Maparyan, 2012: 29). We relish in how womanism both readily recognizes the strength, tenacity, and resilience of Black women as it "necessarily focuses on [our] unique experiences, struggles, needs, and desires" (Hudson-Weems, 2020: 14). Yet, it also centers our mothering, family, and community and believes "until [our] entire people are free, [we are] not free" (Hudson-Weems, 2020: 39). In this, we recognize that to free others, we must be in a supportive place, physically, mentally, and socially, to do the work of aiding our people, which, as Dillard (2006) underscores, allows our spirituality to be visible. Our positionalities within this worldview provide both a lens for understanding our counter-narratives and the spiritual impetus to prioritize our mental and emotional well-being and initiate our exodus from institutions that have limited our ability to flourish as Black women scholars.

Hudson-Weems (2020) has explained that while Africana Womanism encompasses eighteen characteristics, two of them, *self-namer* and *self-definer*, are foundational. As self-namers, we understand how our authenticity and identity are retained. Although others attempt to characterize, mislabel, or assume qualities about us, we focus on our gender, collective identity, and culture, thus embracing ourselves as self-definers. We also make mention of the characteristics *spiritual*, *whole*, *strong*, *ambitious*, *respected*, and *mothering*, as we invoke them in situating our narratives. We recognize the symbiotic relationship between the spiritual and natural worlds and acknowledge that a higher being exists. As such, we are whole women who see the different parts of our lives, whether family, home, community, or career, as working together toward a collective agenda that constitutes who we are. We are steadfast and unyielding, and we recognize that our strength comes from our lineage and forms a bedrock of survival. Ambitiously, we take responsibility for our future and are resourceful and self-reliant. We demand respect because we have a keen awareness of our self-worth. Lastly, we embrace our role as mothers and see ourselves as "fulfilling the role of supreme Mother Nature – nurturer, provider, and protector" (Hudson-Weems, 2020: 48). We do not feel restricted or bound by the mother role; instead, we are committed to the craft of mothering and value this role as part of who we are and what this role represents for the advancement of all our people.

Methodology

As a methodology, narrative inquiry is employed to collect personal accounts of individuals' experiences (Bell, 2005; Davies & Davies, 2007) and frames those experiences within broader social, cultural, and institutional milieus (Caine, Estefan & Clandinin, 2019). Cousin (2009) underscores that narrative inquiry "is particularly useful if you want to know something about how people make sense of their lives through selective stories they tell about noteworthy episodes" (p. 93). Writing within the context of our exoduses, these narratives helped us examine our positions as actors and storytellers, describe the institutional contexts, and map some portions of the sequencing and tensions of our lived experiences (Riley & Hawe, 2005). In doing this, we analyzed components of *why* we self-emancipated from our institutions through narrative vignettes. We also made sense of the need for our departures through the lens of womanism. We ground this in the Deweyan epistemic position that knowledge arises from a person's active engagement and adaptation to their environment; such social and material interactions are not merely natural "but rather [are] always negotiated and filtered through experience" (Dewey, 1958).

Throughout our stories, we use pseudonyms for the institutions and all individuals mentioned. We used data from personal and professional journals, personal dialogues, digital communications, and institutional artifacts to construct our narratives. Rather than emergent themes, these narratives tell our stories within the framework of temporality, sociality, and spatiality, thus eliciting a deeper understanding of those experiences (Clandinin 2006, 2007, 2013). We wield our narratives as emancipatory methodology as we tell our exodus stories.

Our Former Institutions

Both institutions are located in the Midwest. I (Jean) was employed at Mainview University, a small, private, liberal arts institution. According to Mainview's 2018/19 Factbook, 10 percent of undergraduate students were

Black, and I was employed as the only full-time Black faculty. Similarly, my (Larissa's) institution, Redtown University, is a private, liberal arts university. Redtown differs from Mainview in that it is a Christian higher education institution, which means that embedded in its mission and vision is a commitment to faith. According to Redtown (official university website, 2018), the university's Black student population is a little over 10 percent. I, too, was the only Black woman faculty member and only the second in Redtown's more than 125-year history.

Our Exodus Narratives

Jean: Othermothering for the Childless
Single Black Woman, No Children (SBWNC) is hyperbole in academia. Black women in the academy – regardless of their partnership status, number of biological children, 80 percent approval rates on student evaluations, publications per year, university and community service – are always othermothering. In an academic setting, Black female faculty seek out, cultivate and sustain relationships with Black students in othermothering (Beauboeuf-Lafontant, 2002, 2005; McArthur & Lane, 2019). I neither taught undergraduate students nor had much opportunity to interact with them because I instructed evening classes when most of them had already left campus's academic areas. That is why my encounters with Shay, Roberto, and Marcus, all undergraduates, reminded me that, undoubtedly, the SBWNC would never exist for Black women in the academy because othermothering is essential. My initial contact with these students became sustained relationships throughout my tenure at Mainview.

Can I give you a hug? Maria was a Spanish professor at Mainview, and we had shared a floor in the same apartment building. In short order, we became fast friends. While walking by her office one day, she enthusiastically waved me in, noting that she wanted me to meet someone. I was hesitant because she was with a student, Shay, and, judging from Shay's body language, the conversation was intense. After introductions, Shay exclaimed, "So, you are Dr. Swindle! I heard you were here!" Both Shay and Maria invited me to stay. The advising session continued, and Shay sat back in her chair and asked, "Dr. Swindle, can I be real?" to which I responded, "Of course." Shay relaxed, code-switched, turned to me and began relating specifics about her recent study abroad in Sweden and her difficulty with financial aid. Shay, a first-generation African-American female, was also a financial contributor to her household and the principal caregiver to a diabetic stepfather.

Shay had worked to save money for the trip and had found alternative care for her stepfather. After being told her program would be fully funded, the university administration informed her that financial aid would only partially cover the study abroad experience; Maria and I offered suggestions. We formed a plan for Shay to present her evidence-based case to the appropriate Mainview personnel. I worked with her on a backup plan and let her know some recourse options. Finally, she exclaimed, "See there! This is what I'm talkin' about. This is what I needed! The lady in the Study Abroad office just told me to advocate for myself. I am like, 'What does that even mean?' She just kept saying the same damn thing." By this time, the five-minute walk I customarily took after sitting for two hours at my desk had turned into a 40-minute counseling and strategizing session. Finally, I rose to make my departure, and Shay jumped to her feet. She looked at me with tears in her eyes and asked, "Dr. Swindle, thank you so much. It is so good to see you on campus. Can I give you a hug?" And, just like that, I was othermothering.

No, ma'am. No one told me I had to do that   Marcus was a Black male whose Haitian parents had immigrated to the US and, after his parents' divorce, he found himself living with his mother and older sister while working and attending college full-time. We initially met at a district-wide scholarship banquet for underrepresented students. So, when I saw him studying in a corner one evening later in the semester, I greeted him, and we chatted for a bit. He wanted to apply to medical school. Although Mainview did not offer a pre-medicine track, he confidently communicated that his advisor and the professors in his major were customizing courses and advising him along that path.

I was thrilled! *When are you taking the MCAT? Who are you shadowing this summer? Who have you shadowed before? Have you considered some international experience to add to your dossier? Which doctors have you asked to write recommendations? How much money for med school application fees and possible travel have you saved?* I was beaming because I already envisioned another *brotha* in the medical field! Then, I saw it – Marcus, a second-semester sophomore, had not been told to take his MCAT before his senior year, that medical school applications were expensive, that shadowing a doctor was advantageous, and the list went on. He looked up at me, face contorted with doubt, and responded, "No, ma'am. No one told me I had to do that." At 10 p.m., standing beside a worried Marcus in one of Mainview's College of Arts and Science buildings, I texted a friend who was the head of pediatrics at one local hospital. She responded, and within five minutes, Marcus and I had a lunch date with her for the next week. And, just like that, I was othermothering.

See, that is why I can talk to you. You talk to me like my mom and dad do I had attended the ceremony at his district's offices when Roberto was awarded a partial scholarship to Mainview. His favorite teacher, Miss U, was one of my Urban Education master's students, and the three of us made instant connections. Beginning his freshman year, when I came across opportunities from which Roberto could benefit, I would always shoot him an email. So when Roberto sent me a message asking to meet about an advising issue, I said sure. I was puzzled because I knew he already had an advising session with the Elementary advisor, Beth. On the appointed day and time, Roberto and I met, headed over to the student union, and grabbed our coffee and some window seats. I listened as he talked about his degree change from Secondary to Elementary Education and his declaration of an official minor – Human Development. Roberto explained to Beth that interest in human development surfaced because he had been impacted after serving at a camp for children with disabilities the previous summer, and she told him to follow his heart and minor in Human Development.

I sipped my coffee a bit more slowly and counted back from ten. *Ten-nine-eight-seven-six-five-four-three-two-one.* I audibly exhaled, looked at him, and established, "Roberto, there is no way in hell you are going to minor in Human Development!" I code-switched (Hill, 2009) and continued:

> You can obtain two endorsements along with your teaching credential within your scholarship window. Human Development adds nothing to your teaching credential, but a Special Ed and ESL endorsement would. You are first-gen, contribute to your household income, and got bills to pay – those endorsements mean a higher starting salary for you and make you more marketable [in their capitalistic terms] and give you more options [in our liberatory terms]. As a gay, Latino male, you need to secure a position and have a platform so you can follow your passion! Don't get it twisted – some of us have to build a platform while others have had ones built for them. The latter can follow their passions in undergrad. You have to be about the business of working smarter – not harder – and taking advantage of everything at your disposal to make that happen.

I was enraged. Beth had a daughter in the Elementary Education Program who was obtaining multiple endorsements, yet she had advised Roberto to forgo endorsements and minor in Human Development. I was angry because what would never have been acceptable for her child was fine for Roberto. I finished. Roberto looked up at me and exclaimed, "See there, Dr. Swindle, that is why I knew I had to come and talk to you. You talk to me like my mom and dad do." And, just like that, I was othermothering.

I knew the significance of being visible and available to students of color; leaving was difficult, but being the only one could also be overwhelming. Hudson-Weems (2020) explains that, as Black women, mothering means committing to "loving and caring for [our] own, which extends to the entire African family" (p. 8). The mother in me knew that Shay needed a road map with explicit directions, plus a backup route (Kelly et al., 2019), Marcus needed a gentle nudge and a bit of "walking along beside him" (Gasman et al., 2017), and Roberto needed a comprehensive read of his situation in simple, raw terms because he deserved nothing less than equitable academic advising (Lawton, 2018). The mother in me embraced them as our children and not just some students.

Larissa: The Magical Negro Whisperer

Faculty often sought me out for advice for their Black and Brown students, as I was the only Black female faculty member at Redtown. While I was open to talking with sincere peers, I was always wary of random faculty members who only engaged with me when they had an issue with a non-white student. My apprehension was two-fold. First, it was as if they viewed themselves as the main character in the academia storyline. I only existed in the same space with them to aid in their success, and not my own, similar to that of the magical negro movie troupe found in such movies as *Ghost, The Shawshank Redemption,* and *The Legend of Bagger Vance* (Glenn & Cunningham, 2009; Hughey, 2009). Secondly, they seemed to think I was The Oracle with magical powers from *The Matrix,* as if all racialized woes could be cured and generations of compounded systemic racism could be superseded with a few words from me.

Each situation typically unfolded in the same way. After a faculty gathering, a "concerned" professor would approach me at their wit's end. Rarely did they intend to assure success for this particular student of color (Harper & Wood, 2016; King, 2005), improve their culturally responsive teaching, tap into their empathy reserves (Ladson-Billings, 1995, 2014; Noguera, 2019; Warren, 2014), or have an in-depth discussion about racial disparities of students at colleges and universities (Harper, Patton &

Wooden, 2009; Means, Hudson & Tish, 2019). Instead, it seemed like they wanted to *act* like they were doing something to absolve themselves of any guilt of being racially incompetent. It was as if they wanted to say they consulted with me, the Magical Negro Whisperer, so they could feel or say that they had done everything they could have.

This was indeed the impression I received from Dr. Glinton. After a faculty meeting, she bee-lined over to me and explained that she needed my help because several of her Black students were consistently late for her class. She had made several general proclamations about the importance of being on time, but they had not changed their behavior. She simply did not know what to do about this and wanted to know if I had any ideas about ending her 'Negro problem' of tardiness.

To provide context, Dr. Glinton was a long-term faculty member. Redtown's ethos centered on relationships, especially those between faculty and students. Most undergraduate classes still met face-to-face several times a week because of this focus, and particular emphasis was placed on making sure every student felt like they belonged. It was not uncommon for students to have dinner at their professor's house or babysit their children. Many white students were legacy, and several faculty members were alumni, so the personal connections extended generationally, although these experiences were not the typical testimony of Black or Brown students. In fact, Dr. Glinton, as a senior faculty member, had openly boasted about how she went the extra mile in developing relationships.

However, Dr. Glinton framed this lateness issue as if she had never worked with students before in her life. Moreover, she *seemed* to center the student's needs by vocalizing that she was worried they were missing critical information to ensure their success in class. Yet, she reinforced an age-old stereotype that Black people were always late and essentially asked how she could save the Black students from themselves. Instead of "displaying disgust, an emotion that is socially unacceptable and tantamount to racism," Dr. Glinton "display[ed] pity for them, a more socially acceptable emission that still objectifies and sentimentalizes the Black other while deflecting racist culpability" (Matias & Zambylas, 2014: 320).

I gave her the benefit of the doubt and took her inquiry at face value, just in case I was reading the situation wrongly. I thoughtfully responded, "Try talking to your students directly. Ask them to stay after class one day and bring up your observation. Show interest in their lives and their other activities. Bring up your worry about them missing pertinent information at the beginning of class. Through this practice, you will not only begin to address your concern, but you can strengthen your relationship with these students." She seemed to be taking in this information. Hopeful that I was making a difference, I continued, "You know, Dr. Glinton, the fixation on time is a westernized social construct. There is literature that supports this notion, and you might find it applicable to this situation and beyond." She nodded and leaned in to hear more. I continued, "If you are sharing pertinent information only at the beginning of class, perhaps switch it up and use the first few minutes for decompressing and re-centering as a group and then sharing the important details that are essential later in the class period when you know all students are there." Dr. Glinton gave me the biggest smile. She then proclaimed, "Okay! If you think of anything to help my situation, let me know!"

Despite providing her with three strategies, Dr. Glinton had not heard a single word. Her performance was done – she had consulted the Magical Negro Whisperer – and she could disregard my advice and the Black students' needs with a good conscience. This narrative featured my inter-action with one professor but was representative of my role with the institution regarding diversity, equity, and inclusion (DEI). While I was often told that my expertise was valued, it only had worth if it continued to center whiteness. If my advice did not conform to white norms, it was ignored. I often felt used, as if I was nothing more than a prop in a poorly written play about racial progressivism. I was the Magical Negro Whisperer who helped keep the peace among the Black and Brown folk so that Redtown could appear to make strides toward equity. As a womanist, I needed to see my self-worth through my own eyes and my culture and understand that my gifts would be stifled at this university. Furthermore, I knew if I stayed, I would constantly have to reckon "with my cultural consciousness and authentic existence" (Hudson-Weems, 2020: 46). It was clear that my veritable intent toward a more just society was wholly incompatible with that institution. I deserved more, and incidents like this solidified my resolve to leave the institution.

Jean: Academic Assault Gone Awry – Meeting Madness, Messiness, and Menace
I was indescribably excited to secure a tenure-track position and manage my program, a "grow your own," urban education initiative with the local school district. It was no surprise then that I hit the ground running. When introductions to partners were not forthcoming, I made the calls and set up the coffee dates. When colleagues could not introduce me to local schools, I made the connections and visited them alone. When I was told "No"

multiple times after asking, "Do we have a process for this," I simply figured things out and established the processes within the scope of my program. When I asked, as a new junior faculty member, who would be my faculty mentor, I was told, "We are working on that." And, *that* never materialized. And, so it went. For the most part, I was alone in figuring out my job, working out the specifics of an extant urban education program, and navigating new terrain. After six months, I had visited sixteen of the forty-two schools in the district, made connections with other teacher educators across the state, revamped parts of the urban education curricula, and taken a group of undergraduate students of color to a conference on teacher leadership.

I received accolades from other faculty and partners outside the university who were impressed by my strides and the traction the urban education program was getting. Members of Mainview's senior leadership team would spot me around campus and stop to comment that they had heard such great things about my work from university partners. The dean and faculty outside my department were complementary and supportive, often expressing that I was what the department needed. While most faculty in my department were friendly, I sensed some jealousy but dismissed it. I had realized that the faculty in my department were nice, but not welcoming. Since my arrival, only one faculty member had reached out and welcomed me; he showed concern about my adjustment to the Midwest, life outside campus, and needs beyond knowing how to order supplies. He ensured that I received social invitations when I had been left off the list and graciously received me in his home on numerous occasions. When Maria had sounded the alarm and rallied the troops on day three of my arrival because our property manager had given me keys to a filthy apartment, he joined other Mainview faculty (all outside our department) who dropped what they were doing for an entire afternoon to help me clean and scrub the place from floor to ceiling!

Albeit in solitude – by design and not choice – I forged ahead with my job duties and made the most of my time. One balmy February, as I was hunkered down working in my office, I received an invite from the provost's secretary for a meeting in thirty minutes. I reasoned the secretary had sent the message in error. By happenstance (or maybe not), my department head was outside my office. I asked if he knew anything about the meeting, and he barked, "Well, when they summon you, you just go." His response was quizzical, but I had previously noticed irregularities in his behavior. Thirty minutes later, I arrived at the impromptu meeting and joined the provost, dean, and department chair at a round table. And, I wondered, "What the hell is going on?"

The *goings-on* was my yearly evaluation with a hell of a lot of irregularities. I had not received a written evaluation, self-assessment, or other components that should have accompanied the process. I listened as the provost criticized my department and asked what I thought of my colleagues. I listened to the chair and the dean's silence. I listened as the provost asked me to explain one – repeat *one* – comment from a student on my teaching evaluations that stated I was condescending. For them, this singular comment trumped all the other overwhelmingly positive student feedback: Students surmised that my teaching and expertise had raised the bar for the program, my class challenged them, and I held high expectations, and, as their professor, I supported them as they rose to meet those expectations. The intended *coup de grâce* was when the chair exclaimed that I did not work well with others. When I asked him to elaborate, he stated, "Well, with me, for example. In meetings, your body language tells me that you don't agree with me!"

Utter befuddlement ushered me into a liminal space of questioning whether this was actually occurring or if I had somehow been transported to a twilight zone. I did the equivalent of five-finger breathing in my head and responded. First, I defended my colleagues and their work by noting structural and administrative barriers that prohibited collaboration, efficiency, and productivity. Second, I named each faculty and staff member in the department and detailed an instance when I – junior faculty who had only arrived six months previously – had worked with them to resolve issues and connect them with resources. Third, I illustrated four occurrences when I had sought help and had not received it, but had nonetheless resolved the problems. I asked if they needed additional examples. Next, I requested clarification of the evaluation process and counter-questioned if such an unscripted meeting was typical after six months. Finally, I queried if they had further questions or concerns for me. With semi-bowed heads, they replied no, and I left.

I returned to my office with an unwavering resolution – my exodus had begun. The provost, assistant provost (when he learned of the meeting), and dean later apologized to me and confessed that they had been wrong and shortsighted. Three months later, the provost offered me the department chair position, yet I remained resolute. Over the next year, I arduously worked and grew the program at the graduate and undergraduate levels. While I taught and developed new courses, secured renewed partnerships (and monies for the institution), and wrote two grants – the only ones in the department – I persisted in that resolution. I worked and served as if I were never leaving, while building a curriculum vita that would allow me to. Finally, I penned my resignation letter in month twenty on the job, with no prospects in sight, and in month twenty-two, made my exodus after accepting one of two tenure-track offers.

Independent of this microaggression-laden encounter, I already knew what has often been reported – that many colleges and universities in the United States are negative, hostile, and frigid environments for Black faculty who often experience both institutional and personal forms of racism at work (Banks, 1984; Goodnough, 2009; Johnsrud & Des Jarlais, 1994; Johnstrud & Sadao, 1998; Killough et al., 2017; McKay, 1997; Turner & Myers, 2000; Smallwood, 2007; Stanley, 2006). The National Center for Education Statistics (2017) affirms a steady attrition rate of Black professors from assistant to full professor ranks. In 2015, Black faculty represented 7 percent of assistant, 6 percent of associate, and a mere 4 percent of full professor tenured faculty (p. 255). This attrition is in the context of already consistently low numbers of Black faculty at major educational institutions that, for example, varied in 2017 from 6.8 percent at the University of Alabama to 2.7 percent at the University of California Berkeley. While I knew that academia is often a revolving door for many Black faculty, this encounter felt like both a personal and a professional assault. Stanley (2006) underscores that Black faculty are presumptively and repeatedly viewed as incompetent by their peers. Tuitt et al. (2009) and Whitfield-Harris (2016) assert that Black faculty are required to valid-ate their authority to students and credibility and value as a faculty member to colleagues. This often entails showing evidence of expertise in a field where white colleagues are not obligated to prove the same. Yet, from an Africana womanist perspective, as a self-definer and embracing the notion of being strong (Hudson-Weems, 2020), I rested in my emotional and mental power to stay the course and enact an exodus plan – one that centered well-being and self-respect as guideposts. There were additional macro- and microaggressions, exclusions, and attempts to undermine my work, yet support from my village and resolve to leave the Mainview while concomitantly achieving success during the process were essential pre-cursors to my exodus.

Larissa: Killing Us Softly with Midwest Niceness
Like most higher learning institutions, racial diversity was a public-facing center point of Redtown. From marketing pictures to the strategic plan, it looked like Redtown had, wanted, and valued all kinds of students.

In truth, the student body *was* reasonably diverse for the Midwest, a region that historically has some of the least diverse campuses (Franklin, 2012). As a born and raised Midwesterner, though, I knew the small talk with neighbors and the sweet smiles found on so many faces in small-town America often hid bigotry, intolerance, and racial disparity that dates back generations and is still ever-present today (Campney, 2019; Gordon, 2019; Meriwether, 2020; Vega, 2015).

It did not take me a long time to realize that Redtown had very little commitment to its students of color. As a private, faith-based institution, they had little interest in recognizing any diversity beyond race, and even in this, the commitment was shallow. During my second year at Redtown, I was appointed the head of the faculty diversity committee (a story for another time), and I was eager to lend my expertise to this area. Naively, I believed that the university desired to meet all its students' needs but just did not know how to address them. If I could help bridge the gap in policy and practice, it would be a win for the students and the institution.

In the middle of fall semester, I was approached by a white female colleague who I considered a trusted co-conspirator (Love, 2019). She was part of the faculty review committee, the body that oversaw tenure and promotion. The committee's composition was typical, meaning all white and mostly male (National Center for Educational Statistics, 2017). That year the committee had the additional task of updating the required documents. My colleague saw this as an opportunity to address the faculty's accountability to students of color and proposed that a diversity, equity, and inclusion statement be added. She described how the committee was 'lukewarm' about the idea and made several excuses. However, this did not deter her, and she independently crafted a mock-up based on best practices in the field. She presented her draft at their next meeting, and the committee reluctantly considered it. They finally concluded they would include this new requirement if two accommodations were made. The first was that tenured faculty members were exempt from completing it, which meant they would not have to be accountable. The second was that the blanket term of 'diversity' be language-specific toward students' 'race,' 'gender,' and 'socio-economic status.'

My colleague explained that she agreed to these terms, as it was at least a move in the right direction. Ethically though, she was disturbed. She shared that, behind closed doors, the committee decided to be so exact in the language as to exclude student populations that did not align with their belief system, namely LGBTQ+ students. She knew these details would not be disclosed when this motion was taken to the faculty senate's broader audience. At face value, she knew that the proposal appeared to be a step toward equity in holding the faculty accountable, albeit incremental and self-serving (Bell, 1980; Taylor, 1999). In reality, it was an act of carefully constructed discrimination through the intentional omission of a vulnerable group. She felt morally obligated to intervene but, in Midwest fashion, did not want to call it out directly. As the leader of the diversity committee, we agreed that I would introduce a more inclusive version when the time came.

As I prepared to interlope, I decided to talk to one of the other members of the committee with whom I had a working relationship. He was surprisingly forthcoming. He said several on the committee did not want to take diversity too far, and many of the conservative members, himself included, were uncomfortable with embracing all "lifestyles." Over the decades, they have seen the campus change and, although it was hard, they had learned to accept some differences in the student body. He applauded "the old white guys" for expanding their minds to at least being inclusive of people of color, women, and those with limited financial means, because, as he put it, "I can recall a time not too long ago that these groups would not be accommodated so freely." Finally, he stated, "our campus might not be right for every student," suggesting that instead of faculty changing, students should and, if not, choose a different university. He warmly said all of this with a smile on his face, as if the conversation was about finding the best "fit" for a student rather than blatant bigotry.

Although I was appalled by his response, I was glad I was now aware of his stance, and it gave me insight on how to approach the topic. I knew engaging in a discussion of the rights of LGBTQ+ students would go nowhere, and I would need to be crafty. As predicted, the diversity statement proposal was presented as a huge step forward. The senate, unaware of the behind-the-scenes schemes to exclude certain swaths of students, praised it. During the discussion, I proposed the diversity statement be panoptic to allow faculty the academic freedom to interpret how they met diversity, strategically leaving out the sordid details to which I had been privy. My addendum was met with little resistance, the change was adopted, and the open-ended diversity statement requirement passed. Our co-conspiring had worked!

Or so we thought. The monthly faculty senate meetings occurred without incident until the final wrap-up meeting of the year. At that time, the faculty review committee proposed what they called 'small tweaks' to the new requirements that had passed months before. It was now devoid of the diversity statement altogether. I pointed this out, and they explained that the committee had reconsidered what they had presented earlier in the year. Although it was proposed, amended, and voted upon, they now felt it was suggested too early. They excused the removal as a way to make room for a potential new hire, a Director of Diversity, and they did not want to potentially appease their vision. The 'old white guys' had cleverly wrapped their bigotry in Midwest niceness – as if the removal was because they were politely holding the door open for the new person of color. I knew that if I deviated from regional tradition – that is, avoid conflict, uphold the confidence of my colleague, and smile – I would be seen as an aggressive, contentious Black woman (Ashley, 2014; Jones & Norwood, 2016), and the conversation would go nowhere. The diversity statement was no longer, and that was that.

I was upset for the LGBTQ+ students who would continue to experience discrimination for years to come. While I knew that, as a conservative faith-based institution, Redtown would not be accepting of what they considered non-traditional lifestyles, it was appalling that they also did not wield their faith to operationalize the second greatest commandment, love thy neighbor. Indeed, it was also unethical to accept tuition money from LGBTQ+ students, but not accept them as fellow humans. I also knew I could not thrive at a university where those who held power felt they could deem who was and was not worthy of existence. Yet, I was also thankful because this moment further solidified my decision that Redtown was not my place. I needed to be in an environment that accepted everyone, not just me. Ironically, I felt this almost literally, for my 'otherings,' that is, race and gender, had barely made the cut. I also knew my commitment to making space for others extends far beyond myself (Maparyan, 2012), and I could not flourish in an oppressive environment that did not recognize all humans as worthy because I know, "until we are all free, we are none of us free" (Lazarus, 1883). I could not remain heartless in the heartland.

Discussion and Conclusion

Sojourner Truth whole-heartedly encouraged Black people of the South to relocate toward the West. These migrants, aptly called the Exodusters, were not only fleeing a post-Civil War climate of oppression but were also in search of a place where they could thrive. Truth penned, "I think it is a good move for them. I believe as much in that move as I do in the moving of the children of Egypt going out to Canaan, just as much." (Truth, 1850: 19). While we did not share the same level of optimism as Truth – we knew there was problematic racialized turmoil across higher education institutions – we did believe that there was something better for us within the Academy. Liberating ourselves from universities that did not value us was the ultimate act of womanism. Although we both made the difficult decision to leave our institutions, it was not a decision we took lightly. In truth, we almost succumbed to the pressure of being "strong black women" (Allen, 2018), like the Dora Milaje warriors of Wakanda in the movie *Black Panther* (Coogler, 2018), who stay loyal to the kingdom even at the most adverse times, or the female "tall brown" social workers who nurse the socially deviant back to health in N. K. Jemisin's short story "The Ones Who Stay and Fight" in *How Long 'til Black Future Month?* (2018: 11). Instead, we took the path of ultimate self-care – self-emancipation in search of a promised land. We both found institutions that were further along the pathway of racial justice and showed promising signs that they would support us in the way we needed.

After our exoduses, we were able to reflect carefully on what sustained our mental well-being throughout our journey. First, we both were part of sister circles. Few, Stephens & Rouse-Arnett (2003) explain the type of talk in sister circles as "congenial conversation or positive relating in which life lessons might be shared between Black women" (p. 205). We sought out ways to actively engage with other women who embraced the tenets of Africana womanism, particularly that of *genuine sisterhood*; they believed that our success was theirs and that we were part of the same body. I (Jean) recall one sister circle member who exclaimed, "What is happening to you there [Mainview]? This is not you. You never speak [negatively] like that. Girl, you need to do something because I need my sista' back!" Our sister circles cared enough to listen, advise, and sound the alarm when needed. Exodus 17:12 tells of a battle against the Amalekites, where the Israelites triumphed as long as Moses held up his hands. As he tired and his hands lowered, the Amalekites would begin to win. Aaron and Hur came along beside Moses, each holding up one of his tired hands. With hands held high, the Israelites won the battle. Likewise, our sister circle held up our hands as we fought our battles.

Second, we did not deny the harm our institutions caused. When they showed us who they were, we believed them. In this knowledge, we determined whether we wanted to bear the mental and emotional taxes that remaining in the institutions would warrant. Iteratively, we contemplated the concepts of *strong*, *self-namer*, and *self-definer*, and we were adamant in defining ourselves and being the guardians of our mental and emotional health. Because we knew who we were and accepted what the institutions were, we could assess incompatibility and choose to leave the relationship. In this, we did not make what we were experiencing a secret. We both explicitly communicated with our institution that too little was being done for social justice and that systemic irregularities and institutional cultures were creating more barriers than opportunities. The problem was never that we did not recognize or express ourselves. The issue was that no one of consequence from our institutions was willing to listen.

Last, we never stopped operating in our calling. We remained professionally productive and maintained a high level of teaching, research, and service. Focusing on our work not only gave us purpose during trying times, but it also allowed us to be in the position to have a soft landing at other institutions upon our exodus. In addition, our work served as a counter to Racial Battle Fatigue (RBF), or the social-psychological stress responses (for example, frustration, anger, exhaustion, physical avoidance, psychological or emotional withdrawal, escapism, acceptance of racist attributions), Black faculty often face at predominantly white institutions (Smith, Yosso & Solórzano, 2011). In fact, we were both so productive that our respective campuses were shocked when we informed them we were leaving. They mistook our commitment, aplomb, and dedication as a sign of loyalty to the institution when, in actuality, they were representative of our commitment to our well-beings, our students, and ourselves.

Our reflections serve as a roadmap to higher education institutions interested in attracting and retaining Black women faculty. While there is no silver bullet, implementing support for groups of Black faculty to draw strength from each other, really listening to Black faculty when they express concerns, and valuing Black faculty's contributions beyond how they benefit the institution are all ways that could potentially bolster racial diversity. Furthermore, our narratives point to the need to question hegemonic assumptions and stereotypes when working with Black women faculty: de-tokenize the Black faculty; covet the value, dedication, and commitment to success Black faculty mean for all students, especially students of color; and prioritize DEI from stem to stern, across -isms and stakeholders. In hindsight, we are thankful for our experiences, as we learned so much from them. It is our hope that higher education institutions also glean from what we have shared so that upcoming Black women faculty can have better experiences in the future.

REFERENCES

Allen, M. D. (2018). If you can see it, you can be it: Black panther's black woman magic. *Journal of Pan African Studies*, 11(9), 20–2.

Ashley, W. (2014). The angry black woman: The impact of pejorative stereotypes on psychotherapy with black women. *Social Work in Public Health*, 29(1), 27–34.

Banks, W. M. (1984). Afro-American scholars in the university: Roles and conflicts. *American Behavioral Scientist*, 27(3), 325–38.

Beauboeuf-Lafontant, T. (2002). A womanist experience of caring: Understanding the pedagogy of exemplary Black women teachers. *The Urban Review*, 34(1), 71–86.

(2005). Womanist lessons for reinventing teaching. *Journal of Teacher Education*, 56(5), 436–45.

Bell, D. A. (1980). Brown and the interest-convergence dilemma. In Bell, D. A. (ed.), *Shades of Brown: New perspectives on school desegregation*. New York: Teachers College Press, 91–106.

Bell, J. (2005). *Doing your research project: A guide for first-time researchers in education, health and social science*. 4th ed. Maidenhead: Open University Press.

Caine, V., Estefan, A. & Clandinin, D. J. (2019). Narrative inquiry. In Atkinson, P., Delamont, S., Cernat, A., Sakshaug, J. W. & Williams, R. A. (eds.), *SAGE Research Methods Foundations*. Thousand Oaks, CA: Sage. https://www.doi.org/10.4135/9781526421036771087

Campney, B. M. S. (2019). *Hostile Heartland: Racism, repression, and resistance in the Midwest*. Champagne, IL: University of Illinois Press.

Clandinin, D. J. (2006). Narrative inquiry: A methodology for studying lived experience. *Research Studies in Music Education*, 27(1), 44–54. http://dx.doi.org/10.1177/1321103X060270010301

(2007). *Handbook of Narrative Inquiry: Mapping a methodology*. Thousand Oaks, CA: Sage.

(2013). *Engaging in Narrative Inquiry*. New York: Left Coast Press.

Cone, J. H. (1997). *Black Theology and Black Power*. Maryknoll, NY: Orbis Books.

Coogler, R. (2018). *Black Panther*. Burbank, CA: Marvel Studios.

Cousin, G. (2009). *Researching Learning in Higher Education: An introduction to contemporary methods and approaches*. New York: Routledge.

Davies, B. & Davies, C. (2007). Having, and being had by, "experience": Or, "experience" in the social sciences after the discursive/poststructuralist turn. *Qualitative Inquiry*, 13(8), 1139–59.

Delgado Bernal, D. (1998). Using Chicana feminist epistemology in educational research. *Harvard Educational Review*, 68(4), 555–83.

Dewey, J. (1958). *Experience and Nature*. Garden City, NY: Dover.

Dillard, C. B. (2006). *On Spiritual Strivings: Transforming an African American woman's academic life*. Albany, NY: SUNY Press.

Few, A. L., Stephens, D. P. & Rouse-Arnett, M. (2003). Sister-to-sister talk: Transcending boundaries and challenges in qualitative research with black women. *Family Relations*, 52(3), 205–15.

Franklin, R. S. (2012). Benchmarking student diversity at public universities in the United States: Accounting for state population composition. *Annals of Regional Science*. 49, 355–72.

Gasman, M., Smith, T., Ye, C. & Nguyen, T. H. (2017). HBCUs and the production of doctors. *AIMS Public Health*, 4(6), 579–89.

Glenn C. L. & Cunningham, L. J. (2009). The power of Black magic: The magical negro and white salvation in film. *Journal of Black Studies*, 40(2), 135–52.

Goodnough, A. (2009). Harvard professor jailed. *New York Times*. July 21. https://www.nytimes.com/2009/07/21/us/21gates.html

Gordon, C. (2019). Race in the heartland: Equity, opportunity, and public policy in the Midwest. University of Iowa and Iowa Policy Project.

Harper, S. R., Patton, L. D. & Wooden, O. S. (2009). Access and equity for African American students in higher education: A critical race historical analysis of policy efforts. *The Journal of Higher Education*, 80(4), 389–414. https://doi.org/10.1080/00221546.2009.11779022

Harper, S. R. & Wood, J. L. (2016). *Advancing Black Male Student Success from Preschool through Ph.D.* Sterling, VA: Stylus Publishing.

Hill, K. D. (2009). Code-switching pedagogies and African American student voices: Acceptance and resistance. *Journal of Adolescent & Adult Literacy*, 53(2), 120–31.

hooks, b. (1989). *Talking Back: Thinking feminist, thinking black.* Boston: South End Press.

Hudson-Weems, C. (2020). *Africana Womanism: Reclaiming ourselves.* New York: Routledge.

Hughey, M. W. (2009). Cinethetic racism: White redemption and black stereotypes in "magical negro" films. *Social Problems*, 56(3), 543–77.

Jemisin, N. K. (2018). *How Long 'til Black Future Month?* New York: Orbit Books.

Jones, T. & Norwood, K. J. (2016). Aggressive encounters & white fragility: Deconstructing the trope of the angry black woman. *Iowa Law Review*, 102(5), 2016–69.

Johnsrud, L. K. & Des Jarlais, C. D. (1994). Barriers to tenure for women and minorities. *Review of Higher Education*, 17(4), 335–53.

Johnsrud, L. K. & Sadao, K. C. (1998). The common experience of "otherness": Ethnic and racial minority faculty. *Review of Higher Education*, 21(4), 315–42.

Kelly, B. T., Raines, A., Brown, R., French, A. & Stone, J. (2019). Critical validation: Black women's retention at predominantly white institutions. *Journal of College Student Retention: Research, Theory & Practice*, 23(2) 434–56.

Killough, A. L., Killough, E. G., Walker, I. I. & Williams, O. (2017). Examining the delicate balance of maintaining one's blackness as a black professional on the predominantly white campus. *Journal of Best Practices in Health Professions Diversity*, 10(2), 81–110.

King, J. E. (ed.) (2005). *Black Education: A transformative research and action agenda for the new century.* Mahwah, NJ: Lawrence Erlbaum Associates.

Ladson-Billings, G. (1995). Toward a theory of culturally relevant pedagogy. *American Educational Research Journal*, 32(3), 465–91. https://doi.org/10.3102/00028312032003465

(2014). Culturally relevant pedagogy 2.0: a.k.a. the remix. *Harvard Educational Review*, 84(1), 74–84. https://doi.org/10.17763/haer.84.1.p2rj1314854847sl

Lawton, J. (2018). Academic advising as a catalyst for equity. *New Directions for Higher Education*, 2018(184), 33–43. https://doi.org/10.1002/he.20301

Lazarus, E. (1883). A quote from epistle to the Hebrews. *Jewish Women's Archive*. https://jwa.org/media/quote-from-epistle-to-hebrews

Love, B. L. (2019). *We Want to Do More than Survive: Abolitionist teaching and the pursuit of educational freedom*. Boston: Beacon Press.

Maparyan, L. (2012). *The Womanist Idea*. New York: Routledge.

Matias, C. E. & Zembylas, M. (2014). "When saying you care is not really caring": Emotions of disgust, whiteness ideology, and teacher education. *Critical Studies in Education*, 55(3), 319–37.

McArthur, S. A. & Lane, M. (2019). Schoolin' Black girls: Politicized caring and healing as pedagogical love. *The Urban Review*, 51, 65–80. https://doi.org/10.1007/s11256-018-0487-4

McKay, N. Y. (1997). A troubled peace: Black women in the halls of the white academy. In Benjamin, L. (ed.), *Black Women in the Academy: Promises and perils*. Miami: University of Florida Press, 11–22.

Means, D. R., Hudson, T. D., Tish, E. (2019). A snapshot of college access and inequity: Using photography to illuminate the pathways to higher education for underserved youth. *The High School Journal*, 102(2), 139–58.

Meriwether, A. (2020) What's the deal with 'Midwest Nice?' National Public Radio. January 11. https://bit.ly/3yBq6z9

Merriam-Webster (n.d.). self-emancipation. Merriam-Webster. https://www.merriam-webster.com/dictionary/self-emancipation

Morris, J. E. (2004). Can anything good come from Nazareth? Race, class, and African American schooling and community in the urban South and Midwest." *American Educational Research Journal*, 41(1), 69–112.

National Center for Education Statistics (NCES). (2017). *The Condition of Education 2017*. Washington, DC: US Department of Education. https://nces.ed.gov/pubsearch/pubsinfo.asp?pubid=2017144

Noguera, P. (2019, July 8). Equity isn't just a slogan. It should transform the way we educate kids. The Holdsworth Center. https://holdsworthcenter.org/blog/equity-isnt-just-a-slogan

Ogunyemi, C. O. (1985). Womanism: The dynamics of the contemporary black female novel in English. *Signs: Journal of Women in Culture and Society*, 11(1), 63–80.

Riley, T. & Hawe, P. (2005). Researching practice: The methodological case for narrative inquiry. *Health Education Research*, 20(2), 226–36.

Rocha, J. Alonso, L. López Mares-Tamay, M. J. & Reyes McGovern, E. (2016). Beyond theoretical sensitivity: The benefits of cultural intuition within qualitative research and Freirean generative themes: Four unique perspectives. *The Qualitative Report*, 21(4), 744–64.

Smallwood, S. (2007, October 9). Noose discovered on office door of black professor at Columbia U. *The Chronicle of Higher Education*. October 9. https://bit.ly/3EuB63s

Smith, W. A., Yosso, T. J., & Solórzano, D. G. (2011). Challenging racial battle fatigue on historically white campuses: A critical race examination of race-related stress. In R. Coates (Ed.), Covert racism (pp. 211–237). Boston: Brill.

Stanley, C. A. (2006). Coloring the academic landscape: Faculty of color breaking the silence in predominantly white colleges and universities. *American Educational Research Journal*, 43(4), 701–36. https://doi.org/10.3102/00028312043004701

Taylor, E. (1999). Critical race theory and interest convergence in the desegregation of higher education. In Parker, L., Deyhle, D. & Villenas, S. (eds.), *Race Is ... Race Isn't: Critical race theory and qualitative studies in education*. Boulder, CO: Westview Press, 181–204.

Truth, S. (1850). Narrative of Sojourner Truth. *Documenting the American South*. https://docsouth.unc.edu/neh/truth84/truth84.html

Tuitt, F., Hanna, M. D., Martinez, L., Salazar, M. & Griffin, R. (2009). Teaching in the line of fire: Faculty of color in the academy. *Thought and Action*, 25, 65–74.

Turner, C. S. V. & Myers, Jr, S. L. (2000). *Faculty of Color in Academe: Bittersweet success*. Boston: Allyn and Bacon.

Vega, S. (2015). *Latino Heartland: Of borders and belonging in the Midwest*. New York: New York University Press.

Walker, A. (1983). *In Search of Our Mother's Gardens: Womanist prose*. New York: Harcourt Brace Jovanovich.

Warren, C. A. (2014). Towards a pedagogy for the application of empathy in culturally diverse classrooms. *The Urban Review*, 46, 395–419. https://doi.org/10.1007/s11256-013-0262-5

Whitfield-Harris, L. (2016). The workplace environment for African-American faculty employed in predominantly white institutions. *ABNF Journal*, 27(2), 28–38.

CHAPTER 10

Defying Odds and Certainty: Challenges and Approaches to the Retention, Inclusion and Resilience of African-American Women in Higher Education

Teri Platt

Black women in higher education often confront environments in which they are expected to excel professionally, while simultaneously confront, challenge, and thrive in conditions of workplace discrimination and unequal access to resources. Scholarly examinations of challenges to and strategies for the retention and inclusion of women in higher education must examine the unique experiences faced by Black women at the intersections of race, class, and gender. Beginning in the late 1970s, and continuing throughout the 1980s and 1990s, standpoint (Smith, 1974), critical race (Crenshaw, 1988, 1991), Black feminist (Combahee River Collective, 1979; Collins, 1986, 2000; hooks, 1984, 2000a; Henderson, Hunter & Hildreth, 2010), multiracial feminist (Moraga & Anzaldúa, 1983; Baca Zinn & Thornton Dill, 1996), and anti-racist feminist (Sommersell, 2003) scholarship, examining Black women's experiences at the intersections of race, class, and gender, suggested scholars and practitioners needed to do more than simply add gender, or add race. *Intersectionality*, as an analytical framework (Collins, 2015), has been established as a lens for scholars and practitioners seeking to do more than simply add gender or race to analysis. Utilization of intersectionality as a critical framework can support the evaluation of existing practices and provide structure for inclusive practices that support the retention and inclusion of Black women in higher education institutions.

Such a framework requires researchers to look at the ways in which these interlocking systems of oppression function within Black women's experiences as Black individuals, as women, and as having a particular class location within higher education (Walkington, 2017). An intersectional analytical framework understands intersecting identities such as race, class, gender, sexuality, and ability are relational, rather than isolated from each other. These identities are constructed while underlying and shaping intersecting and interrelated systems of power such as racism and sexism. These intersecting power systems result in a socially constructed and complex set of social inequalities for people, like Black women faculty working in higher education who experience these intersecting identities through their material reality. As social inequalities are also cross-culturally specific and historically situated, social interactions and unequal material realities will vary depending on the space and time of social interactions. Groups and individuals who occupy various spaces within the matrix of oppression have varying points of view of their own and others' experiences with inequalities, which results in knowledge projects reflecting their social location within systems of power (Walkington, 2017). Intersectionality, as an analytic tool, has the power to shape knowledge projects, which challenge the status quo (Collins, 2015). Utilizing intersectionality, one may be better able to understand which patterns persist in Black women's experiences as faculty in higher education, and what suggestions scholars provide for Black women faculty toward successfully navigating their experiences in higher education. This chapter examines sociological scholarship of Black women's experiences as faculty in higher education with a focus on their navigation of three areas: workplace discrimination, unequal access to resources, and strategies for resistance and resilience.

Workplace Discrimination

Workplace discrimination is central to the experiences of Black women working as faculty in higher education. Research in this area reveals the existence of negative stereotypes rooted in racist, sexist, and classist notions from the era of chattel slavery about Black women as undeserving recipients of affirmative action (Spraggins, 1998) and lacking workplace productivity (Wilson, 2012). These stereotypes can translate into fewer educational and employment opportunities and lower wages for Black women faculty in higher education, in comparison to their white male counterparts (Aparicio, 1999; Sotello & Turner, 2002). Negative racial stereotypes disproportionately affect women of color, particularly Black women, in ways gender discrimination alone cannot explain. Black women faculty face a double bind of racial and gender discrimination at every level of academic life. This double minority status leads faculty to view Black women scholars as less capable, leading to fewer full-time, tenured positions for Black women faculty. Common across Black women faculty experiences is the image of "the Mammy," who is expected to give deference not only to white faculty, but also white students, and experience sabotage from their white peers (Wilson, 2012). Combating these issues is further complicated as Black women rarely hold upper-level administrative positions in universities.

Patricia Hill Collins (2000) utilizes Black feminist thought to discuss the saliency of negative stereotypes, what she calls "controlling images," particularly those for Black women. According to Collins, stereotypical images of Black women are part of a "general ideology of domination" (2000: 69) that take on special meanings. Collins theorizes that the elite groups, defined as those who have the capacity and power for domination, holding the instruments of power within their ability to define societal values, can and do manipulate ideas about Black women by exploiting existing symbols, and creating new ones when necessary, to make poverty, sexism, racism, and other forms of injustice appear as normal and inevitable parts of life. Prescient to this review is the image of the Mammy, created to justify Black women's economic exploitation by whites during slavery, and continued into their relegation as domestic workers post-slavery. Collins (2000) describes the Mammy as the constructed image of the Black woman who accepts her racial and gendered subordination, and that against which all Black women's behavior is measured. Black female faculty members can be impacted by Mammy constructs in that they are expected to conform to workplace labor expectations that reinforce exploitative social concepts of racial and gendered subordination.

Negative stereotypes of the Mammy continue to impact perceptions of Black women faculty in higher education and impact their ability to navigate institutional spaces in ways that mirror their professional counterparts. For Black women, the Modern Mammy construction expects Black women to give deference to their white and male counterparts, allows for students, along with colleagues, to question their professional competence, and then expects Black women faculty to comfort those who question their abilities (Seo & Hinton, 2009; Wilson, 2012). Black women professors are also sabotaged by white administrators, who often take the side of offended white students in introductory courses covering racism and sexism, even within Sociology departments (Wilson, 2012). When Black women's assertions are aimed toward their own benefit, negative stereotypes come forward, more powerful colleagues and administrators label these women as aggressive, and Black women's progress in academia is stunted.

Facing both de jure segregation in the South, and de facto segregation in the North, Edghill (2007) reports Black women were hopeful that access to education would lead to equal access in employment with the *Plessy*

v. *Ferguson* ruling of 1896, which called for separate but equal education for
Blacks. Under this ruling, Edghill (2007) discusses Black women's place-
ment in predominantly Black schools as a way of implementing and
enforcing segregation. Here we see the institutionalization of racialized
sexism (Collins, 2000; Cotter, Hermsen & Vanneman 2003; hooks, 2000a;
Morales, 2014; Ramey, 1995; Thomas & Hollenshead, 2001; Thorpe, 2014;
Sotello & Turner, 2002) and racial discrimination against Black women
(Aparicio, 1999; Browne & Misra, 2003; Collins, 2000; hooks, 2000b;
Ramey, 1995; Seo & Hinton, 2009; Thorpe, 2014; Sotello & Turner,
2002).

During economic expansion, Black men gained access to marginalized
faculty positions in higher education, while Black women were restricted
from such opportunities. During periods of economic decline, linked to
economic globalization, Edghill (2007) finds that, in the interest of the
capitalist class, Black women provided the opportunity for labor that was
cheaper than their male counterparts. Therefore, while they could gain
access to white campuses, they were relegated to race-specific positions like
service-based positions with low or no prestige. Aparicio (1999) found
Black women described race-specific positions as a "ghetto appointment"
where a "person of color [is] hired to do the Black stuff" (p. 125). This
research supports Thomas & Hollenshead (2001) who also find that Black
women's labor as faculty is both the cheapest and least valued, and as such,
will then be used to educate Black women graduate students whose cheaper
labor will be further exploited in race-specific positions, like serving as staff
for race-focused initiatives and programs, within the institution of higher
education. The historical analysis Edghill (2007) provides, and Aparicio's
(1999) interviews with Black women faculty, how Black women's experiences with racism and sexism in academia can be historically traced back to
their initial participation in higher education, which outlines the devaluation of Black women's labor and why Black women faculty are still paid
less than their white and male counterparts (Browne & Misra, 2003;
Cotter, Hermsen & Vanneman, 2003; Edghill, 2007).

Seo & Hinton's (2009) findings support Pierce's (1995) conclusion that
Black women are both racialized and gendered in professional settings.
Although not focused specifically on Black women faculty and graduate
students' experiences, Pierce's findings are useful in understanding that
Black women lawyers, like Black women faculty and graduate students in
higher education, experience a "double bind," or double minority status, as
both gendered and racialized individuals. In these instances, Black women
faculty are trapped in negative race and gender stereotypes where they are

considered as both aggressive and less competent by their (often white) male colleagues and students when being assertive (Aparicio, 1999).

In addition to a double bind, Black women faculty are expected to mentor students of color more than are their white and male counterparts. This leads to the overextension and exhaustion of Black women faculty, and most certainly impacts their ability to expeditiously complete requirements toward tenure (Glover, 2006; Seo & Hinton, 2009). For Black women working in higher education, the Modern Mammy is a negative stereotype that relegates Black women faculty into race-specific, lesser-paid, overworked, and unappreciated mentoring positions (Seo & Hinton, 2009; Wilson, 2012). Negative stereotypes also impact Black women's faculty placement in overworked and underappreciated courses that teach race-specific content. This can lead to unequal pay, limited access to resources, and limited mentorship opportunities for Black women in new job placements within higher education (Edghill, 2007).

Limited Access to Resources

In addition to research on workplace discrimination, other research has examined Black women's limited access to resources in higher education. Some of this work focuses on women in female-dominated occupations. For example, Cotter, Hermsen & Vanneman (2003) utilize crowding, devaluation, and human capital theories to examine occupational gender segregation effects across multiple racial or ethnic categories. Comparing whites, Blacks, Latinos, and Asians, the authors examine how the processes of occupational segregation for workers in female-dominated occupations, and those of all workers in highly segregated labor markets, may affect earnings. The authors find the observed segregation effects (that is, those in segregated occupations earn less money) most negatively affect Black women. Moving beyond the Black–white binary, the authors find both individual and contextual effects can benefit women from all racial or ethnic groups; women in predominantly male professions, or in less gender-segregated professions, earn more than women in predominantly female professions. Therefore, Black women within academia may earn more than Black women in other occupations, but still earn less than their white, and male, counterparts within academia as they experience gender and occupational segregation effects. Cotter, Hermsen & Vanneman (2003) found that Black women are the only group particularly penalized relative to white women, may face more intense racism than Latinas and Asian women, are more occupationally segregated, and are concentrated in highly segregated labor markets. These patterns are attributable to the negative racialization of Black women and its associated negative stereotypes (Collins, 2000; hooks, 2000b; Ramey, 1995; Seo & Hinton, 2009; Spraggins, 1998; Sotello & Turner, 2002).

Race-specific positions also undermine the access to authority for Black women faculty at all levels of higher education, including with students (Huston 2006; Henderson, Hunter & Hildreth, 2010). Both Aparicio (1999) and Sotello & Turner (2002) discuss Rosabeth Kanter's (1978) concept of tokenism for women of color academics. Although they do not focus specifically on Black women faculty, Sotello & Turner (2002) point to the disproportionately low numbers of women of color who, as tokens, are contextually stereotyped, so their mistakes are more visible and on display within their workplace, while the pressure to be perfect is greater. As tokens, Black women find it harder to gain credibility, are more isolated and peripheral, have fewer opportunities to be sponsored, face misperceptions of their role and identity in their departments, and face more personal stress (Sotello & Turner, 2002: 76). This can be particularly difficult in the Science Technology Engineering and Mathematics (STEM) fields where Black women graduate students are found to drop out, at least in part, due to a lack of faculty mentors and extreme isolation (Borum & Walker, 2012; Charleston et al., 2014).

Being positioned as a token recreates for Black women in academia an "outsider within" status wherein Black women's once intimate proximity to the white families that employed them lent them a unique view of whiteness that most others in the Black community, and those in the white community themselves, never had (Collins, 1986; Henderson, Hunter & Hildreth, 2010). Accompanied with the knowledge that no matter how valued whites in power viewed them to be, Black women knew they would and could never really be considered equal to whites. In academia, this standpoint of Black women as outsiders uniquely situates them for more nuanced analysis, particularly when in touch with their marginalization. Black women are, thus, strangers and "marginal intellectuals" (Collins, 1986: 15).

Strategies for Resilience and Resistance by Black Women Faculty and Opportunities for Institutional Support

Many studies on Black women faculty experiences in higher education include discussions about strategies that can be used by Black women faculty to navigate issues of inclusion and offer recommendations for higher education administrators to support the retention and inclusion of Black women faculty (see Aparicio, 1999; Ramey, 1995; Sotello & Turner, 2002). Three strategies for the inclusion, retention, and resilience of Black women faculty that draw from in an intersectional framework, and can provide actionable responses, are individual and institutional support for peer mentoring relationships; the need for space and opportunities for Black women faculty to identify and resist institutional practices that may marginalize them and their professional expertise; and individual recognition and institutional support for self-care activities. The sections that follow provide discussions about how these individual level and institution supported strategies can advance the goal of retention and inclusion of Black women faculty in higher education.

Institutional Support for Peer Mentoring

Peer mentoring relationships with established faculty can help Black women faculty navigate their chilly reception, negative department climate, norms and expectations, and the assumption by their peers that Blacks are incapable of theorizing (Henderson, Hunter & Hildreth, 2010). Further, these relationships can help Black women faculty to psychologically resist the raced and gendered minefield of academia via validation, emotional support, friendship, and mutuality. Peer mentoring relationships appear fundamental for Black women faculty's resistance against internalizing their marginalization as they also provide feedback, share information, and give advice on work-related issues (Henderson, Hunter & Hildreth, 2010). However, no single mentor can provide all the support new Black women faculty need, so sharing the burden of mentorship across a collaborative and supportive group both in and out of their own departments is necessary. Aparicio (1999) suggests that Black women faculty maintain their relationships with their dissertation advisors from former campuses, and cultivate mentoring relationships through networking with other Black women faculty in national and professional associations who can keep them in the loop about informal and formal events and panels where they may collaborate with other Black women scholars. Institutions can support Black women faculty with these activities by providing funding for membership fees and travel to participate in national and professional meetings, sponsoring research-related working groups for Black women scholars so that collaborations can be encouraged. Campuses can fund and host events and workshops that provide opportunities for the development and maintenance of professional relationships.

Most research finds that mentoring relationships are important for Black women faculty working toward tenure in predominantly white institutions (PWIs), and result in positive effects toward professional and personal success as academics (Edghill, 2007; Henderson, Hunter & Hildreth, 2010; Rosa, 2013). However, Gardner (2014) finds no statistically significant difference in Black women scholar's perceptions of personal and professional success between those who were mentored and those who were not. Efforts to resist isolation are evident through the support of similarly situated scholars without judgment and against the climate of competition, by making allies and connecting with communities of color as an individual strategy of resistance, and through self-care (Thorpe, 2014). Administrative leadership can support newer, Black women professors navigate their new departmental climate, culture and expectations, and mentor them through the department's tenure processes (Aparicio, 1999; Seo & Hinton, 2009; Henderson, Hunter & Hildreth, 2010). Black women also resist isolation by creating academic groups with faculty in other departments (Rosa, 2013). Higher education administrators can support and strengthen mentoring programs by formalizing the mentoring relationships through institutionally sponsored initiatives that prioritize establishing supportive and positive connections. Utilizing a feminist and multicultural mentoring model (Chesney-Lind, Okamoto & Irwin, 2006) which recognizes the power differential that can exist between mentors and mentees and emphasizes open and honest communication that is responsive to the unique needs of women faculty can help Black women faculty resist these traditional hierarchies within higher education. The mentoring relationship in the feminist and multicultural model is built on collaboration on joint projects. The mentor and mentee work side by side on projects, and mentees are encouraged to bring their unique perspectives and contributions. In a higher education setting, mentoring relationships aligned with this model legitimize the professional voices and perspectives of mentees, provide insights for navigating institutional settings, and promote a sense of belonging, thus supporting faculty retention and inclusion.

Utilizing Black Feminist Thought and intersectionality as theoretical frameworks provides a nuanced understanding of the importance of mentoring relationships through the understanding of how Black women scholars navigate the intersections of race, class, and gender. The multicultural and feminist mentoring model that addresses the specific needs of women of color described by Chesney-Lind, Okamoto, & Irwin (2006) provides a framework for Henderson, Hunter & Hildreth (2010) who utilize

Black feminist thought (Collins, 2000) to establish a framework for better understanding how Black women faculty benefit from mentoring relationships. Further, the four main themes of Black feminist thought, the importance of self-definition, the significance of self-valuation and respect, the necessity of self-reliance and independence, and the centrality of a changed self to personal empowerment (Collins, 2000: 35–7), can be used as strategies of resistance against racism and sexism in higher education.

Speaking Truth to Power

Speaking truth to power is another strategy of resistance that Black women faculty are encouraged to engage in (Sotello & Turner, 2002; Shields, 2012). Scholars of intersectionality have called for faculty of color, and those belonging to majority groups, to speak the truth to power regarding Black women faculty experiences with racism, sexism, and classism within the academy. Henderson, Hunter & Hildreth (2010) suggest Black women faculty live Black Feminist Thought by asserting their self-valuation and self-definitions as capable scholars, which will bring an awareness of the interlocking nature of race, gender, and class oppression, and crystallize the importance of including Black women's culture as a strategy of resistance. Defiance and resistance to oppressive practices can create liberatory spaces for manifestations of resilience by Black women faculty and opportunities for authenticity. However, speaking truth to colleagues about experiences can be difficult because they could be re-interpreted and can lead to retaliation (Henderson, Hunter & Hildreth, 2010). Through their self-definition as capable scholars, Black women also, indirectly, resist sexist and racist teaching evaluations (Chesney-Lind, Okamoto & Irwin, 2006) by keeping their focus on their work, carefully documenting teaching successes and professional development workshop attendance, and planning pedagogy which reflects their dedication and investment in student learning (Henderson, Hunter & Hildreth, 2010). To help Black women faculty resist their experiences at the intersections of race–class–gender, campus administrators, policy makers (Sotello & Turner, 2002), and white women allies (Shields, 2012) need to understand and acknowledge how the race and gender composition of their departments affects their successes or failures. Diversity in experiences and perspectives among faculty can advance scholarly inquiry for research and teaching, support the recruitment of academic and professional talent to increase market competitiveness, and support diverse viewpoints that can lead to innovation, improved processes, and greater effectiveness.

Allyship and institution-based support takes many forms like the following: (1) increased individual and institutional understanding of the historical experiences of diverse populations within their organizations; (2) established processes to respond to concerns that may be raised about individual and institutional practices that affirm or exacerbate racism, sexism, and classism; (3) spaces and opportunities for constructive dialogue that does not rely on the adversely affected groups or individuals to teach others and alter institutional practices; and (4) a culture that demonstrates that all community members are valued for their professional expertise and contributions to the institution (Spencer, 2008). At the administrative level, colleges and universities can ally in resistance by supporting formal mentorship programs that include, but are not limited to, pairing new Black women faculty hires with established Black women faculty, or other women of color (Henderson, Hunter & Hildreth, 2010), and by providing professional development to assist new Black women faculty to overcome challenges of multiple marginalization based on their race, class, and gender (Sotello & Turner, 2002). The burden cannot solely rest with Black women faculty to legitimize their work and worth in institutions of higher education.

Institutional Support for Self-Care Practices

Although creating and maintaining a healthy work–family balance and engaging in self-care are suggested as crucial strategies of resistance (Thomas & Hollenshead, 2001; Sotello & Turner, 2002; Thorpe, 2014), many suggestions focus on individual efforts but opportunities exist for institutions to support self-care practices as a way of promoting inclusion and retention of faculty. Findings suggest Black women faculty do engage in individual strategies of self-care, which can include choosing when to serve on committees and when to protect the work–family balance. Institutions support self-care activities by providing campus programs and policies that preserve work–family balance, and by offering options such as family care leave, mental health days, counseling. Campus policies that support decisions by faculty not to respond to campus correspondence after hours and on weekends also support self-care efforts (Henderson, Hunter & Hildreth, 2010). Black women faculty also engage in individual resistance when they respect each other's work, seek advice from mentors and select committees and tasks that are meaningful and overlap research, service to community, and instruction, leaving the campus as often as possible, or leave to find new departments with more supportive senior faculty (Aparicio, 1999; Chesney-Lind, Okamoto & Irwin, 2006; Seo & Hinton, 2009; Henderson, Hunter & Hildreth, 2010).

At the institutional level, promoting a welcoming environment by increasing the representation of Black women faculty, graduate students, and other scholars of color is another crucial strategy of inclusion and retention in which faculty and administrators in higher education can engage (Sotello & Turner, 2002; Seo & Hinton, 2009). Borum & Walker (2012) suggest that institutional culture must be addressed to ensure the well-being and academic success of Black women faculty. One way this can be achieved is by seeking greater parity in racial and gender representation among faculty and students of color. This would also require that departments place careful consideration on job candidates that match the racial, ethnic and gender composition of their graduate students. Future research must also attend to strategies that will address institutional issues beyond a welcoming environment and toward substantive programming that will educate departments on racial microaggressions commonly experienced by Black women faculty (Aparicio, 1999; Sotello & Turner, 2002) and graduate students (Morales, 2014; Borum & Walker, 2012).

Lastly, and perhaps most importantly, Sotello & Turner (2002) suggest a four-step strategy of resistance toward a healthy work–family balance that accommodates conflicts of commitment for Black women faculty. First, departments must identify and acknowledge institutional norms and policies that place Black women faculty at a disadvantage resulting from family or community commitments. Once identified, departments can then develop and promote new policies that support, rather than penalize, community and family involvement. Departments should then include women of color in identifying these problems and possible solutions. Finally, departments must examine family-friendly initiatives used by private corporations and evaluate their appropriateness for higher educational settings (Sotello & Turner, 2002: 86).

Conclusion

Challenges persist in higher education that undermine the efforts of many Black women faculty to thrive in academia. However, actions taken by administrative leadership can expand access to resources, promote the inclusion of faculty with diverse experiences within institutional settings, and establish practices that support faculty retention and resilience. Three areas explored in this chapter are challenges associated with workplace discrimination, the hurdles of unequal access to resources, and specific strategies for resilience and resistance. The retention, resilience, and inclusion of Black women faculty requires intentional efforts on the part of individual administrators who commit institutional resources to develop sustainable programming and support.

Actions by individual faculty to combat, challenge, and resist the impacts of negative stereotypes and assumptions are identified in the chapter, but these individual efforts must be affirmed and supported by administrators through funded support for the establishment of regional and national professional networks of scholars; initiatives that promote inclusive campus cultures that value racial, gendered, and class diversity; faculty mentoring programs that foster inclusion in campus culture as well as professional advancement; and processes that are responsive to articulations of concern about discrimination, marginalization, oppression, and exclusion. The absence of committed actions to support the professional success and inclusion in the culture and practices of institutions can leave scholars feeling stagnated, oppressed, and like outsiders, which leads to departures from academia.

Black women faculty still hold uniquely oppressed positions as they continue working together, and with non-Black and male allies, to navigate institutional and individual barriers of higher education. Assumptions and stereotypes about the professional abilities, academic preparedness, and overall fit within academic units can undermine the efforts of Black women faculty to advance and thrive in academia. Intersectionality can serve as an analytical framework for evaluating experiences at the intersection of race, class, and gender, as well as a foundation for providing recommendations for individual and institutional practices that support retention, resilience, and inclusion of Black women faculty. Additionally, integrated theoretical approaches must be developed to understand how power dynamics at the intersections of race, class, and gender continue to shape and impact Black women faculty experiences within higher education.

REFERENCES

Aparicio, F. R. (1999). Through my lens: A video project about women of color faculty at the University of Michigan. *Feminist Studies*, 25(1), 119–30.

Baca Zinn, M. & Thornton Dill, D. (1996). Theorizing difference from multiracial feminism. *Feminist Studies*, 22(2), 321–31.

Borum, V. & Walker, E. (2012). What makes the difference? Black women's undergraduate and graduate experiences in mathematics. *The Journal of Negro Education*, 81(4), 366–78.

Browne, I. & Misra, J. (2003). The intersection of gender and race in the labor market. *Annual Review of Sociology*, 29, 487–513.

Charleston, L. J., George, P. L., Jackson, J. F. L., Berhanu, J. & Amechi, M. H. (2014). Navigating underrepresented STEM spaces: Experiences of black women in US computing science higher education programs who actualize success. *Journal of Diversity in Higher Education*, 7(3), 166–76.

Chesney-Lind, M., Okamoto, S. K. & Irwin, K. (2006). Thoughts on feminist mentoring: Experiences of faculty members from two generations in the academy. *Critical Criminology*, 14, 1–21.

Collins, P. H. (1986). Learning from the outsider within: The sociological significance of black feminist thought. *Social Problems*, 33(6), 14–32.

(2000). *Black Feminist Thought: Knowledge, consciousness, and the politics of empowerment*. New York: Routledge.

(2015). Intersectionality's definitional dilemmas. *Annual Review of Sociology*, 41(1), 1–20.

Combahee River Collective (1979). A black feminist statement. *Off Our Backs*, 9(6), 6–8.

Cotter, D. A., Hermsen, J. M. & Vanneman, R. (2003). The effects of occupational gender segregation across race. *The Sociological Quarterly*, 44(1), 17–36.

Crenshaw, K. W. (1988) Race, reform, and retrenchment: Transformation and legitimation in antidiscrimination law. *Harvard Law Review*, 101(7), 1331–87.

Crenshaw, K. (1991). Mapping the margins: Intersectionality, identity politics, and violence against women of color. *Stanford Law Review*, 43(6), 1241–99.

Critzer, J. W. & Rai, K. B. (1998). Blacks and women in public higher education: Political and socioeconomic factors underlying diversity at the state level." *Women & Politics*, 19(1), 19–38.

Edghill, V. E. (2007). Historical patterns of institutional diversity: Black women in race-specific positions on predominantly white college campuses. Dissertation. Howard University.

Gardner, D. R. (2014). The impact of mentoring on the self-perceived personal and professional success of African American women graduates of a Midwestern University. Doctoral dissertation. Western Michigan University.

Glover, W. F. (2006). Navigating the academy: The career advancement of black and white women full-time faculty. Dissertation. College of William and Mary. https://dx.doi.org/doi:10.25774/w4-7jwj-jg31

Henderson, T. L., Hunter, A. G. & Hildreth, G. J. (2010). Outsiders within the academy: Strategies for resistance and mentoring African American women. *Michigan Family Review*, 14(1), 28–40.

hooks, b. (1984). *Feminist Theory: From margin to center*. Boston: South End Press.

(2000a). Rethinking the nature of work. In hooks, b. (ed.) *Feminist Theory: From margin to center*. 2nd ed. Cambridge, MA: South End Press, 96–107.

(2000b). Educating women. In hooks, b. (ed.) *Feminist Theory: From margin to center*. 2nd ed. Cambridge, MA: South End Press, 108–16.

Huston, T. A. (2006). Race and gender bias in higher education: Could faculty course evaluations impede further progress toward parity? *Seattle Journal for Social Justice*, 4(2), 591–611.

Kanter, R. M. (1978). *Men and Women of the Corporation*. New York: Basic Books.

Moraga, C. & Anzaldúa, G. (1983). *This Bridge Called My Back: Writings by radical women of color*. 2nd ed. New York City: Kitchen Table, Women of Color Press.

Morales, E. M. (2014). Intersectional impact: Black students and race, gender, and class microaggressions in higher education. *Race, Gender & Class*, 21(3), 48–66.

Pierce, J. L. (1995). *Gender trials: Emotional lives in contemporary law firms*. Berkeley, CA: University of California Press.

Ramey, F. H. (1995). Obstacles faced by African American women administrators in higher education: How they cope. *Western Journal of Black Studies*, 19(2), 113–19.

Rosa, K. D. (2013). Gender, ethnicity, and physics education: Understanding how black women build their identities as scientists. Doctoral dissertation. Columbia University.

Seo, B-I. & Hinton, D. (2009). How they see us, how we see them: Two women of color in higher education. *Race, Gender & Class*, 16(3–4), 203–17.

Shields, S. A. (2012). Waking up to privilege: Intersectionality and opportunity. In Muhs, G. G., Niemann, Y. F., González, C. G., Harris, A. P. (eds.) *Presumed Incompetent: The intersections of race and class for women in academia*. Boulder, CO: University Press of Colorado, 29–39.

Smith, D. E. (1974). Women's perspective as a radical critique of sociology. *Sociological Inquiry*, 44(1), 1–13.

Sommersell, N. V. (2003). Anti-racist feminist theory and women of colour in the graduate classroom. Master's thesis. University of Toronto.

Sotello, C. & Turner, V. (2002). Women of color in academe: Living with multiple marginality. *The Journal of Higher Education*, 73(1), 74–93.

Spencer, M. S. (2008) A social worker's reflections on power, privilege, and oppression. *Social Work*, 53(2) 99–101. doi: 10.1093/sw/53.2.99

Spraggins, R. E. (1998). Fly girl in the buttermilk: The graduate experiences at a predominantly white institution of black women who attended various undergraduate environments. Doctoral dissertation. Syracuse University.

Thomas, G. D. & Hollenshead, C. (2001). Resisting from the margins: The coping strategies of Black women and other women of color faculty members at a research university. *The Journal of Negro Education*, 70(3), 166–75. https://doi.org/10.2307/3211208

Thorpe, C. W. (2014). Black women in higher ed caring for each other. *Women in Higher Education*, 23(8), 15–17.

Walkington, L. (2017). How far have we really come? Black women faculty and graduate students' experiences in higher education. *Humboldt Journal of Social Relations*, 1(39), 51–65.

Wilson, S. (2012). They forgot mammy had a brain. In Muhs, G. G., Niemann, Y. F., González, C. G., Harris, A. P. (eds.) *Presumed Incompetent: The intersections of race and class for women in academia*. Boulder, CO: University Press of Colorado, 65–77.

CHAPTER II

Black Talent: Practical Retention Strategies

Tyra M. Banks

Introduction

In the wake of the Black Lives Matter movement, which has highlighted racial inequities in American society, educational institutions have sought to affirm their commitment to equity and inclusion by forming committees to address diversity needs. Academic institutions understand the importance of a diverse workforce, but diversity is not reflected in their faculty positions at a proportion that represents the US population. According to the National Center for Education Statistics, in fall 2018, only 6 percent of all full-time faculty in degree-granting postsecondary institutions were Black, compared to 75 percent being white. They also report that Black professors are also disproportionately hired in the capacity of adjunct or non-tenure track positions and are not well represented in the higher ranks of the professoriate in tenure track positions (NCES, 2020).

Many organizations have prioritized increasing the number of talented Black academics, however, they have been unsuccessful in retaining them (Shore, Cleveland & Sanchez, 2018). Academic institutions often fail at keeping Black faculty when the strategy focuses solely on the number of diverse candidates hired. As Griffin (2019) precisely states, "increasing faculty diversity in the most vulnerable academic positions does not solve the overall problem; rather, it creates new, pernicious inequities." Faculty of color are not given adequate support and opportunities to thrive. Unfortunately, the inherent oppression embedded in the normative culture of higher education encourages exclusion and creates an unsupportive environment. When faculty of color accept faculty positions, continuing to pursue an academic career can challenge their mental and physical well-being as they attempt to compete in a toxic environment. Despite their qualifications and valuable contributions, feelings of isolation and lack of progression fuel the disconnectedness with their institutions (Zambrana et al., 2015). As a result, the retention of Black talent becomes a struggle for academic institutions. Identifying the needs of Black faculty, and implementing support systems based on those needs, attracts talent and increases the potential for retention. Developing new retention strategies with equitable consideration of the unique needs of Black faculty facilitates positive outcomes.

In theory, diversity adds value to academic communities. Exposure to different perspectives in the classroom, especially when the faculty is diverse, better prepares students to be successful in a global society (Antonio, 2002; Umbach, 2006). Hiring Black professors allows Black students opportunities to see themselves represented in academia, and white students' opportunities to see Black people in positions of expertise and authority. This type of exposure challenges the implicit bias and stereotypical belief that underperformance is inherent in Black people as a whole. Providing diverse representation in the classroom creates counter-narratives that help establish ecosystems that reflect equity and inclusion of Black faculty. For the purposes of this chapter, an ecosystem is the influence of the interconnection between person (physical, psychosocial, and cultural attributes), environment (physical and context), institution (that is, policies, practices, and climate), and community. In practice, academic institutions reinforce ecosystems in which climate, policies, and practices are institutionalized in dominant white culture. Faculty of color are expected to assimilate into an environment that reinforces inequitable and exclusionary practices, but are not given adequate support and opportunities to thrive in it.

Theoretical Framework

When considering issues of diversity, equity, and inclusion (DEI), social capital theory (SCT) and critical race theory (CRT) provide frameworks for analysis and developing solutions for retaining Black talent in higher education. SCT reinforces the importance of social networks in which knowledge, behaviors, and skills are shared (Coleman, 1988). Social networks greatly influence a person's access to information, support, and advice (Benbow & Lee, 2019). These essential networks are platforms through which people learn about, and prepare for opportunities. Through these networks, individuals gain social capital, which enhances their capabilities and allows them to utilize the resources and opportunities presented before them.

Tajfel (2010) argues that individuals who identify with a social group are able to position themselves to gain social capital. In higher education, Black faculty may find it difficult to draw on the social capital of their white counterparts. Although they identify as faculty members, they do not identify as part of the white social category or have a sense of belonging within that social group. Identity is a joint accomplishment between an individual and their context, developed by participation in accessible activities embedded within communities of practice. According to Lave & Wenger (1991), a community of practice encompasses access and use of resources, activities of the community, its norms, practices, and the interaction and shared resources between members of the community. The spectrum of participation flows from peripheral participation to full participation and mastery. Generally, people learn through practice and participation. In this respect, learning how to navigate higher education systems is embedded in the culture and social practices of the members of the higher education community. When members of the community are not given opportunities to participate, they have reduced chances of learning the cultural norms of the higher education landscape and understanding the university as a system.

While SCT leans on relationships within personal and institutional networks, CRT further explores how these institutions support oppression and deny an equal opportunity for underrepresented groups (Delgado & Stefancic, 2017). CRT is grounded on the premise that race and racism are fundamental structures that underpin how US society functions and perpetuates racial inequities (Bell, 1992). In higher education, CRT frames the ways in which marginalized groups experience race and racism within the educational system, inside these constructs, as they navigate the "normative culture" (Bell, 1992). The focus is on the institutional and individual racial inequities that are embedded in the fabric of the educational system (Delgado & Stefancic, 2017).

There are several tenets that guide this theoretical framework: (a) The *centrality of racism* – racism is so ingrained in the infrastructure of our landscape, that it looks ordinary and natural. (b) *Experiential knowledge* – the acknowledgment that people of color have lived experiences that are legitimate and critical to understanding and analyzing racial disparities in education (Solórzano & Yosso, 2001). Through stories or counternarratives, real lived experiences of people of color *counter* or challenge white dominant culture as the norm and serve as a strength-based approach to confront the validity of stereotypes (Delgado & Stefancic, 2017). (c) *Intersectionality* – the understanding that while racial identity centers on race and racism, other forms of oppression (for instance, sexism, homophobia, or ableism) intersect, as a person can identify with many social categories. The term "intersectionality" was coined by Kimberlé Crenshaw (1991), who explained how various identities intersect, with an exponential effect on lived experiences. (d) *Interest convergence* is grounded in the premise that the interest of Blacks in achieving racial equality will only advance when that interest converges with the interests of those in power (Bell, 1980). (e) *Race as a social construct* – race and races are invented categories, created by society without the merit of biological or genetic reality (Delgado & Stefancic, 2017).

This theory challenges power structures that define "normative culture" and refutes the marginalization and "othering" of non-whiteness. Othering is "a process whereby individuals, groups, and communities are deemed to be less important, less worthwhile, less consequential, less authorized and less human, based on historically situated markers of social formation such as race, class, gender, sexuality and nationality" (Yep, 2002: 18). Oppressive interactions with administration, other faculty, and peers, lend insight into the ways in which othering creates isolative environments, thus limiting opportunities for them to thrive on their campuses.

Theory of Change

Historically, institutionalized racism has caused Black and Hispanic populations to feel excluded from opportunities to forge successful pathways in academia as reflected in societal norms (Better, 2008). Their white counterparts are positioned to take advantage of opportunities by virtue of being white in a society that values their contributions, based on the merit system designed in their favor (Putman, 2017). By contrast, Black faculty are burdened with the pressure to assimilate to the culture of academia in an attempt to "fit in" and attain the same validation of merit awarded to their white peers. Additionally, Black faculty are expected to perform without adequate structural support or access to social networks, which can have a detrimental effect on their career potential. In essence, Black professors are placed and unsupported in environments that are influenced by racist policies and practices, making it twice as hard to ascend the ranks of the professoriate. Therefore, they are left vulnerable and may find their existence in academia less desirable, leading them to consider career choices outside the academy.

Research shows that structural and social barriers are primary reasons higher education struggles to retain Black talent (Wolfe & Dilworth, 2015;

Daniel, 2007). Structural barriers include lack of financial and human resources dedicated to DEI, exclusionary discourse reflected in policies and practices, lack of intentional recruitment of Black professors in tenure track positions, racism in promotion and tenure review, a lack of policies and procedures in place to address macro and microaggressions, and a lack of clear pathways to leadership. Social barriers consist of lack of access to exclusive networks, lack of mentorship and/or sponsorship, and limited opportunities to engage in collaboration. Providing pathways and resources that reifies a discourse of diversity, equity, and inclusion would signal to those who have been consistently marginalized that the opportunities are available for them.

Institutions are in a position to offer equitable solutions through opportunities and resources to increase the job satisfaction of Black faculty. To facilitate organizational change, institutions must intentionally interrupt the exclusionary patterns and practices embedded in the dominant white institutional culture. Once leadership commitment is established, administration can take the recommended actionable steps to support Black faculty structurally and socially, and ultimately, increase the rate of retention. Being intentional in developing equitable DEI practices prior to the hiring process cultivates a supportive ecosystem that strengthens feelings of belonging and ultimately, job satisfaction for Black faculty (Laden & Hagedorn, 2000).

Practical Strategies for Black Faculty Persistence

Structural Support Systems

Provide financial support to form a diversity, equity, and inclusion (DEI) committee and charge it to review the institution's or department's commitment to these aims.

Creating a committee with dedicated funding to focus on the institution's or department's commitment to DEI can be instrumental in facilitating an inclusive environment for all. Many institutions form committees that rely on volunteers (often comprised of "diversity hires") to lead these efforts (O'Meara et al., 2021). However, when volunteers are tasked with serving on these committees in addition to their workloads, efforts to enact change are arduous and slow. Although well meaning, volunteers have other job responsibilities that take precedence over the fulfillment of committee obligations. Therefore, it is essential to hire dedicated people to handle strategic planning and timely execution of equitable DEI policies and practices. This committee should set institutional or departmental priorities and create action plans with key performance indicators (KPIs) for the year. Annual reviews of KPIs allow critical assessment of progress and provide an opportunity to adjust plans as necessary. Providing the above resources is the beginning of establishing trust and signals a commitment to actionable change to DEI for future and current Black talent.

Review and revise mission/diversity statement and departmental policies and procedures to reflect a discourse of inclusion.

The University's mission statement reflects the institution's values, expectations of student learning, and organizational priorities. It is a telltale statement as to what the institution deems important and conveys a discourse of shared values and goals of an institution (Wilson, Meyer & McNeal, 2012; Morphew & Hartley, 2006). As the rise in diverse students in higher education has emerged over the last decade, universities have begun to include diversity language to demonstrate performative alliance with diversity initiatives. However, the statements are generally broad and often written from a white dominant culture point of view (Sensoy & DiAngelo, 2017).

The mission statement should be analyzed and revised to include language that decenters white culture as standard and provides equitable ways to include the voices of all members of the community. Eliminating exclusive discourse is essential in changing negative attitudes and ideologies that drive racist policies and procedures (Iverson, 2007). Having a mission statement that is explicitly inclusive signals to Black faculty that their voice is valued within the organization. It also communicates to internal and external stakeholders (that is, current and potential students, faculty, and staff) an administrative commitment to DEI. Similarly, departmental policies should be aligned with the mission of the university. Likewise, university and departmental policies and procedures should be reviewed and revised to reflect a discourse of inclusion. Appropriate revision of these artifacts is an essential first step as these documents set the tone for institutional and departmental climate and culture.

Dedicate a search committee to recruit Black faculty actively and intentionally.

Being intentional in seeking Black talent further strengthens the institution's commitment to DEI. When recruitment efforts are anchored with equitable policies and practices, the probability of increasing faculty of color on campus increases. Although focusing on numbers alone does not solve the retention problem, it adds inclusivity into the ecosystem.

According to critical mass theory, hiring only one Black faculty within a department promotes tokenism. Tokens are not treated as people with unique characteristics and abilities, but as representatives for their category. As a numeric rarity, tokens are monitored more closely and their performance is judged based on their race (Kanter, 1977). For example, a Black professor is prejudged and seen as a representative of their race rather than being seen as a respected colleague and peer. When white people perform well, their success is attributed to their intelligence. By contrast, when Black people perform at a level of success, notions of luck or highly motivated exceptions overshadow their abilities. As a result, Blacks have to continuously work hard to provide a counter-narrative that proves their capabilities. The physical and mental exhaustion resulting from chasing this validation makes academia less desirable and challenges persistence (Griffin, Bennett & Harris, 2013). Additional hires within a department tilt the demographics toward a critical mass that creates opportunities. Increasing the number of Black faculty members enhances the capacity to build social capital that will be helpful in gaining the skills required to negotiate the dominant culture networks (Zambrana et al., 2015), as well as build on a support system that will reduce isolation. To facilitate reaching that critical mass, institutions should seek out scholars of color from minority serving institutions (MSIs) and public universities (Gasman, Abiola & Travers, 2015). Departments that do not reach a critical mass in hiring faculty of color do not reap the full benefits of diversity as intended (Elam et al., 2009).

Communicate transparency in the promotion and tenure review process.
Promotion and tenure are symbols of success in the academy. However, it is difficult for Black faculty to gain success in the process, as appraisals of merit in promotion and tenure decisions are often subjective (Delgado, 1995). For faculty of color, the tenure review process can be confusing. Historically, marginalized faculty have been left out of the information loop when it comes to the informal rules of negotiating white dominant spaces. Understanding the unwritten rules, values, and political dynamics of institutional culture are necessary to move through the professoriate process efficiently (Laden & Hagedorn, 2000). Deficient networks limit faculty's requisite knowledge around these informal practices that support the promotion and tenure process. Lack of opportunities to learn how to navigate these hidden obstacles that are embedded in racist institutionalized practices prevent faculty of color from climbing through the ranks at a rate that is comparable to their white peers (Griffin, 2019; Zambrana

et al., 2015). As interpretation of policies and procedures for this process is subjective (Delgado, 1995), promotion and tenure committees need to acknowledge and place value on all scholarly contributions. Providing a list of KPIs of promotion and tenure, at initial hire, prepares one for expectations, hidden or otherwise. Offering this information early will also serve as a guide to structuring access to networks that will support the career trajectory of faculty of color. Administration must commit to facilitating a transparent, non-biased promotion and tenure review process in order to provide equity (O'Meara et al., 2021; Shore, Cleveland & Sanchez, 2018).

Research that does not subscribe to the social norm of the dominant white culture is not considered scholarly and not given the appropriate merit it deserves. Faculty who participate in scholarship focused on race and culture are not given the proper value, based on discriminative practices (Laden & Hagedorn, 2000; Griffin, Bennett & Harris, 2013; Joseph & Hirschfield, 2010). Scholarship such as this not only fills gaps in the research, it also dispels stereotypes within academia (Griffin, Bennett & Harris, 2013). Additionally, scholarly contributions on platforms outside the normal culture of higher education (for example, social media and blog posts), should also be considered a value add to the promotion and tenure process as these mediums have a broad reach and high impact.

Within the promotion and tenure process, proper merit should be awarded to Black faculty who engage in supportive mentorship relationships with Black students. Often, Black faculty are charged with the added responsibility of informally mentoring and providing support to Black students. Although not appropriately compensated or given proper release time from teaching, many fill their time with contributing to the perseverance of Black students. Faculty members feel compelled to engage in these activities due to their shared identity and affinity with the students' experience (Loveless-Morris & Reid, 2018; Pittman, 2012).

Researchers Jimenez et al. (2019) have found that more faculty of color participate in DEI service activities (for example, mentoring students of color, participating in DEI committees, or undertaking community service), yet their engagement does not support them in the promotion and tenure process. Great importance is placed on research and publishing, but faculty are not given sufficient time to engage in the higher-valued criteria of promotion. Time spent engaging in supportive relationships takes time away from other duties and conflicts with opportunities for career development. Diversity service should be recognized by providing appropriate release time that will allow faculty to engage fully in research activities for publication (Sensoy & DiAngelo, 2017). Institutions need to reconsider this process to ensure equity and to advance the diversity and inclusion agenda.

Create policies and procedures to address macro and microaggressions in the workplace.

Microaggressions are offensive statements or actions aimed at a marginalized group that may be unintentional, but nonetheless reinforce stereotypes. Society has been culturally trained to ignore them, as they are often subtle and easy to miss. Over time, the microaggressions infiltrate a recipient's psyche and affect how they see themselves in relation to others. The serial perpetuation of stereotypes contributes to unconscious biases and reinforces discriminatory practices. Often, Black faculty are on the receiving end of microaggressions in the form of negative assumptions (Banks, 1984; Pittman, 2012; Stanley, 2006). Whether it is from white faculty or white students, these microaggressions can have detrimental effects on the recipient's physical and mental well-being. Assumptions based on negative stereotypes, such as being less qualified, force faculty members to constantly prove that they are deserving of the faculty position (Banks, 1984; Fries-Britt & Griffin, 2007; McGee & Martin, 2011; Steele, 2011). When left unaddressed, microaggressions can also negatively impact job satisfaction (DeCuir-Gunby & Gunby Jr, 2016).

The first step in addressing microaggressions is to provide employees with anti-bias training that supports them in recognizing and confronting their own biases, and removing them from their unconsciousness (Carter, Onyeador & Lewis Jr, 2020; Griffin, 2019). Once an offender becomes aware of their biases, they are able to deconstruct their stereotypical views of marginalized groups and contribute to an inclusive work environment. While Human Resources may have avenues for reporting discrimination, many do not have appropriate procedures in place that deliver consequences for infractions. There must be real accountability for those who are appropriately informed, yet continue to perpetuate micro-aggressive behaviors and discriminatory practices.

Develop Pipelines to leadership.

Equally crucial in addressing the lack of retention of Black faculty is the scarcity of Black faculty in leadership positions within higher education. Lack of diverse leadership impacts how people participate and feel included within organizations. As mentioned earlier in this chapter, social capital is essential for a Black faculty member to climb the promotion ladder, including leadership positions (Benbow & Lee, 2019; Gasman, Abiola &

Travers, 2015). Having access to these networks validates them as a qualified candidate. When there is a deficiency in network connections, faculty members are unable to participate in opportunities that are afforded to their white counterparts (Lave & Wenger, 1991). When individuals from underrepresented groups see themselves in leadership, they feel part of the organization. They begin to identify as a member of the professoriate and start to position themselves for potential opportunities (Tajfel, 2010). Institutions should seek out Black faculty with the potential for leadership development. As with intentional recruitment of Black faculty, institutions should seek out scholars of color from MSIs, public universities, affinity groups, and organizations for leadership positions. Developing a pipeline to leadership creates a structural support system that positions faculty to access the required social capital for advancement (Benbow & Lee, 2019), and demonstrates institutional commitment.

Social Capital Support Systems

Facilitate community-building within the department, institution, and community at large.

Faculty of color encounter unique challenges when becoming socialized into an academic institution. In particular, tokenism, isolation, and undervalued scholarship interests have all impacted how Black faculty experience academia. Participation within a community can provide the proper socialization that is required to reduce feelings of isolation and othering, and is able to facilitate access to opportunities to participate fully as a faculty member within the institutional environment. There are several types of communities of practice that can be developed to facilitate community-building within the department, the institution, and the community at large. Intentionally creating communities of practice that develop mentoring practices, learning communities, and collaborative opportunities for research can increase job satisfaction, allowing full participation in academia (Laden & Hagedorn, 2000; Zambrana et al., 2015; Loveless-Morris & Reid, 2018). It is within these relationships that knowledge regarding the norms and practices of the community is shared. Communities of practice provide platforms to facilitate accumulation of social capital and assist Black faculty in accessing resources that are afforded to their white peers.

Effective mentoring and learning communities enhance opportunities to learn through participation and development of a shared identity. Each provides built-in opportunities to acquire social capital (Loveless-Morris &

Reid, 2018). Pairing new faculty with senior faculty to co-teach a course forms a community of practice that facilitates supportive interactions between peers and supports mentorship relationships. These interactions can be influential in reinforcing a positive academic career path for Black faculty.

Faculty tasked with research production would benefit from opportunities to reach across campus to work on initiatives that would otherwise be unavailable to them. Individuals and departments often research in silos, which are by their nature isolating. Gaining access to a community of scholars equips faculty with the social capital to advance their career trajectory (Zambrana et al., 2015). Providing dedicated time and space to collaborate with other faculty both inter- and intra-departmentally expands a community of practice, creating access to a broader network that encourages participation.

When faculty situate themselves within a context where they feel heard and accepted, they become equipped to persevere in adverse environments later. Affinity groups consist of individuals with a shared interest, characteristic or identity. In essence, they are a community of practice that provides a sense of community, a source for mentorship, and overall professional support (Abdullah, Karpowitz & Raphael, 2016). Oftentimes, this is where faculty of color can be themselves without the lingering threat of feeling "othered." In this safe space, faculty can explore issues of shared experiences and affirm their feelings and responses to being part of a white-centric community. These groups are important tools for influencing participation in a way that affords a community member access to opportunities to learn. Black faculty often seek outside resources to create safe spaces to process macro- and microaggressions experienced in their work environments. Financial and structural support for the organic formation of affinity groups within an institution demonstrates institutional commitment to equity and inclusion.

Institutions of higher education must take intentional and explicit action to retain talented Black faculty successfully. Commitment to DEI alone will not bring about change. Without considering equity and inclusion, policies and procedures geared toward diversity can actually reinforce inequities and exclusion, further marginalizing Black faculty on campus. Investing in systemic change benefits all stakeholders in the community. Providing structural and social support lays the groundwork for redefining the culture of academia. Challenging the status quo can be an uphill battle, but it is necessary to enact change. Creating an inclusive campus environment that is welcoming and values the contributions of Black faculty sets the foundation for success.

What are you intentionally doing to retain Black talent?

Below is a checklist of practical strategies that can be enacted today. Following these practical steps facilitates an ecosystem of equity and inclusion, where all faculty can thrive.

Practical strategies for structural support of Black Faculty persistence

- Form a committee for an annual review of the institution's commitment to DEI.
  ○ Dedicate funds for proper creation and execution of an action plan.
  ○ Set priorities and KPIs for the year.
  ○ Create an action plan based on the KPIs.
  ○ Review and adjust goals as necessary.
- Ensure congruency between mission statement and action plan.
- Review and revise institutional and departmental policies and procedures to ensure reflection of equity and inclusion.
- Dedicate a search committee to recruit Black faculty actively and intentionally.
  ○ Hire more than single Black faculty members to aim for a critical mass.
- Critically review promotional criteria and tenure policies to ensure equitable and inclusive practices.
  ○ Practice transparency in the promotion and tenure review process.
  ○ In the review process, impart value to all scholarly contributions outside the cultural norm (for example, non-peer-reviewed publications, such as social media and blog posts).
  ○ Provide merit for participation in scholarly engagement that is not traditionally considered (that is, informally supporting and mentoring Black students).
- Provide a safe, centralized reporting system for macro- and microaggressions with accountability in place.
- Develop pipelines to leadership.
  ○ Identify and support Black faculty for leadership positions such as department chair, dean, chief academic officers, provosts, etc.
  ○ Establish search committees to seek out potential leadership candidates at HBCUs, affinity groups, and non-academic organizations.

Practical strategies to increase social capital to support Black faculty persistence

- Create communities of practice to facilitate increased social capital and build community within the department, institution, and the community at large.
  - Develop mentoring and professional learning communities that pair new faculty with senior faculty to co-teach a course, forming a community of practice.
    - Facilitates supportive interactions with peers.
    - Supports mentorship and/or sponsorship relationships.
  - Support affinity groups
  - Intentionally expand inter- and intra-departmental networks and facilitate research initiatives by providing opportunities for interest clusters.

REFERENCES

Abdullah, C., Karpowitz, C. F. & Raphael, C. (2016). Affinity groups, enclave deliberation, and equity. *Journal of Deliberative Democracy*, 12(2). https://doi.org/10.16997/jdd.258

Antonio, A. L. (2002). Faculty of color reconsidered. *The Journal of Higher Education*. 73(5), 582–602. https://doi.org/10.1080/00221546.2002.11777169

Banks, W. M. 1984. Afro-American scholars in the university. *American Behavioral Scientist* 27(3), 325–38. https://doi.org/10.1177/000276484027003005

Bell, D. (1992). Racial realism. *Connecticut Law Review*, 24(2), 363–4.

Bell Jr, D. A. (1980). *Brown* v. *Board of Education* and the interest-convergence dilemma. *Harvard Law Review*, 93(3), 518–33.

Benbow, R. J. & Lee, C. (2019). Teaching-focused social networks among college faculty: exploring conditions for the development of social capital. *Higher Education: The International Journal of Higher Education Research*, 78(1), 67–89.

Better, S. (2008). *Institutional Racism: A primer on theory and strategies for social change*. Plymouth: Rowman & Littlefield.

Carter, E. R., Onyeador, I. N. & Lewis Jr, N. A. (2020). Developing & delivering effective anti-bias training: Challenges & recommendations. *Behavioral Science & Policy*, 6(1), 57–70.

Coleman, J. S. (1988). Social capital in the creation of human capital. *American journal of sociology*, 94, S95–S120.

Crenshaw, K. (1991). Mapping the margins: Intersectionality, identity politics, and violence against women of color. *Stanford Law Review*, 43(6), 1241–99.

Daniel, C. (2007). Outsiders-within: Critical race theory, graduate education and barriers to professionalization. *Journal of Sociology & Social Welfare*, 34(1), 25–42.

DeCuir-Gunby, J. T. & Gunby Jr, N. W. (2016). Racial microaggressions in the workplace: A critical race analysis of the experiences of African American educators. *Urban Education*, 51(4), 390–414.

Delgado, R. (1995). Rodrigo's tenth chronicle: Merit and affirmative action. *Georgetown Law Journal*, 83, 1711–48.

Delgado, R. & Stefancic, J. (2017). *Critical Race Theory: An introduction*. New York: NYU Press.

Elam, C. L., Stratton, T. D., Hafferty, F. W. & Haidet, P. (2009). Identity, social networks, and relationships: Theoretical underpinnings of critical mass and diversity. *Academic Medicine*, 84(10), S135–S140. https://doi.org/10.1097/acm.0b013e3181b370ad

Fries-Britt, S. & Griffin, K. (2007). The black box: How high-achieving blacks resist stereotypes about black Americans. *Journal of College Student Development*, 48(5), 509–24.

Gasman, M., Abiola, U. & Travers, C. (2015). Diversity and senior leadership at elite institutions of higher education. *Journal of Diversity in Higher Education*, 8 (1), 1–14.

Griffin, K. A. (2019). Redoubling our efforts: How institutions can affect faculty diversity. In Espinosa, L. L., Turk, J. M., Taylor, M., & Chessman, H. M. (eds.), *Race and Ethnicity in Higher Education: A status report*, 273–9.

Griffin, K. A., Bennett, J. C. & Harris, J. (2013). Marginalizing merit?: Gender differences in Black faculty D/discourses on tenure, advancement, and professional success. *Review of Higher Education*, 36(4), 489–512.

Iverson, S. V. (2007). Camouflaging power and privilege: A critical race analysis of university diversity policies. *Educational Administration Quarterly*, 43(5), 586–611.

Jimenez, M. F., Laverty, T. M., Bombaci, S. P., Wilkins, K., Bennett, D. E. & Pejchar, L. (2019). Underrepresented faculty play a disproportionate role in advancing diversity and inclusion. *Nature Ecology & Evolution*, 3, 1030–3. https://doi.org/10.1038/s41559-019-0911-5

Joseph, T. D. & Hirschfield, L. E. (2010). "Why don't you get somebody new to do it?" Race and cultural taxation in the academy. *Ethnic and Racial Studies*, 34, 121–41.

Kanter, R. M. (1977). Some effects of proportions on group life: Skewed sex ratios and responses to token women . In Rieker, P. P. & Carmen, E. (eds.) *The Gender Gap in Psychotherapy*. Boston: Springer, 53–78. https://doi.org/10.1007/978-1-4684-4754-5_5

Laden, B. V. & Hagedorn, L. S. (2000). Job satisfaction among faculty of color in academe: Individual survivors or institutional transformers? *New Directions for Institutional Research*, 27(1), 57–66.

Lave, J. & Wenger, E. (1991). *Situated Learning: Legitimate peripheral participation*. Cambridge: Cambridge University Press.

Loveless-Morris, J. A. & Reid, L. S. (2018). Learning communities: Opportunities for the retention of faculty of color. *Learning Communities Research and Practice*, 6(1), A6.

McGee, E. O. & Martin, D. B. (2011). "You would not believe what I have to go through to prove my intellectual value!" Stereotype management among academically successful black mathematics and engineering students. *American Educational Research Journal*, 48(6), 1347–89.

Morphew, C. C. & Hartley, M. (2006). Mission statements: A thematic analysis of rhetoric across institutional type. *Journal of Higher Education*, 77(3), 456–71.

National Center for Education Statistics (NCES). (2020) Institute of Education Sciences. Washington, DC: US Department of Education. https://nces.ed.gov/pubsearch/pubsinfo.asp?pubid=2020144

O'Meara, K., Culpepper, D., Misra, J. & Jaeger, A. (2021). *Equity-Minded Faculty Workloads: What we can and should do now*. Washington, DC: American Council on Education.

Pittman, C. T. (2012). Racial microaggressions: The narratives of African American faculty at a predominantly white university. *The Journal of Negro Education*, 81(1), 82–92. https://doi.org/10.7709/jnegroeducation.81.1.0082

Putman, A. L. (2017). Perpetuation of whiteness ideologies in U.S. college student discourse. *Journal of Intercultural Communication Research*, 46(6), 497–517.

Sensoy, Ö. & DiAngelo, R. (2017). "We are all for diversity, but . . .": How faculty hiring committees reproduce whiteness and practical suggestions for how they can change. *Harvard Educational Review*, 87(4), 557–80.

Solórzano, D. G. & Yosso, T. J. (2001). From racial stereotyping and deficit discourse toward a critical race theory in teacher education. *Multicultural education*, 9(1), 2–8.

Shore, L. M., Cleveland, J. N. & Sanchez, D. (2018). Inclusive workplaces: A review and model. *Human Resource Management Review*, 28(2), 176–89. https://psycnet.apa.org/doi/10.1016/j.hrmr.2017.07.003

Stanley, C. A. (2006). Coloring the academic landscape: Faculty of color breaking the silence in predominantly white colleges and universities. *American Educational Research Journal*, 43(4), 701–36. https://www.jstor.org/stable/4121775

Steele, C. M. (2011). *Whistling Vivaldi: How stereotypes affect us and what we can do*. New York and London: W.W. Norton.

Tajfel, H. (ed.). (2010). *Social Identity and Intergroup Relations*. Cambridge: Cambridge University Press.

Umbach, P. D. (2006). The contribution of faculty of color to undergraduate education. *Research in Higher Education*, 47(3), 317–45.

Wilson, J. L., Meyer, K. A. & McNeal, L. (2012). Mission and diversity statements: What they do and do not say. *Innovative Higher Education*, 37(2), 125–39.

Wolfe, B. L. & Dilworth, P. P. (2015). Transitioning normalcy: Organizational culture, African American administrators, and diversity leadership in higher education. *Review of Educational Research*, 85(4), 667–97.

Yep, G. A. (2002). The violence of heteronormativity in communication studies: Notes on injury, healing, and queer world-making. *Journal of Homosexuality*, 45 (2–4), 11–59. https://doi.org/10.1300/J082v45n02_02

Zambrana, R. E., Ray, R., Espino, M. M., Castro, C., Douthirt Cohen, B. & Eliason, J. (2015). "Don't leave us behind" The importance of mentoring for underrepresented minority faculty. *American Educational Research Journal*, 52 (1), 40–72.

CHAPTER 12

Bearing a Black Woman's Burden: Autoethnography for Provoking Perspective-Taking and Action in Predominantly White Academic Spaces

Kathy-Ann C. Hernandez

> *Yesterday, I grieved alone.*
> *I said the name George Floyd out loud, but not his name alone.*
> *I grieved at this death memorial to those who had gone before,*
> *Yesterday, I grieved alone.*[1]

After George Floyd died, I lost my scholarly voice. As a scholar intent on giving a voice to issues that exist at the intersections of race and class in my scholarship and practice, I found myself unable to write or speak. While the now infamous video of the knee on the neck of another Black man exhaling his last breath on a city street played in a constant loop on television screens all across America and the world, I could not watch. The emotions were too raw; the hurting was too deep. I did not need to experience in visual detail, the embodiment of what we, Black people, have been experiencing for too long in the legacy of systemic racial injustice in American society. In a sense, the civil rights activist Reverend Al Sharpton summed up the significance of the moment well in his speech at a memorial service: "George Floyd's story is the story of Black folks ... You kept your knee on our neck" (Johnson & Tapp, 2020).

As a Caribbean-born Black and Hispanic woman who migrated to the United States to pursue graduate study, I have not always felt the suffocating presence of that metaphoric knee on my neck. I came to the United States from the twin island Republic of Trinidad and Tobago to pursue graduate studies. In those early years, the dichotomy between my Black Caribbean experience and the African-American experience was clear and striking – "us" versus "them" (Hernandez & Murray, 2015; Robinson,

---

[1] I published this poem on *Medium* a few months after the death of George Floyd (Hernandez, 2020). The first and last stanzas are presented here to capture some of the sentiments expressed in this chapter.

2011). I had been raised in a country where my Blackness was not at the center of my identity. Yet, in the US, I gradually came to understand my positioning in the racial and social hierarchy. Some scholars have described the residual and potent ways in which Blacks are still treated in the US as one of the most violent depictions of a caste system: Wilkerson (2020) defines a caste as "the granting or withholding of respect, status, honor, attention, privileges, resources, benefit of the doubt, and human kindness to someone on the basis of their perceived rank or standing in the hierarchy" (p. 70). For others like me, born in countries where we were members of the dominant group before migrating to the US, the process of coming to terms with this different construction of Blackness, and the attendant inequities that accompany it, is a challenging one (Hernandez, Ngunjiri & Chang, 2014: Hernandez & Murray-Johnson, 2015).

In this chapter, I explore my journey into claiming this space and marking it as the birthplace of my research agenda and scholarship. Moreover, drawing on my work as one of the co-authors of *Collaborative Autoethnography* (Chang, Ngunjiri & Hernandez, 2013), I show how employing a Transformative Collaborative Autoethnographic (TAM) framework can be a practical strategy to provoke perspective-taking in diverse settings, with a view to changing individuals and the communal spaces they occupy.

Reconstructing Blackness

The journey in my reconstruction of Blackness has involved navigating difficult experiences of racial discrimination, prejudice, and marginalization through different chapters of my life in my new US home. I married an African-American man who was born and raised on the streets of West Philadelphia. I became the mother of two Black girls, who are painfully aware of what it means to be numbered among the few students of color in school. And, shortly after obtaining my doctoral degree, I began my tenure as a faculty of color among the handful of us at a predominantly white institution (PWI).

My academic journey as a scholar began with an interest in investigating the very socio-identity markers – race and gender – that are central to the positioning of Black experiences in US schools and society, with a focus on Black males (Hernandez, 2004, 2011). This research focus revealed disturbing trends, which have not abated. Black males, at the intersection of their gendered and racial identities, face multiple challenges at various stages of their life trajectory: beginning in the early years, schools often function in ways that keep them out of the school to university pipeline (Smith & Harper, 2015; US Department of Education Office of Civil Rights, 2014), encounters between them and police are likely to be violent and may even end in death (Mapping Police Violence, 2020; United States Census Bureau, n.d.), and they are likely to end up incarcerated (The Sentencing Project, 2018; Western, 2006). In the age of camera phones, we have instant access to the visual footage of some of these violent encounters with police, including the killings of Oscar Grant, Michael Brown, Stephon Clark, Tamir Rice, and George Floyd, among others (Campbell & Valera, 2020). Even when such encounters end in arrests that place Black men in the judicial system, they face additional challenges. Bryan Stevenson, Civil rights activist and founder of the Equal Justice Initiative, has astutely noted that we have a racially skewed judicial system that unfairly penalizes those who are poor and/or persons of color: "we don't protect people who are poor and we don't protect people of color in the same way we protect other people" (Equal Justice Initiative, 2015). Consequently, Black are disproportionately represented among those who are incarcerated. (Western & Pettit, 2010).

Once outside the sterile environment of graduate school where my research agenda was no longer something out there, I became more intimately invested in understanding the reality in which I found myself – a foreign-born Black Hispanic woman in a predominantly white academic landscape. (Hernandez, Ngunjiri & Chang, 2014). Black women, as part of the larger group of women of color, continue to be underrepresented in lead administrative and faculty positions in higher education (McChesney, 2018). According to data from the National Center for Education Statistics (2020a) the majority of full-time faculty are white, whereas only about 25 percent of faculty are Black, Asian/Pacific Islander, Hispanic, American Indian/Alaska, Native or multiracial. When it comes to the smaller subset of female faculty of color, the numbers are even more telling. In 2018, of all full-time faculty in degree-granting postsecondary institutions 35 percent were white females, whereas only 3 percent were Black females (National Center for Education Statistics, 2020b).

As I familiarized myself with the literature and the experiences of others like me, I recognized common themes in the challenges we faced in successfully navigating these spaces. Our intersecting identities shape our experiences of misogyny and racism and position us as outsiders within the very spaces that continue to oppress: we are outsiders-within (Collins, 2000). Within PWIs, Black women often face diminished productivity, and struggle to achieve a quality work–life balance (Hills, 2019);

"invisibility, salary inequities, lack of support from administrators regarding students and stereotypical comments and racist behaviors from colleagues as well as students" (Wilson, 2012: 70). The recognition of themes in the literature that mirrored my own experience was the impetus for adopting more inward-looking research methodologies that centered on the Black ways of knowing as well as the female experience in discourse as legitimate and valued (Hernandez, Ngungiri & Chang, 2014). I, along with other scholars, embarked on a mission of using our scholarship to advance perspectives of those like us who encounter the tension of learning how to exist in spaces where our political standpoint necessitates that we continually challenge the culture, even as we deftly manage it for our advancement. We became tempered radicals (Meyerson, 2008) – choosing to provoke change in line with our values and identities while simultaneously navigating these white spaces so we could flourish. We had to learn how to "rock the boat" while making sure that we did not fall out of it (Meyerson, 2008).

In a close examination of our experiences as foreign-born women of color in higher education, I, along with two other women of color chose to lay bare the challenges we experienced positioned in a PWI (Hernandez, Ngunjiri & Chang, 2014). Specifically, we explored how the intersection of our gender and cultural ethnic identity as immigrant women of color complicated our efforts to "identify, fulfill, and negotiate our roles in traditionally white-male dominant academia" (p. 2). What we uncovered were ways in which our experiences as immigrants were in some ways distinct from our native-born sisters but also ways in which they were remarkably similar. As a distinction in our status as women of color from countries where we were in the majority, a persistent challenge for us remained in how to reconfigure our identities in this new context, while still remaining true to who we were. As we told our stories, one consistent theme was the social pressures that we felt continuously "coalescing to divest us of our cultural/ethnic status and our spirited resistance to becoming anything other than our personal self-definitions" (p. 10). For example, our early socialization status provided us with unique abilities to view our experiences through both majority and minority lenses. However, we recognized that these lenses are now multifocal, and we must find ways to reconfigure our identities to become superficially minoritized.

On the other hand, we also share similar experiences as native-born women of color in these spaces. Common themes that emerged from our study were: receiving harsher student evaluations than our white peers; reluctance to express passionate viewpoints for fear of being dismissed as another "angry Black woman"; grappling with issues of credibility based on our identity and accents; and recognition that we were vulnerable to marginalization on the basis of our intersecting identities (Crenshaw, 1991), that is, just because of who we were. In order for us to be able to cope effectively and advance in the academy, we adopted an activist agenda. We chose to engage in acts of resistance in our political stand-points, our teaching, our scholarship, and our service work within the institutions. In sum, we used practical wisdom to position ourselves along the spectrum of activism – resisting quietly and staying true to one's self; turning personal threats into opportunities; broadening impact through negotiation; leveraging small wins; and organizing collective action (Meyerson, 2004). We sought to provoke institutional change while remaining true to who we were.

During the course of my tenure at this university, I was so intent on managing this intricate act of survival, advocacy, and scholarship that I had not given myself space to weigh the cost of it all to my well-being. All of that changed in 2020 after George Floyd died. Suddenly, I found myself with a full-frontal assault at the nexus of my gendered and racial-ethnic selves. While, from the outside, it seemed like I was flourishing profession-ally (rising to the ranks of tenured full-professor), in the ways that mattered personally (connecting with others) in my institutional space in deep and meaningful ways (Seligman, 2011), I was not.

On the day that George Floyd died, May 25, 2020, the combined weight of living in the space of this oppression and still continuing to produce scholarship that gave voice to this work became too heavy for me to bear. I became vocally paralyzed: I tried in vain to say or write something, anything, but the words would not come. Within my institutional context, things continued as usual. The phones did not stop ringing and emails continued to fill up my inbox. One of my colleagues called me the day after his death to discuss the minutiae of administrative matters without so much as mentioning it, and all I wanted to do was scream at her. Yes, routine work needed to be addressed, but for my Black body the life energy was draining out of me. I found myself clutching my own "bruised and bloodied heart" gasping for breath, and I needed space to adjust and recalibrate – to rest a while.

A Black Woman's Burden

What I was experiencing was *racial trauma* – a form of race-based stress ignited "from dangerous events and real or perceived experiences of racial discrimination ... [which] involves ongoing individual and collective injuries due to exposure and re-exposure to race-based stress" (Comas-Díaz, Hall & Neville, 2019: 1). The experiences that give way to racial trauma are everyday occurrences for individuals who belong to one of any racial-ethnic minority (for example, Latinxs, Asian-Americans, Indigenous peoples, Black Americans). However, Black Americans are more likely than any other racial ethnic group to face issues of discrimination that are historic, individualistic, and systemic (Chou, Asnaani & Hofmann, 2012). Education professor William Smith has used the term "racial battle fatigue" (RBF) to describe the ways in which this repeated exposure to stressful racial issues in daily life can affect the individual (Smith, 2004). RBF can manifest itself in multiple physiological, psychological, and behavioral symptoms: tension headaches, insomnia, ulcers, difficulty thinking or speaking, mood swings, and even social withdrawal (Smith, 2004; Smith, Yosso & Solórzano, 2006). In particular, Black women, by virtue of belonging to more than one historically marginalized group, are especially vulnerable to racial traumas that have negative effects on their mental and physical health (Pascoe & Smart Richman, 2009; Williams & Williams-Morris, 2010; Kaholokula, 2016). This positioning in academic and corporate settings, and the wider society, affects our ability to survive and flourish.

For Black women, the tensions of navigating their professional and personal self-identities in white spaces, and the aforementioned challenges they face, come at a tremendous cost to their overall sense of well-being. Personally positioned as mothers, partners, wives, aunts, and fictive maternal figures, the traumas they experience in navigating the instincts that compel them to care cannot be understated (Graham, 2007). For example, when George Floyd cried out for his mother, that call reached the ears of women all over the world. As other women writers have commented (Oglesby, 2020; O'Neal, 2020), that call reverberated to women of all ethnicities who shared the bond of motherhood. But, whereas all women could perhaps empathize at a womb level with what it feels like to hear a son or daughter call out for "momma," Black mothers face a complex concoction of gut-wrenching pain which can only be felt by those who have borne or cared for Black children and are insiders to navigating Blackness in white spaces (Longman, 2020).

I felt that churning in my own stomach and heaviness in my chest, as I thought about my Black daughters. Even at a time when I was voiceless, it was imperative that I find my voice for the demands of Black motherhood. I needed to find the words to explain to a ten- and a twelve-year old what had happened and why. It was necessary to triage my own trauma, to meet the urgent needs of my daughters for care and for healing. The questions I struggled with the most were: "How do I explain what has happened without traumatizing them? How do I tell the story without damaging their emerging self-concept?" and "How do I continue to nurture in my children the seeds of discomfort at racial injustice and injustice in all its forms and a desire to become a champion in the struggle long after I was gone? This was a heavy and immediate load to bear. I saw the need to redouble my efforts to craft a curriculum for them in answer to all these questions. For mothers of a Black or Brown hue, these critical conversations also known as "the talk" are essential and urgent parts of the parenting arsenal for raising their children in the United States (Sanders & Young, 2020). My commentary and activism in the public sphere would have to wait.

But, more than the actions I needed to take in the present, there was a deep troubling in my spirit. As I continued to work within the context of my institution with the burden of it all weighing down on me, I was voiceless-unwilling to explain to those of another hue why or in what ways I was not okay. I was weary. There were no words – it had to be felt.

Some of my white colleagues did reach out and ask if there was some way they could help: perhaps they might assist with some of my course work, or review and edit some of my papers. A close friend sent me a thoughtful text message – she was sorry for being silent – sorry for it all. All of these were appreciated. I realized that it took courage to step outside the comfortable space of white privilege to confront the dark truth of racism and offer a helping hand. However, these courageous gestures also made me wonder what it was like to inhabit the space of being a white woman in the academy at that moment. What internal dialogues were they having? In what ways, if any, were they being confronted with the realities of the intersection of their race and gender? And how might we take actions to close the divide in ways that might transform us and the spaces we inhabit for the better? As I have argued elsewhere, to facilitate this kind of transformation, it is necessary for us "to step out of the comfort of our monolithic lens and embrace the perspective of the other – because this is the space in which the real work of diversity and inclusion can begin" (Hernandez, 2017: 331–2).

In the rest of this chapter, I discuss an approach to autoethnography that is inspired by a working model of autoethnography for transformation. My colleagues and I (Hernandez, Chang & Bilgen, 2022) advance this as a useful strategy for affecting this kind of transformational change.

What is Autoethnography

Autoethnographic (AE) research methods invite researchers to center themselves in scholarship that is birthed in their experiences. The growing presence of this research method as a legitimate form of social inquiry over the last several decades finally allowed researchers freedom to position themselves unapologetically in their scholarship. We are connected to, and should connect our lives to, our research (Ngunjiri, Hernandez & Chang, 2010). Moreover, this approach to social inquiry is well suited to the ways of knowing of women and marginalized groups (Ngunjiri, Chang & Hernandez, 2017; Stead & Elliott, 2012).

Autoethnography can be defined simply as the study of self (Reed-Danahay, 1997: 9). The researcher positions self as both researcher and participant in the study. The autoethnographic eye turns the traditional research paradigm of the researcher's *etic* – an outsider looking in – inside out. Instead, AE positions the researcher's *emic* – the insider perspective– and *etic* perspective side by side. Researchers are then able to bring their full selves to the investigation of an experience with which they are intimately aware. AE then affords an unparalleled exploration of an experience with the added benefit of the researcher's skill set of social inquiry; it is the path to exploring our lives situated in context from a first-person point of view (Holman Jones, Adams & Ellis, 2016). As Ronald J. Pelias asked, "How could a person study speech anxiety without ever having embodied such anxiety?" (cited in Holman Jones, Adams & Ellis, 2016: 29). However, more than being confessional tales or storytelling, Denzin (1992) writes that "the tale being told should reflect back on, be entangled in, and critique this current historical moment and its discontents" (p. 25). Spry (2001) describes it as an inherently critically reflexive approach to discourse that targets the intersection of peoples, cultures, and identities.

AE is also well suited to investigate sensitive social issues in depth. To this end, individuals have used it to explore the grieving process they experienced after the loss of a loved one (Hanauer, 2020; Matthews, 2019). Other topics have included living with an eating disorder (Chatham-Carpenter 2010); navigating the complexities of being a white mother to a Black son in a racialized US Society (Miheretu & Henward, 2020); a personal journey in embracing natural curly hair as a rebirthing process from internalized racism (Norwood, 2018); and a reflection on the backlash of microaggressions that followed the publication of an article about the experiences of being a Black woman in the academy (William-White, 2011).

A variant of AE, that has pervaded much of my work in company with other scholars, is collaborative autoethnography (CAE). Unlike AE, which is a solo process of investigation, CAE invites others into a sharing and meaning-making community to investigate social issues that are personal, yet speak to common human experience. In the book of the self-same name, we define CAE as "a qualitative research method in which researchers work in community to collect their autobiographical materials and to analyze and interpret these data collectively to gain a meaningful understanding of sociocultural phenomena reflected in their autobiographical data" (Chang, Ngunjiri & Hernandez, 2013: 24). Like AE, CAE has been used to investigate critical social issues including what it means to be a Black person in the United States (Hernandez & Murray-Johnson, 2015), navigating the white academic landscape as women of color (Hernandez, Ngunjiri, Chang, 2014), investigating the physical and emotional experiences of women who have experienced perineal trauma (third and fourth degree tears) during childbirth (Priddis, 2015), and exploring the risk and benefits for white woman conducting research on race in higher education (Davis & Linder, 2017) to name a few.

The Transformative Element of Autoethnographic Work

AE/CAE is more than a research method. In addition to providing opportunities to increase our understanding of pertinent social phenomena, the critical dialogic element of autoethnographic work is transformative. Whereas, AE allows for a level of probing that can facilitate intrapersonal change, the communal aspect of CAE allows for both intrapersonal and interpersonal transformation through communal dialogue and probing. This dialogue, rather than debate, is characterized by open engagement and reflection on a topic with others to arrive at a deeper understanding of an issue (Sawyer & Norris, 2009). In CAE, the dialogue is enriched "as autoethnographers work together, building on each other's stories, gaining insights from the group sharing, and providing various levels of support as they interrogate topics of interest" (Chang, Ngunjiri & Hernandez, 2013: 23). Collective dialogue and meaning-making "has the potential to break down silos and build theoretical bridges across disciplines and perspectives" (Ngunjiri, Chang & Hernandez, 2017: 111–12).

These elements of critical self-reflection and dialogue align with some of the best thinking about facilitating change in adult learners. Jack Mezirow's (2006) *transformative learning* theory details a multi-step process through which transformation can take place as individuals interact in learning settings. Building on the influences of such thinkers like Kuhn (1962), Freire (1970) and Habermas (1971), and his own empirical investigations with adult learners (1978), Mezirow proposed an early definition of transformative learning as:

> The emancipatory process of becoming critically aware of how and why the structure of psycho-cultural assumptions has come to constrain the way we see ourselves and our relationships, reconstituting this structure to permit a more inclusive and discriminating integration of experience and acting upon these new understandings. (Mezirow, 1981: 6)

Whereas this early definition emphasized changes to the individual, Mezirow's later work elaborated on how transformation within the individual becomes a catalyst for transforming existing and future relationships (Kitchenham, 2008).

Put simply, transformative learning can happen when individuals get new information that causes them to reflect on and evaluate past ideas and thinking. Through the process of taking in this new information and reflecting on it, their thinking begins to change. This inner change has the capacity to impact their existing and subsequent relationships. In AE, the individual undergoes this transformation as they turn the lens inward. At the intrapersonal level, they can engage in critical self-dialogue with themselves that leads to new insights and perspectives with the potential to affect interpersonal relationships (Hernandez & Ngunjiri, 2013). In the case of CAE, there are immediate additional benefits that come to participants who gather in community to explore shared experiences.

A focus on transformation has not often been the focal point of autoethnographic work. In fact, one common observation of CAE researchers in retrospect is that, though not often the stated purpose of the study, CAE resulted in transformation at various levels. In particular, a very visible artifact of transformation that can take place in individuals and relationships within a CAE project is the community-building that it has engendered. This has been my experience working along with a team of co-autoethnographers over several years. Our scholarly investigations have allowed us to form a sisterhood of scholarship and scholarly products across our similarities and differences (Hernandez, Chang & Ngunjiri, 2017). But more than the scholarship we have produced as evidence of our journey together, are the changes that have taken place in us as we learned to embrace the differences in our Caribbean, African, and Korean immigrant identities, as well as our distinct disciplinary perspectives (psychology, leadership studies and anthropology, respectively).

The community-building element of CAE that facilitates transformation has been noted by other researchers as well. For example, Lapadat et al. (2010) experienced this kind of synergy when they first started to do collaborative research as part of a class project. This, and other beginnings, resulted in the cultivation of communities of practice that continued to work together beyond the class to produce several articles (Lapadat et al., 2010, Longman, Hernandez & Robalino, 2016). Similarly, other researchers have commented on the transformative byproducts of their CAE work (Longman, Chang & Loyd-Paige, 2015). This was the case in an extended CAE study designed to investigate the influence of mentorship and sponsorship on the leadership identity development of emerging leaders of color (Hernandez & Longman, 2020). For this study, we used the definition of mentorship as a developmental relationship with someone who provides career support, which may include psychosocial support and role modeling (Murphy, Gibson & Kram, 2017). On the other hand, sponsorship is increasingly being viewed as a unique kind of developmental relationship where individuals "cultivate strategic alliances with individuals capable of propelling them into leadership positions and protecting them from other contenders" (Hewlett, 2013: 18). What we found was that "the CAE process of shared community building that had taken place over the course of the study had evolved as a catalyst for creating a relational dynamic as potent as the targeted areas of mentorship and sponsorship" (Hernandez, 2021: 69). Moreover, the collaborative nature of the CAE process provided support that enabled individuals to further their leadership identity development.

In many CAE projects, individuals often come together to investigate a common phenomenon or choose projects in which they occupy similar spaces based on demographic markers. For example, in one such project, several participants investigated their shared experiences with mothering (Geist-Martin et al., 2010). However, there are also examples of CAE projects that draw individuals together who do not share in the experience under investigation and/or are experiencing it from a position of difference. This was the case for one woman of color, Shametrice Davis, and a white woman, Chris Linder, who used CAE to explore the complexity of their experiences and emotional reactions to each other being committed to an anti-racist research and activism agenda (Davis & Linder, 2017). In some other cases, one or more of the researchers may not even share in the experience under investigation. For example, in a CAE project investigating the experience of living with an eating disorder, two co-authors contributed autobiographical data from their own experience of living with this condition, while the third author was enlisted to provide the research expertise for the project (Ellis, Kiesinger & Tillman-Helay, 1997). What these studies have revealed is that, in engaging with others in this kind of intimate sharing around deeply personal issues, we are changed. It is for this reason that CAE is well suited for applications in which the primary purpose can be facilitating transformational learning.

Collaborative Autoethnography for Transformation

The critically dialogic element of CAE is particularly useful for creating understanding among people of diverse identities (Zuniga et al., 2007). In shared spaces where Black and white women co-exist, a CAE model can be implemented with the set goal of facilitating transformational learning – learning to see with the eye of the other. Drawing from my ongoing collaborative work (Hernandez, Chang & Bilgen, 2022), I offer the following scenario as a transformational learning opportunity to provoke perspective-taking with a view to facilitating personal, communal, and organizational change. The scenario below has been crafted specific to the experiences of women of color and white women in academic spaces. However, it can be adapted for various groups drawing on a centering experience.

> **Step 1. Participants:** A lead researcher who is familiar with AE or CAE methods invites a diverse pool of female participants to be a part of the exploration, discovery and transformation process to understand better the unique spaces female faculty occupy in response to a triggering racial event, for example, the death of George Floyd.
>
> **Step 2. Purpose and Question:** Participants agree on the focus and scope of the transformative CAE project and formulate an overarching question. The question might focus more specifically on one topic aligned with the triggering incident: a question about racism, white privilege, motherhood and mothering, racial trauma, or flourishing in the academy. For example, an overarching question might be as follows:

In what ways did the death of George Floyd trigger thoughts within you about racism as a Black or white woman within the academy?

> **Step 3. Study and Objectives:** Participants prepare the transformative CAE study design. The group specifies the type of CAE design (see Chang, 2008; Chang, Ngunjiri & Hernandez, 2013; Hernandez,

Chang & Bilgen, 2022), the various tools that will be used in data collection and analysis, and ethical concerns (see Hernandez & Ngunjiri, 2013). The two-fold study objectives are articulated. First, to understand the topic and, second, through the immersion and exploration of the topic to experience and facilitate transformation at the personal, group and/or organizational or institutional level.

Step 4. Data Collection Methods: Data collection takes place relative to the two-fold study objectives. Data is first collected in response to the research question. Participants can be asked to write independently about what they felt or experienced in response to the triggering event, and to reflect on what they think the other might have felt or experienced. Selected independent writings are then shared among participants for reading and formulating probing questions for the writer. The group then gathers for a focus group discussion. These steps can be repeated until a point of saturation is reached. Data is then collected relevant to the transformational objectives. Participants write a reflection piece on how and in what ways, if any, they have experienced changes at the personal and/or group level:

What ideas and thoughts were confirmed through the process?

What ideas and thoughts were not confirmed through the process?

What do I now know that I did not before?

What changes if any would I like to make going forward as a result of this learning experience?

Step 5. Data Analysis: Participants examine the data to understand what they learned about the topic under investigation and to focus on the transformation experienced at each of the various levels in a three-phase process.

Phase 1: At the personal level, participants compare initial and later autobiographical writings to discover in what ways their thinking has changed through the CAE process.

Phase 2: At the group level, participants examine what was learned and how the group changed through the critical dialogic process of meaning making, multivocality and working across differences.

Phase 3: Participants analyze how their shared experience might be used to effect changes within their organizational context. Can these experiences be replicated with different sub-groups? Can the findings be shared with a larger audience within the institution? What are the implications for making changes within the organization?

Step 6. Audit, Action and Evaluation: The team audits the CAE project and creates a plan of action emanating from the project with a timeline for implementation, and evaluation as well as for dissemination of the result of their collaborative work as needed.

This kind of collaborative work can provide rich benefits at the personal, group, and individual level. Ideally, it should not be rushed and may work well as a semester or immersion retreat project. The targeted end products for this work would be the transformational objectives with action steps beyond the study. Other deliverables of a report or presentations can be done as ancillary to this primary purpose.

Burdens and Blessings

In June of 2020, I found refuge in returning to my early love for creative writing to process my emotions around the death of George Floyd and wrote the poem, "About Yesterday." It was a means of catharsis – to lay bare the hurt. In doing so, not only was I able to process this traumatic experience, but it also allowed me to chronicle the transformation in my own thinking about the next steps in advancing work that addresses the issues that Black bodies face in white spaces. Bridging the divide that positions people of color as outsiders within predominantly white spaces requires collaborative action. It requires us to engage in the hard work inherent in inviting the other into the sacred space of our lived experiences – to continue the courageous work of dialoguing, informing, sharing, and even wrestling with the commonalities and differences in our lived experiences. It has applications for individual, community and institutional transformation (Hernandez, Chang & Bilgen, 2022).

I am convinced that it is this level of perspective-taking that will allow us to become intimately aware of the experiences of the other. From this vantage point, as Ellis (2004) asserts, "in the same way autoethnography requires you to go inside yourself, it also requires you to understand the other people. If you do, then you can't just dismiss their point of view" (p. 218). Even if the outcome of such encounters is "to agree to disagree," we do not leave these interactions the same (Davis & Linder, 2017).

Autoethnography has the capacity to change us as relational individuals within communities. As I have discussed in this chapter, it can allow us to engage in the deeply transformative work of critically examining the inner struggles we face within our various selves. CAE in particular can allow for the examination of our experience of an event relative to the experience of others who are different from us, facilitating communal learning and transformation. Its application is not specific to gender or race. However, in the context of this chapter, it is this latter aspect of CAE that has the potential to allow women of color and white women to reach across the academic chasm and bear each other's burdens as they work to change the very spaces they inhabit.

There is important work to do! There is important work to do!
To join the gathering crowd, to rebuild, restore, and re-craft
a Black anthology that burns away at poplar roots
and plants instead baobab trunks,
stately tales of a people beautiful, resilient, and strong, whose lives do matter.
Yesterday, I grieved alone,
But today, we rise up!

REFERENCES

Campbell, F. & Valera, P. (2020). "The only thing new is the cameras": A study of U.S. college students' perceptions of police violence on social media. *Journal of Black Studies*, 51(7), 654–70. https://doi.org/10.1177/0021934720935600

Chang, H. (2008). *Autoethnography as Method*. Walnut Creek, CA: Left Coast Press.

Chang, H., Ngunjiri, F. & Hernandez, K. C. (2013). *Collaborative Autoethnography*. Walnut Creek, CA: Left Coast Press.

Chatham-Carpenter, A. (2010). "Do thyself no harm": Protecting ourselves as autoethnographers. *Journal of Research Practice*, 6(1) Article M1.

Chou, T., Asnaani, A. & Hofmann, S. G. (2012). Perception of racial discrimination and psychopathology across three U.S. ethnic minority groups. *Cultural Diversity and Ethnic Minority Psychology*, 18(1), 74–81.

Collins, P. H. (2000). *Black Feminist Thought: Knowledge, consciousness, and the politics of empowerment*. New York: Routledge.

Comas-Díaz, L., Hall, G. N. & Neville, H. A. (2019). Racial trauma: Theory, research, and healing: Introduction to the special issue. *American Psychologist*, 74(1), 1–5. http://dx.doi.org/10.1037/amp0000442

Crenshaw, K. (1991). Mapping the margins: Intersectionality, identity politics, and violence against women of color. *Stanford Law Review*, 43(6), 1241–99.

Davis, S. & Linder, C. (2017). Problematizing whiteness: A woman of color and a white woman discuss race and research. *Journal of Dialogue Studies*, 4, 49–68. https://bit.ly/2UfbuW7

Denzin, N. K. (1992). The many faces of emotionality. In Ellis, C. & Flaherty, M. G. (eds.) *Investigating Subjectivity: Research on lived experience*. London: Sage, 17–30.

Ellis, C. (2004). *The Ethnographic I: A methodological novel about autoethnography.* Walnut Creek, CA: AltaMira Press.

Ellis, C., Kiesinger, C. & Tilmann-Healy, L. M. (1997). In Hertz, R. (ed.), *Reflexivity and Voice.* Thousand Oaks, CA: Sage.

Equal Justice Initiative. (2015). Bryan Stevenson talks to Oprah about why we need to abolish the death penalty. November 28. https://bit.ly/32tkZW1

Freire, P. (1970). *Pedagogy of the Oppressed.* New York: Herter and Herter.

Geist-Martin, P., Gates, L., Wiering, L., Kirby, E., Houston, R., Lilly, A. & Moreno, J. (2010). Exemplifying collaborative autoethnographic practice via shared stories of mothering. *Journal of Research Practice,* 6(1), M8–M8.

Graham, M. (2007). The ethics of care, black women and the social professions: implications of a new analysis. *Ethics and Social Welfare,* 1(2), 194–206. https://doi.org/10.1080/17496530701450372

Habermas, J. (1971). *Knowledge of Human Interests.* Boston: Beacon.

Hanauer, D. (2020). Mourning writing: A poetic autoethnography on the passing of my father. *Qualitative Inquiry,* 27(1), 37–44. https://doi.org/10.1177/1077800419898500

Hernandez, K. C. (2004). Motivation in context: An examination of factors that foster engagement and achievement among African American and African Caribbean high school students. *Dissertation Abstracts International,* 65 (10-A), 3690. (UMI. No. 3151006). Doctoral dissertation, Temple University.

(2011). The Other Brother. *Journal of Black Masculinity,* 1(2), 92–116.

(2017). Embracing the perspective of the other. In Longman,K. A., Loyd-Paige, M., Hernandez, R., Hernandez, K. C., & Ash, A. (eds.) (2017) *Diversity Matters: Race, ethnicity and the future of Christian higher education.* Abilene, TX: Abilene Christian University Press, 325–33.

(2020). About yesterday. *Journal of Journeys.* June 12. https://medium.com/@drhvaluewhatmatters

(2021). Collaborative autoethnography as method and praxis: understanding self and others in practice. In Fourie, I. (ed.). *Autoethnography for Librarians and Information Scientists,* Abingdon and New York: Routledge, 61–76.

Hernandez, K. C., Chang, H. & Bilgen, W. (2022). *Transformative Autoethnography for Practitioners: Change processes and practices for individuals and groups.* Gorham, ME: Myers Education Press.

Hernandez, K. C., Chang, H. & Ngunjiri, F. W. (2017). Collaborative autoethnography as multivocal, relational, and democratic research: Opportunities, challenges, and aspirations. *a/b: Auto/Biography Studies,* 32(2), 251–4. doi: 10.1080/08989575.2017.1288892

Hernandez, K. C. & Longman, K. A. (2020). Changing the face of leadership in higher education: "Sponsorship" as a strategy to prepare emerging leaders of color. *Journal of Ethnographic and Qualitative Research,* 15(2), 117–36.

Hernandez, K. C. & Murray-Johnson, K. K. (2015). Towards a different construction of blackness: Black immigrant scholars on racial identity development in the United States. *International Journal of Multicultural Education*, 17(2), 53–72. https://doi.org/10.18251/ijme.v17i2.1050

Hernandez, K. C. & Ngunjiri F. W. (2013). Relationships and communities, In Adams, T., Ellis, C. & Holman-Jones, S. (eds.). *Handbook of Autoethnography*, Walnut Creek, CA: Left Coast Press.

Hernandez, K. C., Ngunjiri, F. W. & Chang, H. (2014). Exploiting the margins in higher education: A collaborative autoethnography of three foreign-born female faculty of color. *International Journal of Qualitative Studies in Education*, 28(5), 533–51. doi: 10.1080/09518398.2014.933910

Hewlett, S. A. (2013). *(Forget a Mentor) Find a Sponsor: The new way to fast-track your career*. Boston: Harvard Business Review Press.

Hills, D. D. (2019). "Admirable or ridiculous?": The burdens of black women scholars and dialogue in the work of solidarity. *Journal of Feminist Studies in Religion*, 35(2), 5–21. doi: 10.2979/jfemistudreli.35.2.02

Holman Jones, S. H., Adams, T. E. & Ellis, C. (eds.). (2016). *Handbook of Autoethnography*. Abingdon and New York: Routledge.

Johnson, T. & Tapp, T. (2020). George Floyd memorial: Al Sharpton decries Trump Bible photo, says "Get your knee off our necks." *Deadline*. June 4. https://bit.ly /3mrkDGq

Kitchenham, A. (2008). The evolution of John Mezirow's transformative learning theory. *Journal of Transformative Education*, 6(2), 104–23. https://doi.org/10 .1177/1541344608322678

Kaholokula, J. K. (2016). Racism and physical health disparities. In Alvarez, A. N., Liang, C. T. H. & Neville, H. A. (eds.), *The Cost of Racism for People of Color: Contextualizing experiences of discrimination*. Washington, DC: American Psychological Association, 163–88. https://doi .org/10.1037/14852–008

Kuhn, T. (1962). *The Structure of Scientific Revolutions*. Chicago: University of Chicago Press.

Lapadat, J. C., Black, N. E., Clark, P. G., Gremm, R. M., Karanja, L. W., Mieke, L. W., & Quinlan L. (2010). Life challenge memory work: Using collaborative autobiography to understand ourselves. *International Journal of Qualitative Methods*, 9(1), 77–104.

Longman, K. A., Chang, H. & Loyd-Paige, M. (2015). Self-analytical, community-building, and empowering: Collaborative autoethnography of leaders of color in higher education. *Journal of Ethnographic and Qualitative Research*, 9(4), 268–85.

Longman, K. A., Hernandez, K. C. & Robalino, G. (2016) How a collaborative autoethnography of sponsorship enhanced ethnic-minority participants' leader identity. Paper presented at the International Leadership Association Annual Meeting. Atlanta, Georgia: November.

Longman, M. (2020). What black mothers want you to know about George Floyd's death. *Refinery29*. June 9. https://r29.co/3ySBHtL

Mapping Police Violence (2020). https://mappingpoliceviolence.org

Matthews, A. (2019). Writing through grief: Using autoethnography to help process grief after the death of a loved one. *Methodological Innovations*, 12(3). https://doi.org/10.1177/2059799119889569

McChesney, J. (2018). Representation and pay of women of color in the higher education workforce. Research report. College and University Professional Association for Human Resources (CUPA-HR). www.cupahr.org/surveys/research-briefs

Meyerson, D. E. (2004). The tempered radical: How employees push their companies – little by little – to be more socially responsible. *Stanford Social Innovation Review*, Fall, 13–22.

(2008). *Rocking the Boat: How tempered radicals effect change without making trouble*. Boston: Harvard Business Review Press.

Mezirow, J. (1978). Perspective transformation. *Adult Education Quarterly*, 28(2), 100–10. https://doi.org/10.1177/074171367802800202

(1981). A critical theory of adult learning and education. *Adult Education*, 32(1), 3–24.

(2006). An overview of transformative learning. In Sutherland, P. & Crowther, J. (eds.), *Lifelong Learning: Concepts and context*. London: Routledge.

Miheretu, K. R. & Henward, A. S. (2020). I am Roha's Emaye: A critical autoethnography of mothering in liminal spaces. *Genealogy*, 4(2), 35. https://doi.org/10.3390/genealogy4020035

Murphy, W. M., Gibson, K. & Kram, K. E. (2017). Advancing women through developmental relationships. In Madsen, S. R. (ed.). *Handbook of Research on Gender and Leadership*. Northampton, MA: Edward Elgar Publishing, 361–77.

National Center for Education Statistics (NCES) (2020a). Race/ethnicity of college faculty. Washington, DC: US Department of Education. https://nces.ed.gov/fastfacts/display.asp?id=61

(2020b). Characteristics of postsecondary faculty. *The Condition of Education 2020*. Washington, DC: US Department of Education. https://nces.ed.gov/pubsearch/pubsinfo.asp?pubid=2020144

Ngunjiri, F. W., Chang, H. & Hernandez, K. C. (2017). Multivocal meaning making: Using collaborative autoethnography to advance theory on women and leadership. In Storberg-Walker, J. & Haber-Curran, P. (eds.) *Theorizing Women and Leadership: New insights and contributions from multiple perspectives*. Charlotte, NC: Information Age Press, 103–19.

Ngunjiri, F. W. & Hernandez, K. C. (2017). Problematizing authentic leadership: A collaborative autoethnography of immigrant women of color leaders in higher education. *Advances in Developing Human Resources*, 19(4), 393–406.

Ngunjiri, F. W., Hernandez, K. C. & Chang, H. (2010). Living autoethnography: Connecting life and research. *Journal of Research Practice*, 6(1), E1.

Norwood, C. R. (2018). Decolonizing my hair, unshackling my curls: An autoethnography on what makes my natural hair journey a Black feminist

statement. *International Feminist Journal of Politics*, 20(1), 69–84. https://doi
.org/10.1080/14616742.2017.1369890

Oglesby, C. (2020). "I need white mamas to come running." *CNN*. Opinion.
May 29. https://cnn.it/3sHhkPx

O'Neal, L. (2020). George Floyd's mother was not there, but he used her as
a sacred invocation. *National Geographic*. May 30. https://on.natgeo.com
/33Kei2d

Pascoe, E. A. & Smart Richman, L. (2009). Perceived discrimination and health:
A meta-analytic review. *Psychological Bulletin*. 135(4), 531–54. https://doi.org
/10.1037/a0016059

Priddis, H. S. (2015). Autoethnography and severe perineal trauma – An unexpected journey from disembodiment to embodiment. *BMC Women's Health*,
15, 88. https://doi.org/10.1186/s12905-015-0249-3

Reed-Danahay, D. E. (ed.) (1997). *Auto/Ethnography: Rewriting the self and the
social*. London and New York: Routledge.

Robinson, E. (2011). *Disintegration: The splintering of black America*. Westminster,
MD: Anchor.

Sanders, S. & Young, K. (2020). A black mother reflects on giving her 3 sons 'the
talk' . . . again and again. *NPR*. June 28. https://n.pr/3H4otNv

Sawyer, R. D. & Norris, J. (2009) Duoethnography: Articulations/(re)creation of
meaning in the making. In Gershon, W. S. (ed.), *The Collaborative Turn:
Working together in qualitative research*. Rotterdam: Sense Publishers,
127–140.

Seligman, M. E. (2011). Flourish: a visionary new understanding of happiness and
well-being. *Policy*, 27(3), 60–1.

Smith, E. J. & Harper, S. R. (2015). *Disproportionate impact of K-12 school
suspension and expulsion on Black students in southern states*. Philadelpha:
University of Pennsylvania, Center for the Study of Race and Equity in
Education.

Smith, W. A. (2004). Black faculty coping with racial battle fatigue: The campus
racial climate in a post-civil rights era. In Cleveland, D. (ed.) *A Long Way to
Go: Conversations about race by African American faculty and graduate students*. Peter Lang Publishing, 171–90.

Smith, W. A., Yosso, T. J. & Solórzano, D. G. (2006). Challenging racial battle
fatigue on historically white campuses: A critical race examination of race-
related stress. In Stanley, C. A. (ed.), *Faculty of Color: Teaching in predominantly white colleges and universities*. Bolton, MA: Anker Publishing,
299–327.

Spry, T. (2001). Performing autoethnography: An embodied methodological
praxis. *Qualitative Inquiry*, 7(6), 706–32. https://doi.org/10.1177
/107780040100700605

Stead V. & Elliot (2012). Women's leadership learning: A reflexive review of
representations and leadership teaching: *Management Learning*, 44(4), 373–
94. https://doi.org/10.1177/1350507612449504

The Sentencing Project. (2018). Report to the United Nations on Racial Disparities in the U.S. Criminal Justice System. *The Sentencing Project.* April 19. https://bit.ly/3yNMGF3

Western, B. (2006). *Punishment and Inequality in America.* New York: Russell Sage Foundation.

Western, B. & Pettit, B. (2010). Incarceration & social inequality. *Daedalus.* 139(3), 8–19. https://bit.ly/3EmKsxk

Wilkerson, I. (2020). *Caste: The origins of our discontents.* New York: Random House.

William-White, L. (2011). Dare I write about oppression on sacred ground [emphasis mine]. *Cultural Studies ↔ Critical Methodologies,* 11(3), 236–42. https://doi.org/10.1177/1532708611409535

Williams, D. R. & Williams-Morris, R. (2000). Racism and mental health: The African American experience. *Ethnicity & Health,* 5(3–4), 243–68. https://doi .org/10.1080/713667453

Wilson, S. (2012). They forgot mammy had a brain. In Muhs, G. G., Niemann, Y. F., González, C. G., Harris, A. P. (eds.) *Presumed Incompetent: The intersections of race and class for women in academia.* Boulder, CO: University Press of Colorado, 65–77.

Zuniga, X., Nagda, B. A., Chesler, M., Cytron-Walker, A. (2007) Intergroup dialogue in higher education: Meaningful learning about social justice. *ASHE Higher Education Report,* 32(4), 1–128.

CHAPTER 13

Programs with Promise

Antija M. Allen, Justin T. Stewart, and Nyesha James

Introduction

Thus far, this book has provided you, the reader, with the varied, yet common, experiences of Black faculty in higher education. The authors have suggested several strategies and made recommendations for faculty, leaders in higher education, and those responsible for diversity, equity, and inclusion (DEI) work at their institutions. This final chapter highlights what we the editors are referring to as "programs with promise." The focus is not on perfection as much as potential. Whether it is a small initiative or a large-scale program, if it makes an impact on Black (or diverse) faculty then it is worth sharing with others. The goal is to provide examples of programs that you can replicate, utilize a modified version of, or simply be inspired by. Peer institutions are excellent sources from which to draw on successful integration of diversity and equity issues (Barnett, 2020). This chapter will share only a handful of the numerous programs possible that focus on DEI for faculty in higher education.

Eligibility

The programs or initiatives had to have had a positive impact with Black (or diverse) faculty in the areas of retention, inclusion, and/or mental wellness. Institutions of all types and sizes were welcome. Although not required, all the representatives are members of the BIPOC community. The editors sat down virtually with representatives from institutions across the US and simply asked them to tell us about their programs with promise.

Programs with Promise

Virginia Union University

Terrell L. Strayhorn, PhD
Provost & Senior Vice President, Academic Affairs
Professor of Urban Education
Director, Center for the Study of HBCUs

MarQuita A. Carmichael, M.Div., D.Min
Assistant University Pastor/ Assistant Director of Religious Life

Virginia Union University (VUU) is a private HBCU located in Richmond, Virginia. According to the institutional website,[1] Virginia Union University was founded in 1865 to give newly emancipated slaves an opportunity for education and advancement. The University is the result of the merger of four institutions: Richmond Theological Seminary, Wayland Seminary, Hartshorn Memorial College, and Storer College. It is nourished by its African-American heritage and energized by a commitment to excellence and diversity. Its mission is to (1) Provide a nurturing intellectually challenging and spiritually enriching environment for learning; (2) Empower students to develop strong moral values for success; and (3) Develop scholars, leaders, and lifelong learners of a global society. The institution's core values are referred to as I.N.S.I.D. E. VUU, which stands for: Innovation, Spiritual Formation, Integrity, Diversity & Inclusion, and Excellence.

When approached about this chapter, Dr. Strayhorn was excited to share how beneficial programs organized by Dr. Carmichael have been to faculty. Being that the institution has a solid spiritual foundation, it came as no surprise that Dr. Carmichael serves as the Assistant University Pastor and Assistant Director of Religious Life. She shared several spiritually based initiatives with me including some that are student led, but still beneficial to faculty as well. One frequent and significant way spirituality is experienced in the lives of Black Americans is as an aid to manage and regulate a variety of stressors (Graham, 2016). The following programs have been especially helpful to VUU faculty, staff, and students who have been faced with numerous societal, academic, personal, and professional challenges especially in recent years with the largely publicized killings of

---

[1] www.vuu.edu

both Breonna Taylor and George Floyd along with the COVID-19 pandemic.

Panther P.A.W.S.

What stood out the most for faculty was something created by Dr. Carmichael, known as Panther P.A.W.S. This is a two-minute centering exercise that she leads regularly during faculty meetings (face to face and virtual). P.A.W.S. stands for Pause, Attend, Wait, and Start again. She explains what she means when she says Pause, Attend, and Wait. Dr. Carmichael states that she tells faculty to give themselves permission to take two minutes.

Dr. Strayhorn acknowledges that faculty have a busy schedule both during and after work, so having this built into something that is already scheduled is vital. In previous chapters of this book, you have seen how overloaded Black faculty are with work. Imagine if they had some time during the day to pause (or PAWS). Dr. Carmichael also shares recorded guided meditations with faculty, which allows them to do them on their own at any point during their day. Although research has shown that meditation can be psychologically beneficial in coping with stress and trauma, Dr. Carmichael emphasizes that the focus is on spiritual wellness.

In the earlier chapters of this book various authors discussed traumatic experiences related to their time as faculty members. Trauma is described as a sensory experience, an experience not only of the mind, but also the body. To relieve some of the trauma responses, one must be able to identify how the body physically responds under stress. Meditation creates the opportunity to identify physical sensations and provides time for the brain to make a different choice. Njia (Nyesha James) has created a guided meditation and journal prompting to be used individually or collectively (see pages 229–232 for the full document). Guided meditations like those developed by Dr. Carmichael and Njia can both aid in relieving the trauma that many Black faculty experience in both their personal and professional lives.

Desk Side Ministry

Faculty and staff can complete a form asking for prayer and someone from campus ministries will literally "minister desk side."

Weekly Chapel Service

In Ekwonye, Sheikhomar & Phung (2020), the authors studied how spirituality can be a psychological resource to academic related stress and found that attending church services helps people stay focused, increases relaxation, and increases their sense of confidence about the future. Each week VUU streams a chapel service on both their Facebook and YouTube pages. They advertise it on their various Instagram profiles. Having the virtual service allows them to reach faculty, staff, students, and alumni from all over the globe. Although chapel attendance is mandatory for students, but not for faculty, faculty still attend regularly and faithfully each week. Since the service is recorded, it can be viewed at any time by VUU's nearly 14,000 Facebook followers. On average, there are several hundred views as tracked by both Facebook and YouTube.

Faith-Filled Fridays
This is open to faculty, staff, students, and alumni. They are asked the question of the day, such as "what are you grateful for?", or, if you could ask the Lord a question, what would it be? While some answer with words, others respond with a song. These are recorded and shared on the various VUU Instagram profiles.

VUU Campus Ministries offer several other initiatives that have been beneficial to the campus community including Mindfulness Mondays, Inspirational Tuesdays, the prayer line, wellness classes, Zumba, yoga, and a "lunch & learn," to name just a few. More information about these programs and others can be found on their Instagram profiles.[2]

North Hennepin Community College

Dr. Rassheedah Watts, Associate Vice President of Equity & Inclusion, Chief Diversity Officer

North Hennepin Community College (NHCC) is a public community college located in Brooklyn Park, Minnesota. According to the institution's website,[3] NHCC was founded in 1966 and is one of the largest and most diverse colleges in the state of Minnesota. It is a member of the Minnesota State Colleges and Universities system or Minnesota State System. Their mission is to engage students and change lives by creating opportunities for students to reach their academic goals, succeed in their chosen professions, and make a difference in the world. Although, according to recent facts and data found on the North Hennepin Community

---

[2] www.instagram.com/vuuasstpastor and www.instagram.com/vuucampusministries
[3] www.nhcc.edu

College website, students of color make up 49 percent of the population, faculty of color only make up for 14 percent, while 38 percent are staff of color. This is not broken down further by race, but it does provide context as to why Dr. Rassheedah Watts saw a need and found a way to address topics of inclusion that addressed the needs of Black employees (faculty included) within the college and the Minnesota State System.

In the chapters preceding this one, you have read how Black faculty in PWIs are often the only one or one of very few. Through the experiences shared, you have seen just how lonely it can be and have read about the effects of tokenism. The impacts of working in an environment where you feel you do not belong and are not understood cannot only impact inclusion, but also affects mental health. Most importantly to institutions, it can have a direct influence on faculty retention. In 2016, the Harvard Graduate School of Education (HGSE) piloted their Faculty Retention and Exit Survey with several campuses of a large public university system (Matthews & Benson, 2018). They have now distributed this nationwide. The results of the pilot were intriguing because they showed that, although salary is often noted as playing a major role in faculty retention, it was not true for 71 percent of the departing faculty. In fact, the data showed that one in four departures accepted external offers with an increase in salary of less than $6,000. If it was not money, then what was the most cited reason for faculty turnover? A total of 67 percent of departing faculty said the quality of colleagues was a compelling factor in their decision to stay or leave. HGSE suggests that institutions encourage a collegial environment. "The more opportunities you create for faculty to engage each other professionally and personally, the stickier the institution becomes. You build social capital that becomes part of the cost equation when leaving."

Academic Black Table Talk
Dr. Watts is the Associate Vice President of Equity & Inclusion – the Chief Diversity Officer at NHCC – and has launched a program that this author believes is *the* glue that HGSE references that could make not only NHCC, but also all colleges and universities in the state of Minnesota a little bit stickier. Following the murder of George Floyd in Minneapolis in 2020, Dr. Watts developed and implemented "Academic Black Table Talk," a program designed specifically to amplify the voices and experiences of Black faculty, administrators, and staff within the Minnesota State System. Aimed at highlighting the Black experience in the Academy, it is the first such program of its kind. It is also accessible, available, and inclusive to all employees and students throughout the 30+ colleges and universities

within the Minnesota State System. The program is described on YouTube as a monthly webinar series designed to process recent national events, and elevate Black voices, knowledge, and expertise.[4] In the series, Dr. Watts and other Minnesota State Black professionals discuss issues of education, racial justice, equity, and topics salient to Black identity in America. According to Dr. Watts, "Academic Black Table Talk" serves a three-fold purpose: First, it helps connect Black professionals from around the Minnesota State System by providing a shared outlet where experiences can be expressed and processed with others through transparent and frank dialogue. Second, the program serves as an awareness-building tool and learning opportunity for everyone within the State System. Guests and attendees have included students, cabinet members, the Minnesota State Chancellor, and a number of provosts and presidents from throughout the State System. Third, it is a unifying and inclusionary platform designed to provide an equitable space for Black voices, which are often disregarded – a space to be seen and heard in. Since its emergence, the Academic Black Table Talk series has been met with positive responses from those in attendance.

The Academic Black Table Talk series streams live with a chat option for those watching and is recorded for those who cannot watch live. As a Black faculty member at a PWI, I (Antija) found myself feeling more understood and less isolated simply by watching the various videos which touched on topics such as the inclusion of Black History and Black people in higher education, navigating racial battle fatigue, raising mental awareness on campus, and the impact of the Breonna Taylor case.

The series, in part, is a psychosocial resource created in response to the COVID-19 pandemic to mitigate the fear of people being disconnected due to the mandatory transition to working from home. When we (Antija and Justin) asked Dr. Watts if this inclusion initiative would change and move to face to face post-pandemic, she made an excellent point about the distances between the various institutions in Minnesota which can involve more than five hours of travel for some Black faculty located in rural campus locations. Therefore logistically, its current iteration allows for more professionals to be involved and sustains the much-needed social connection and support, though she does not fully rule out the possibility of a face-to-face forum in the future.[5]

---

[4] https://bit.ly/3JbtvcY
[5] There is more information about Dr. Watts and her work at www.drrassheedah.com

Rochester Institute of Technology (RIT)

Dr. Donathan Brown, Assistant Provost and AVP for Faculty Diversity and Recruitment, Associate Professor

Rochester Institute of Technology is a private research university located in Rochester, New York. Founded in 1829, RIT is a diverse and collaborative community of engaged, socially conscious, and intellectually curious minds.[6] Through creativity and innovation, and an intentional blending of technology, the arts, and design, they provide exceptional individuals with a wide range of academic opportunities, including a leading research program and an internationally recognized education for deaf and hard-of-hearing students. Beyond their main campus in Rochester, New York, RIT has international campuses in China, Croatia, Dubai, and Kosovo. With nearly 19,000 students, and more than 135,000 graduates from all fifty states and more than a hundred nations, RIT is driving progress in industries and communities around the world.

The Future Faculty Career Exploration Program
RIT's Future Faculty Career Exploration Program is designed for BIPOC scholars and artists. The rigorous four-day program provides participants a "behind the scenes" glimpse of what it would be like to be a faculty member at RIT. Before COVID restrictions forced the program into a virtual setting for 2021, the program was held in person and participants took an all-expenses-paid trip to Rochester, New York, where RIT is located. While on campus, they take part in various activities and events such as: networking receptions with RIT's President, Provost, Deans, faculty, staff, and students; presenting their research or art to faculty, department chairs and Deans; engaging in one-on-one, panel, and round-table discussions about life in academia; learning about current and upcoming faculty positions; gaining career development insight and advice from RIT faculty and receiving feedback on their research or art, and job talk to improve their candidacy. A vital part of the program provides participants with the chance not only to get to know about the school by touring campus, but also to explore the greater Rochester community.[7]

There are roughly 125 applicants, with around eighteen being accepted. Of those accepted, 17 percent of that population eventually become RIT faculty. For many that have been selected to participate in this program,

---

[6] www.rit.edu   [7] www.rit.edu/diversity/ffcep

this is the first time they are experiencing conversations regarding items such as the rules of engagement for tenure, there having previously been no socialization on these types of topics.

A former program participant, who will be referred to as Dr. C, has taken part in several programs offered at other institutions that are similar to RIT. However, when asked what distinguished RIT from these other institutions, they stated that, at other institutions, "you were mainly in the same room all day while various people came in and talked 'at you'." Additionally, the faculty, many times, did not seem invested in the process – either missing meetings with the participant or showing a lack of enthusiasm when speaking with the participant. Dr. C stated that was not the case with RIT, where it felt like everyone involved was welcoming and prepared to meet them. Participants went to various locations meeting faculty and staff in different departments. This is why it should have come as no surprise that when the opportunity arose to serve as a faculty member at RIT, they accepted.

While enthusiastic about the program in its ability to be inclusive and celebrate diversity, Dr. C felt that the ball was dropped, so to speak, after they were actually hired. This is not uncommon, as you have read in previous chapters. Dr. C is a social and outgoing individual who started some informal groups in order to meet with other faculty of color. Dr. C also mentioned that there were other informal opportunities to gather with other faculty of color. Although, these informal gatherings and groups can aid in inclusion, if you have a faculty member who is less social and more introverted, can they be reached in these informal ways? Dr. C noted that they were in discussion with the FFCEP to explore ideas for inclusion and retention of faculty of color. The first step would most definitely be to find a way to formalize the aforementioned groups, which would make them easier to access for new faculty. The FFCEP's openness to having this conversation about how to improve the post-program experience is a testament to the RIT culture.

The Pennsylvania State University

Penn State Outreach and Penn State Online Education

Karen Armstrong, M.S., Counseling; Doctoral Candidate, Educational Equity in Higher Education Director of Inclusion, Equity & Diversity

According to its website, Pennsylvania State University is a multi-campus, land-grant, public research university that educates students from around the world and supports individuals and communities through integrated programs of teaching, research, and service.[8]

Penn State Outreach's mission states that they will make a positive impact on society by engaging diverse audiences in the design and delivery of compelling content and meaningful programs that are grounded in faculty expertise. Through their work they are committed to being an inclusive and engaged university for Pennsylvania and beyond.[9] Tracey DeBlase Huston leads the Outreach aspect of the organization. Karen Armstrong steers diversity, equity, inclusion and belonging for both the Online and Outreach divisions of the university. Working in such pivotal areas of the university, Outreach and Online Education, which are led by two women, is a demonstration of applying equitable leadership in theory and practice.

According to the Penn State Online Education website, the Office of the Vice Provost for Online Education is led by Dr. Renata S. Engel. The office controls all aspects of Penn State World Campus as well as the development and coordination of the vision, strategies, policies, and practices for online education that Penn State offers. It houses academic affairs, student affairs, faculty development, enrollment management, and administrative and strategic operations. These are all units that support Penn State World Campus and online education. In addition, the office is supported by cross-unit services in marketing, information technology, finance and operations, human resources, and development.[10]

It is important to note that Pennsylvania State University is a large institution and the initiatives and programs that take place on the campuses that Ms. Armstrong leads or is responsible for do not necessarily happen in other areas of the institution. This is not to say they are not also carrying out programs dedicated to diversity, equity, and inclusion, it is just to note that this section solely focuses on the Outreach and Online Education area.

In addition to being a DEI expert, Ms. Armstrong has experience as a faculty member at the University of Bridgeport and served as a faculty consultant at Florida State College at Jacksonville. She stated that those experiences shaped her role as a director.

Connections Events
Because of the size of the institution and various campus locations around the state of Pennsylvania, they have always held virtual events, even pre-COVID.

---

[8] www.psu.edu/this-is-penn-state/mission-and-values
[9] www.outreach.psu.edu/about/vision-mission   [10] https://online-education.psu.edu/about

They refer to these as *connection events*. A connection event could be experts coming and talking about the impact of racial trauma for faculty and staff. For example, the experience of repeatedly seeing people murdered, or becoming nervous at the sight of police, or being stopped by them, is what Ms. Armstrong explains needs to be recognized as trauma. Traumatized individuals should not be expected to come in and do their lesson plan or work with their students (or whatever their role may be) without authorities first acknowledging that they may be experiencing trauma on a regular basis just because they exist. This is why connection events are held. This is just one of the things done to open up a space for conversation around the reality of this trauma and any area of trauma related to marginalization. These events are open to faculty and staff only; something different is conducted for the students. It is important to note that these events, which allow faculty and staff time to process, all take place during the working day and last on average one hour. Ms. Armstrong states that they do not want them to process this with their students. That is why they build in these opportunities to connect. All the connection events and initiatives that follow are strategic, deliberate, and mindful. According to Ms. Armstrong, they all have outcomes that they specifically want to happen to foster belonging. It is also important to add that the programs and initiatives that will be discussed in this section are for the most part either low-cost or free. This is vital information because at times cost is an issue when it comes to implementing DEI initiatives and programs.

Expert Speakers and Speaker Series
Led by an expert guest speaker, these events are held on Zoom and last from an hour to an hour and a half. Attendees are allowed to unmute themselves and share what their experiences are. Penn State is a PWI that does not have many BIPOC employees across the university in general. Ms. Armstrong explains that because we are so marginalized it is important to share these experiences and then to affirm them in order to recognize that what faculty and staff are saying is true and real.

Book Club
This event is described as something a little lighter to open the door for many white faculty and staff who feel unsure of how to have conversations about race, want to help but do not know how, and/or are not sure about marginalized people in general. Books that are available in the library are commonly used, eliminating any costs involved. Fictional works are the only focus and Ms. Armstrong says that is deliberate because it is a lot easier, for example, to hate a character. This then initiates a discussion

about hate – what it looks like, feels like, and how it impacts you. When we use works of fiction, the employee is not afraid to judge because it is characters that are being discussed, and that is a goal of the club because it allows participants to be able to recognize what they really feel and think. The book club looks at a lot of different topics, not just BIPOC. One book that they covered was *This Is How It Always Is: A Novel*, a book about the experience of a transgender child (Frankel, 2017). Having conversations like these yield belonging. According to Davis (2004), more radical reading effects are produced when empathetic connections are accompanied by critical reflection. Thought and feeling then combine, resulting in a critique of racism and a deeper respect for cultural differences.

Listening Sessions

According to Barnett (2020), for academic leaders to integrate mission and social justice outcomes successfully, they must listen to students, faculty, staff, and other relevant stakeholders. Ms. Armstrong goes into different units and departments to hear what areas of equity, diversity, or training staff say they need. As a researcher would do when conducting a qualitative analysis, Ms. Armstrong looks at themes based on what she hears. One example of a theme is *intersectionality*, understood as the view that as individuals we have more than one aspect: In other words, an individual can be Black, but also a woman, and/or "disabled"; or can be a man, Black, and/or identify as gay. Ms. Armstrong explained that many in marginalized populations at PWIs are often seen as *being* only one of those attributes instead of having one or more of them, which impacts their sense of belonging. Although the listening sessions are geared toward staff, they have been included because it appears to be an initiative that could also be beneficial to faculty as well.

Other Recommendations

DEI Training for BIPOC Faculty

Ms. Armstrong stressed the importance of offering DEI training for all employees in Outreach & Online Education, including BIPOC faculty. Despite their small numbers, there is greater proportional participation in the training from BIPOC staff. She mentioned what has been noted in some of this book's previous chapters, the notion that some administrators have that, because someone is Black, they do not need DEI training: There is often this assumption that they must already know certain things. According to Ms. Armstrong, that is where equity comes in: Some get training because they are assumed not to know, while others do not because it is assumed they already do know. This then impacts BIPOC faculty's opportunities for advancement not just at their current institution, but also at other institutions they may apply to. Lacking DEI training leaves BIPOC faculty less competitive in the job market.

Statements of Solidarity

Ms. Armstrong expressed the importance of presidents of institutions making statements of solidarity. When a president makes such a statement, there is a trickle-down effect that enables others in leadership positions to make similar statements. As a result, events can be held that make those statements more than words.

Njia Guided Meditation Worksheet

At this point, you have likely developed your own working definition of *trauma* and what it means to you and for you. It is imperative to acknowledge that what qualifies as a traumatic experience will vary from person to person. What may be a traumatic experience for you may not be a traumatic experience for another, and vice versa.

Trauma extends beyond the mental memory of the experience. The body remembers the traumatic experience as well because trauma is a sensory experience. It is an experience of not only the mind, but also the body and all five senses.

Consider the following scenarios:

A soldier who served in combat many years ago, moved away from a hustling city for peace and quiet. This soldier returns to the city to visit family after a couple of years. While walking past a construction site, the soldier runs for cover when he hears the jackhammer pounding into the cement.

A little girl grows up in a two-parent home. Her parents do not argue all of the time but when they do, they yell so loud that all of the neighbors can hear. The screaming scares the little girl, so she hides in the closet. As an adult this woman finds that when her partner raises their voice, she immediately shuts down.

Both individuals are experiencing "fight or flight" responses. Their bodies remember the sensations of perceived danger and move to get them out of harm's way. These are two clear examples. Our personal experiences of trauma may not be so obvious and can fall anywhere on the spectrum of traumatic experiences.

Because trauma is a sensory experience, one way to begin to address and relieve some of that traumatic experience is through sensory-based interventions. Some sensory interventions that stimulate the vagus nerve are human contact, breath work, mindfulness, dance, movement, yoga, and journaling.

Below, you will be guided through a small meditation that will help identify and begin to regulate some of the sensory feelings that your body identifies with your traumatic experience.

Guided Meditation

Disclaimer: The exercise below may elicit some unexpected reactions and feelings. Identify a mental health provider or trusted confidant to help process your experience.

❏ Find a quiet, private place free from distractions. You should feel comfortable and safe in this space.
❏ Sit up as straight as possible but without strain.
❏ Place palms loosely on your stomach or resting on your lap.
❏ Take some deep grounding breaths. Breathe slowly in through your nose and out of your mouth until you feel your body has calmed and come into the present. (Some say 3 – 5 breaths, but everyone and every body is different.)
❏ Consider a situation that has brought you discomfort.
❏ Note where you feel that discomfort in your body.
  ❏ Did your muscles tense?
  ❏ Did your breathing rhythm change?
  ❏ Did you feel a lump in your throat?
  ❏ Did you clench your teeth?
  ❏ Do you feel knots in your stomach?
  ❏ What other sensations do you feel?
❏ Mentally note these sensations.
❏ Remind yourself that you are in a safe place.
❏ Breathe into these tense areas; imagining that you are sending your breath to relax any uncomfortable or tense sensation. Do this as long as needed.

This is a good point at which to take a short break and journal your experience. It is encouraged that this be done in a brainstorming format.

Just let the words flow with little concern for making sense, complete sentences, or self-censorship.

Immediately move on in the meditation to bring the body back to balance. We never want to intentionally leave the body in a state of discomfort.

- ❏ Return to your meditative position.
- ❏ Sit up as straight as possible but without strain.
- ❏ Place palms loosely on your stomach or resting on your lap.
- ❏ Take some deep grounding breaths. Breathe slowly in through your nose and out of your mouth until you feel your body has calmed and come into the present. (Perhaps 3 – 5 breaths again.)
- ❏ Consider a situation, person, place, or thing that brings you happiness.
- ❏ Note where you feel this joy in your body.
  - ❏ Do you feel a tingling sensation?
  - ❏ Do you feel the corners of your mouth turn up slightly, like a smile?
  - ❏ Do you feel an increased heartbeat?
  - ❏ Mentally note these sensations.
  - ❏ Stay in this place as long as you like.
- ❏ When you're ready, return to your deep grounding breaths. Breathe slowly in through your nose and out of your mouth.
- ❏ Open your eyes.

If you like, you can journal those sensations of joy.

It is not recommended that you immediately go back and analyze your journaling from the first portion of the meditation. Let it be. A good time to review your journaling is after a few times of practicing this mediation exercise. Analyze not to judge your feelings, but just to notice any change in intensity of the sensation.

Continued practice in this mindfulness practice will also help you identify some of your physical triggers that take you to that fight or flight response, that response to those subconscious triggers. You may have identified sweaty palms and shortened breath as sensations during your time of discomfort. In a real-time situation, you may recognize that your palms become sweaty and your breath quickens. Because you have acknowledged these sensations, it provides a buffer, that is, time for you to step back and regulate your system and choose your response more consciously.

This is just a short exercise that can be used to begin to identify, acknowledge, and regulate some of our discomforts due to traumatic experiences. Seek guidance from a mental health provider to dive deeper into your personal journey of healing.[11]

REFERENCES

Barnett, R. M. (2020). Leading with meaning: Why diversity, equity and inclusion matters in US higher education. *Perspectives in Education*, 38(2), 20–35. doi: 10.18820/2519593X/pie.v38.i2.02

Davis, K. C. (2004). Oprah's book club and the politics of cross-racial empathy. *International Journal of Cultural Studies*, 7(4), 399–419. https://doi.org/10.1177/1367877904047861

Ekwonye, A. U., Sheikhomar, N. & Phung, V. (2020) Spirituality: A psychological resource for managing academic-related stressors. *Mental Health, Religion & Culture*, 23(9), 826–39. doi: 10.1080/13674676.2020.1823951

Frankel, L. (2017). *This Is How It Always Is: A novel*. New York: Flatiron Books.

Graham, A. (2016). Womanist preservation: An analysis of Black women's spiritual coping. *International Journal of Transpersonal Studies*, 35(1), 106–17. https://dx.doi.org/10.24972/ijts.2016.35.1.106

Matthews, K. & Benson, T. (2018). Findings from the first ever multi-institutional survey of faculty retention & exit. Infographic. Harvard University Graduate School of Education. https://bit.ly/3H4H9N3

[11]   This worksheet was created by Nyesha James of Njia: Pathways to Healing.

The Road that Lies Ahead

Justin T. Stewart

Black, Indigenous, and People of Color (BIPOC) in the United States have been historically burdened with the weight of having to prove themselves in an oppressive system. Unsurprisingly, as our best interests were not always a focal point, this system has continuously failed us personally and professionally. With the troubled history and treatment of marginalized people throughout the US, some of these ripple effects have manifested as systemic, institutional, and personal racism. As a result, for POC, certain spaces are more comfortable to exist in than others. For Black and Brown people, living a second-class experience under the thumb of these circumstances, the struggles to be accepted, validated, and feel as though they belong, remain.

While society has progressed and evolved in its train of thought, embracing the dynamics presented through perspectives and different cultures, faculty of color have not yet been able to see or benefit from this new beginning. For Black and Brown professors existing as the racial minority at a PWI, suffering from conscious and unconscious bias has been par for the course, with many feeling relegated to the more subservient role of focusing on advancing the mission of their colleges and universities, while forfeiting their own professional aspirations due to a lack of support. It is for these reasons, and more, that we are not ok. Regardless of what some people may project or lead others to believe, racism is far from being a "moment" that is now in the distant past.

We're Not OK was conceived as a platform for faculty of color to stand on to break their silence on the trials and tribulations of working at PWIs and in academia as a whole. Sharing experiences, presenting research findings, detailing challenges, and devising potential strategies for academia serve as a resource to help others identify and recognize the fact that older models of thinking and operating no longer work. While these conversations may not be new to non-white educators currently experiencing what has been shared, be assured that your voice cannot be silenced, or ignored, any longer. By providing perspective and raising awareness of past and present transgressions, a dialogue can be initiated to decipher the root cause, and work collectively toward a solution. This provides a new starting point to make a change.

In *Caste: The origins of our discontents*, an account of the systemic oppression of Black people in America, Pulitzer Prize-winning author Isabel Wilkerson refers to the country as having a caste system (Wilkerson, 2020). She describes this as an artificial hierarchy that helps to establish standing, respect, and assumptions of beauty and competence, and determines who gets the benefit of the doubt and access to resources. She argues that while caste focuses on the infrastructure of our divisions and the rankings, race is the metric that is used to determine one's place in that. Existing within an infrastructure, the foundation of which is defined and constructed by a caste system, there are cultures that are forced to put in an extraneous amount of effort, in comparison to others, to meet the standard. Generations later, this establishment continues to be perpetuated, further undermining the efforts of marginalized communities that are attempting to seek the validation that will afford them with more opportunities. It has gradually become necessary to employ tactics to be socially acceptable and fit in with white norms.

The pressure to be, or become, what is considered "ideal," is based on definitions from yesteryear when basic human rights were a bit more *selective*. Such "traditional" standards that were previously the norm no longer have room to exist. With society continuing to transition in its ideologies, and the makeup of populations strengthening in diversity, the country is tasked with re-defining its identity in an ever-evolving social and racial climate. The system has to change in order to move forward. This shift should also exist within academia as a renewed culture is developed and erected that reflects the current societal landscape and its progressive nature. The failure to assess and modify their infrastructure, and effectively implement DEI for minority groups, will inevitably lead to their collapse. Get with the program, or get left behind!

A common theme expressed throughout *We're Not OK* is trauma experienced by Black and Brown professors in academia and how they are impacted. For faculty of color that are entering, or currently working in, PWIs, the journey can be tumultuous, burdened by microaggressions, tokenism, imposter syndrome, and isolation, all of which can lead to a diminished sense of self by having their presence minimized and contributions devalued. These attacks, originating from false characterizations of their racial identity, come from the perceived safe spaces of their colleagues and students. When compounded, such obstacles account for the constant mental strain impacting their overall well-being. While these faculty members have persevered through these challenges, implementing maladaptive coping strategies to establish credibility among white colleagues, it has come at the price of sacrificing authenticity. Continuing to be of service within our respective colleges and universities, we have been done a disservice by these same institutions that have failed to expand intentional support for Black faculty, along with other marginalized groups. Existing in these environments where your authentic self is unwelcome, or where you do not feel supported, many faculty of color have elected to leave higher education altogether.

In January 2021, after serving nearly seven years at the Yale Center for Emotional Intelligence, Assistant Director Dena Simmons resigned from her position with immediate effect (Young, 2021). Citing her experiences in the workplace, Simmons expressed dealing with racist and sexist behaviors from colleagues, which left her "feeling threatened, devalued, and tokenized" (Horta & Price, 2021). Expounding further, Simmons referenced numerous microaggressions and described instances of "unconsented hair-touching" and "constant undermining" in her resignation email. This was supported by her colleagues, who witnessed instances and mentioned that Simmons often had to explain to peers why she was not comfortable with hair touching. She described a June 2020 Zoom incident as "a racist attack at an antiracism town hall at the Child Study Center." In response to the attacks on Simmons, apology letters were sent from several faculty members on the call, but she felt that action was required that had not occurred. Simmons took a six-month medical leave following this incident but, compounded with previous attacks, she no longer felt protected by the University and felt it in her best interests to leave the organization permanently and "finally do authentic work at the intersection of racial justice and social and emotional learning without reprimand."

At its conception, this book was not intended for grandstanding on race politics, or as a means to expose PWIs and *cancel* them for questionable practices that are advantageous to specific groups. Nor is it a soapbox on which to stand waving our collective finger or bark about a crooked establishment. If, however, the content of *We're Not OK* has caused discomfort, part of our intention to understand the plights of those that are underrepresented within colleges and universities has been accomplished. This is an opportunity to correct assumptions and learn from "honest mistakes" that can result in being labeled as "one of the good ones." By addressing the historical and contemporary effects of institutional racism there is a chance to improve and develop an environment that welcomes people from different walks of life. The path to belonging starts with feeling connected to an institution and the community within it.

Additionally, our purpose is to stir the pot and encourage conversations on a grander scale. Racial inequity is not specific to Black men and women; it does not apply only to faculty of color; and it is not exclusive to colleges and universities within the United States. It remains an issue that is prevalent in multiple industries locally, nationally, and internationally. The research, observations, and experiences explored in each chapter should enable readers to expand their capacity to learn from and grow with one another. In planting these seeds, institutions should ask why and start, or continue, discussion that will lead to changes that are long overdue. In forging a path for tomorrow, will you be a bridge or a barrier?

Working Toward Sustainable Solutions in DEI

Throughout *We're Not OK*, the authors have articulated the journey of where we've been and where we are in pursuit of DEI. Now, with these new revelations, where are we going from here?

In the wake of the 2020 murders of George Floyd and Breonna Taylor, along with the prominence of the Black Lives Matter movement, there have been concentrated efforts to deliver on finding solutions toward equality and providing a safe space for Black communities on a societal level. Unfortunately, questions have risen regarding the sincerity of these institutions based on what is said versus what is actually being done. At an institutional level, PWIs must make their own shift in broadening its understanding of their Black faculty. Checking a box about increasing numbers does not achieve diversity. The infrastructure, if left unchanged, projects a social order that continues to leave faculty of color at a disadvantage, regardless of their title. Black professors are left spending an inordinate amount of time making white people – from leadership to peers to students – feel comfortable, though that same grace is not always reciprocated.

To avoid simply talking about the problems, strategies, recommendations, and possible solutions have anchored each chapter to aid in taking steps forward. This book has presented an opportunity not only to air grievances, but also to celebrate, and potentially leverage, successes achieved along the way. A conscious decision was made to suggest *what* can be done for faculty of color that creates a diverse, equitable, and inclusive community that will increase their success and retention. Through addressing the issues of the current infrastructure of academia, there remains an opportunity to fix the broken components of the system, and show the ways we can reach that goal collectively. Additionally, Chapter 13 has provided specific real-world examples of initiatives with positive outcomes for retention, inclusion, and/or mental wellness. In conducting interviews throughout the country (Northeast, South, Midwest), we wanted to ensure that we highlighted the new perspectives gained from every region and individuals who are continually rolling up their sleeves to do the necessary work. By presenting models that have been successful demonstrating *how* it can be done, institutions will have more of an outline on which to base their own framework.

If the goal of a PWI is to evolve in its efforts for DEI, it first requires accountability. Honesty and transparency are paramount and must be present in order to usher in these changes. In creating a vision for the future, it is vital to acknowledge the past, and reflect on what is currently happening at your own organization. Through leadership monitoring any inherent bias against social class and cultural signals in faculty of color, there is an opportunity to re-evaluate expectations and welcome new methods of learning. This approach built by the collective will encourage individuality, allowing less restraint in Black professors forging their own paths. Exposing faculty of color to different ways in which they can be engaged in their college or university (mentorship, development programs, networking events, and resource groups) also allows them to shed the monolithic mentality of believing they are restricted to certain spaces, or can only fulfill a single function. A true representation of Black faculty among the ranks of leadership that mirrors society presents a variety of options that can inspire an individual without feeling the need to compromise.

Recognizing that people come from different walks of life, there must be an environment present that stimulates and allows their individuality to flourish. Faculty of color have expressed burnout, needing to work exponentially harder within the classrooms and throughout these institutions, when compared to their white counterparts, to be perceived as qualified. Additionally, tailoring their approaches in teaching students to fit a standard hinders their ability to create an authentic learning experience that they truly own. Working at PWIs, while performing instruction in the classroom, these faculty members must internally battle with the pressures of disproving stereotypical beliefs about competence and capacities that students have projected onto them. Offering professional learning opportunities targeted at the link between student success and faculty development is the utmost priority to improve instructional quality. Facing a lack of cultural competencies, and making concentrated efforts to develop initiatives that support minority groups, will enable these marginalized groups to feel celebrated rather than tolerated. Ideally, we can reach a point where strategies and survival techniques such as code-switching, which can be more of a repellant than a solution, will no longer be necessary.

An institution's foundation is built around its mission statement, a declaration of its purposes and its vision of excellence, which should encompass every individual within its diverse population. Rejecting previous practices of exclusivity and weaving more inclusivity into the fabric of organizational culture will encourage growth within the workplace to bring about transformational and sustainable change. Frankly speaking, the makeup of faculty within higher education does not reflect the changing demographics in the US, let alone the student population. While these structures give the impression of the white population being the majority, the margin by which that is true is steadily decreasing. In moving toward presenting an accurate depiction of this gradual change, representation, especially in leaderships and other positions of power, is a vital step that must continue to be pushed forward. Allowing these small percentages through the door achieves diversity, but with minimal opportunities to advance their careers, these professors are operating beneath low ceilings and are limited in their ability to advance at their institutions.

A man of many titles, American novelist and activist James Baldwin once stated, "Not everything that is faced can be changed, but nothing can be changed until it is faced." In dismantling these structures that were built upon hierarchy and oppression, to create meaningful change, there must be a commitment to the long road ahead. This task is gradual, and not something that can be accomplished in a matter of weeks, months, or years. In fact, due to the ever-evolving nature of society, such work can never truly be complete, as there will always be room for improvement and a need to return to the drawing board. One size neither fits nor fulfills everyone, a fact that must be taken into consideration when developing an approach to make the communities within these institutions more inclusive. Tapping into the unique perspectives of different cultures, bringing them to the table to discuss what is working well and how what is not can be improved, will incentivize individuals to offer insight and feedback, become more engaged and play an active role to drive change. Without factoring these in while restructuring institutions, the calls to action for equality result in nothing more than pandering and paying lip service, which will leave Black faculty with greater mistrust of their institutions and lead toward an exodus. As we look to find and develop sustainable change, will you provide opportunities or obstacles?

Opposition Along the Journey to DEI

Moving forward without expecting any naysayers or forms of resistance would be foolish. There exists a population of people that "don't see color," and believe that racism is no longer a hurdle that modern societies are impacted by. As such, these negative experiences may be deemed as coincidental or that person simply not being the right fit. The concept of inequality is foreign. Additionally, there are individuals that have vastly benefited from the system in its current iteration and are less inclined to promote making a change if it risks forfeiting opportunities they have been afforded as a result. Even with conflict in ideas, when tackled with respect and understanding, healthy conversation can exist for each side to present their case. Ultimately, this journey is meant for the collective, even when opinions are not aligned with the perspectives that have been shared throughout, *We're Not OK*. However, if you solely exist to serve as an obstacle or maintain willful blindness to the perils described, there is no seat for you on this ride or at this table.

Another point of contention comes from intentionality. Mentioned earlier, this period of civil unrest has led to institutions outwardly putting their respective flags in the sand to proclaim how inclusive they are, or intend to be. In 2021, heinous acts of police brutality have continued to take innocent Black lives. What has not gone unnoticed, however, is the silence from some of these institutions, calling into question their intentions. Looking within your organizations, how have you impacted the Black lives that work alongside you for the better? What changes have you implemented to create a healthy environment to not only teach, but also learn and develop? Are you only promoting illusions of inclusivity? Questions such as these differentiate those that have served as advocates, pushing boundaries, and those that are chasing recognition, or a pat on the back, for the "efforts" of their colleges and universities. Theatrics and distractions can only be taken so far until they are revealed. Regardless of what is projected to the masses, and the accolades received from the mainstream, what matters most is changing the lives of these marginalized groups for the better. In the fight to achieve true equality for all, will you be an ally or an adversary?

The Future for Faculty of Color

Paranoia and anxiety have accounted for the insecurities of past generations where African Americans have been perceived, described, and presented as being lesser than their white counterparts. Constant assimilation and integration with another group's culture has only muted the cultural expression of BIPOC faculty. When the world looks at them and chooses to see only one thing, it attempts to rob them of the realization of their full potential.

For faculty of color working at PWIs, the paths to recognition and respect have been long and arduous. Faced with rejection, being made to feel second rate and as if they do not belong, they have weathered the storm and persevered in the face of the hurdles blocking their way. While some have succeeded in their career paths, others have had to try again and again. The road that lies ahead will begin to reveal how much of an asset they are to these institutions of higher education. If the recommendations of this book are acted upon, there will be people and programs across the United States to make sure of that.

If no one else tells them, *We're Not OK* was developed with faculty of color, and those like them, in mind, and it is to them our final comments are addressed. The experiences detailed throughout this book have been a reflection of what is seen, and what is felt.

As institutions work to create an inclusive and energizing environment that embraces diversity holistically and empowers faculty to learn, grow, and have meaningful careers, we will remain committed to sharing your stories and struggles until this has been achieved. While continuing to express the grievances and areas for improvement, we will also celebrate the successes.

Ensuring proper representation is always at the table holds colleges and universities to account in becoming better places. As we continue to advocate transformational change, know that you are an integral and essential part of this process.

Your voice is important. Your individuality is important. Your presence is important.

REFERENCES

Horta, B. & Price, Z. "Threatened, devalued and tokenized": Yale Center for Emotional Intelligence assistant director resigns over workplace racism. *Yale News*. January 26. https://bit.ly/3zhhqhO

Wilkerson, I. (2020). *Caste: The origins of our discontents*. New York: Random House.

Young, J. R. (2021). Citing racism and "years of bullying," Dena Simmons resigns from Yale Center for Emotional Intelligence. *EdSurge*. February 17. https://bit.ly/3qgSa7m

Index